An inspiring story told with lashings of energy and humour.

Ranulph Fiennes

This is the trip I would take if I were younger, braver and lightly but certifiably out of my mind.

Bill Bryson

What do you do after leaving university? Get a boring office job – or drive a black cab 43,000 miles around the world? Ernest Hemingway said always do sober what you said you'd do drunk. These lads did and raised 20 K whilst smashing two world records. Brilliant.

Andy Parsons

High adventure filled with hilarity and mischief – it goes to show what can happen when you combine some serious guts and a daft idea.

Levison Wood

IT'S ON THE METER

Summersdale Publishers Ltd
46 West Street
Chichester
West Sussex
PO19 1RP
UK

www.summersdale.com

Printed and bound by CPI Group (UK) Ltd, Croydon, CR0 4YY

PAPERBACK ISBN: 978-1-84953-825-1
HARDBACK ISBN: 978-1-84953-942-5

Substantial discounts on bulk quantities of Summersdale books are available to corporations, professional associations and other organisations. For details contact Nicky Douglas by telephone: +44 (0) 1243 756902, fax: +44 (0) 1243 786300 or email: nicky@summersdale.com.

IT'S ON THE METER

ONE TAXI, THREE MATES AND 43,000 MILES
OF MISADVENTURES AROUND THE WORLD

PAUL ARCHER & JOHNO ELLISON
AFTERWORD BY LEIGH PURNELL

summersdale

CONTENTS

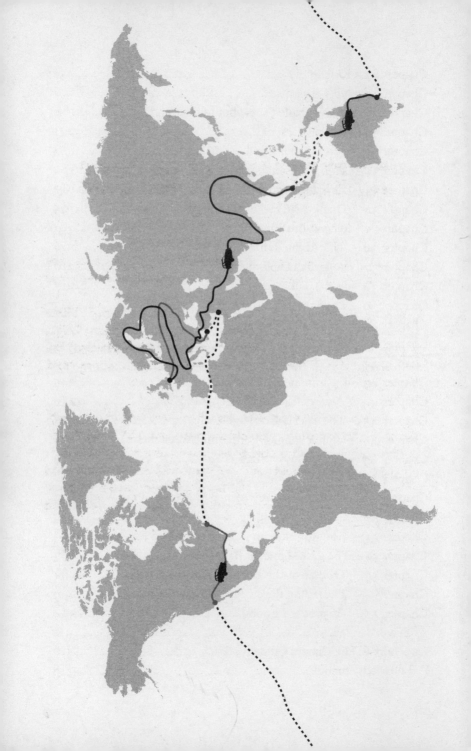

A NOTE FROM THE AUTHORS

This is a story about three of us, by two of us. Throughout the book Johno will be writing in a font like this, and Paul in a font like this.

Writing a book with two voices has been a challenge. Three voices proved beyond our abilities, so our third member, Leigh, is mostly absent from the writing (except for the afterword) but his contribution to the adventure was just as important as ours, if not greater.

This is a story about what happens when three lads in their early 20s go on an adventure in an old banger. It was not noble, it was not smart and should probably be viewed as a series of stories outlining how one should not travel the world, but (unfortunately) all of the events detailed in the book are true. However, some names have been changed to protect people we met along the way.

PREFACE

The soldiers looked unsure of themselves. It seemed unlikely that they had ever been in this situation before.

'JUST LET US OVER THE BORDER, YOU FUU...!'

The nearest soldier jumped backwards, out of reach of the screaming red-faced Australian who lunged out of my car window. The others, less intimidated by the yelling, jostled forward cradling their AK-47s.

How did I end up here? Sitting in a 20-year-old London taxi in the middle of the Baluchistan desert, on the Iran–Pakistan border, with a raging Aussie hitchhiker who was trying to start a fist fight with a bunch of armed conscripts.

Oh, yeah, that's right, I listened to my idiot friend, Paul. But where was he now? He was long gone.

I closed my eyes and tried to zone out from the chaos for a moment.

When I opened them the view hadn't changed. I was still staring out through the filthy cracked windscreen at the rolls of barbed wire that marked the all-important border, our holy grail.

Sweat dripped off my scraggy beard.

I eyed the gauges on the dashboard wearily; the temperature seemed to be holding steady, but the fuel gauge was barely at halfway. Getting across this border relied heavily on this beaten-up, jetlagged taxi not packing up. Beyond this lay 350 miles of Taliban-controlled desert, baking with 50-degree heat. My two best friends were hundreds of miles away and I had been left to navigate this desolate landscape, with its recent spate of kidnappings, drug smuggling and banditry, with a passenger who seemed hell-bent on getting us arrested, or worse.

The Aussie started afresh: 'I'M GONNA KILL YOU, YOU LITTLE FUU...'

How the *hell* did I end up here?

Three years earlier and thousands of miles away, a different black cab raced along the rainy Birmingham expressway:

'Been busy tonight?'

How many times had this guy been made to suffer that question?

I didn't actually care about the answer and he knew it. I was pretty sure he didn't care either, yet the awkward charade played out in its usual way. He replied with the standardised formula that he used when other punters slurred the very same question through the pay hole in the plastic barrier: a non-engaging comment on the traffic, a reference to which club had chucked out the most people, a generic moan about recent roadworks.

'Cool,' I replied, returning to my intoxicated thoughts, only just managing to stop myself from asking him what time his shift would end.

I was dressed up like a Thunderbird. The reason for this escapes me, but I took comfort in the fact that everyone else at the party had also been in fancy dress. I had been just on the right side of tipsy until I'd been roped into that round of shots, and now I was firmly in the 'I reckon that tree is climbable' reckless and excitable stage of inebriation.

The yellow felt of my Thunderbird boots had turned black from the sweat and beer and vomit and blood and dirt and blue alcopop on the club floor. None of these constituents were actually black, yet they had somehow mixed together to form a black slime. I pondered this great unanswerable question for a handful of seconds, until my thoughts returned to how long the taxi was taking to get me home, where my warm bed – and tomorrow's hangover – awaited me. The fare was getting expensive; incredibly so.

I had been discussing earlier that night with my best friend Leigh what to do after we graduated. Ideas began to surface as the beer flowed; he wanted to have a driving adventure somewhere – as 'travelling around the world with a plane ticket that stops in just six places is for pussies' – and I thought that sounded fun.

The taxi driver and I were pootling along the expressway five minutes later and I began to wonder about the longest ever taxi ride. Maybe there was a world record? That would be a world record worth having! Not quite as noble as the fastest 100 m sprint, perhaps, or some of the Arctic adventures or mountain climbing ones... but definitely better than having the world's longest fingernails or spending the longest time in a bathtub of baked beans—

'HOW MUCH!?'

We'd finally pulled up outside my student house and it appeared as though I was in the process of being mugged. I considered contacting Guinness to tell them that I had just broken the world record for the most expensive taxi ride ever.

Once I got inside, I heard Greg snoring in his room and Johno's room was locked. When Johno's room is locked, it's best not to think about what he's doing – let alone disturb him – so I went into the kitchen to raid the fridge.

Living with Paul was sometimes a challenge. He has one of those uniquely loud voices that seem to pierce through all other sounds. A few times over the past year Paul had arrived back home later than me with friends in tow. As they sat up in our squalid living room putting the world to rights, I could hear a low murmur from them all... apart from Paul, whose entire side of the conversation was clearly audible even from the floor above me.

However, tonight was different. There seemed to be a different voice booming down the stairs and through my door. In my sleepiness I wasn't quite sure that I was hearing things right. The voice was saying:

'... living in groups can lead to particular problems...'

I sat up in bed and strained my ears to catch some more of the stranger's conversation.

'... instead of laying eggs...'

Eggs? I shivered as I pulled on my tatty dressing gown. I'd have to investigate.

'... pull it through its mother's fur towards the pouch on her belly...'

I wearily opened my door and climbed the stairs. What was going on up there?

'... last season's joeys are now fast approaching independence.'

I didn't expect the sight that greeted me as I opened the living-room door.

There sat my best friend and housemate, a 20-year-old man, dressed as John Tracy, wolfing down a pizza and glued to a David Attenborough documentary on kangaroos.

I wasn't particularly patient.

'What the hell are you doing, can't you turn it down it a bit?'

His eyes didn't leave the screen.

'Sorry dude, someone's lost the remote... but check out these kangaroos – they're amazing! Did you know the babies live in their pouches until they're nine months old?'

'I really don't care, Paul, I was asleep.'

'Mate!' he said, suddenly turning to face me, 'let's drive a taxi to Australia!'

So, naturally, I did what anyone would do when confronted with a drunken Thunderbird asking them to drive halfway around the world at two o'clock on a Tuesday morning.

I told him to stop being so fucking stupid and to go to bed.

CHAPTER 1

NEVER PLAN AN EXPEDITION IN A PUB

Paul was the first person I ever met at university, and in the three years we were there he had constantly been coming up with crazy ideas and then failing to follow through with them. I had quickly learned that it was much easier just to say yes and wait for him to forget about the schemes than to argue why it wasn't a sensible idea to waterski across the North Sea or turn up to lectures wearing 1950s fancy dress.

So when I sleepily reminded Paul the next morning of his barely coherent ramblings about driving a taxi to Australia, I immediately regretted my schoolboy error. My heart sank as I saw his eyes widen in recollection of the plan and then grow bright with the possibilities. I braced myself for an afternoon's verbal assault.

It had already been a hard day for me. I had checked Facebook a couple of hundred times, caught up with my daily episode of *Neighbours*, made some toast, looked out of the window and played a bit of PlayStation; I was rapidly running out of things to do.

I glanced over at the dusty engineering textbook lying on my desk. Surely things weren't so desperate that I was actually considering doing university work? I tried to think of an alternative but my mind came up blank. I started to reach for the book. Just as my fate was about to be sealed, Paul burst into my room wearing his threadbare, stained dressing gown, bowl of cereal in hand.

'So this taxi idea,' he started, plonking himself down on my bed, 'you in?'

Although there was no way I was getting involved in such a foolish idea I decided to humour Paul a little and ran through all the reasons he wouldn't be able to complete the journey. Somehow through his sheer enthusiasm he managed to counter my every argument.

'How are you going to afford this?'

'I dunno, we'll get sponsors or something.'

'Right, OK. When are you going to have time to do this?'

'We'll do it after our graduation, that gives us two years to plan.'

'Where the hell are you going to get a black cab from?'

'Auto Trader, classifieds, eBay, ask cabbies when we get rides back from nights out; there's loads of places.'

'Wait a minute...' I thought I finally had him, '... you don't know anything at all about cars.'

He faltered for the first time, then quickly recovered. 'Leigh!' he gushed, beaming. 'Leigh says he knows how to fix cars and has wanted to do something like this for ages! Come on it'll be *well* funny.'

I knew he would never go through with it and I had to say something drastic to get him out of my room so I could go back to watching 'Greatest Fails of the Year' on YouTube.

'Alright,' I sighed, 'I'm in. Now leave me alone, I've got an essay to write.'

Only slightly perturbed by Johno not instantly jumping up, pledging his dedication to the project and then celebrating the genius of my idea with a nice cup of tea, I decided to call Leigh. Although not the hardiest of travellers (his most adventurous journey to date was teaching chubby American kids how to climb walls at Camp America), he was a great mate and he could fix cars.

He answered the phone in his dulcet Midlands tones.

'Alright, Dickhead.'

'Alright, good night last night?'

'Yeah great, or I think it was anyway… whose idea was it to do the shots?'

'Dunno. So… err… remember you said you want to go on an adventure? D'ya fancy driving a black cab to Australia when we graduate?'

'Yeah, alright.'

'Sweet.'

'Cool, see you in a bit.'

'See ya… oh Leigh, you said you can fix cars last night, didn't you?'

'Yeah, no problem.'

He hung up. I had a teammate for this adventure – and one who could fix a car at that.

Or at least claimed he could.

Leigh had also once claimed he could snowboard as well, but after one rather painful day resulting in a broken thumb, it emerged that he'd never actually been snowboarding, he was just pretty sure he'd be able to do it.

I put my doubts about his engineering prowess aside – he had said yes in about one second flat, as though a mate calling you up after a night out and asking if you fancied driving to the other side of the world in an iconic form of London transport was a regular occurrence.

It was time to start planning.

The planning process for an expedition of this importance and magnitude is highly complex, so a few days later we packed up a map and a laptop and headed to the pub, where Johno, ex-RAF-pilot-trainee-turned-student and never one to miss out on a pint or adventure, joined us to 'consult'.

Now, here, you'll see, is where we made our first – and possibly gravest – error of the trip: never plan anything in a pub.

We agreed right away that a black cab would have to be the vehicle. There were no options other than possibly a yellow New York cab, and it was agreed that that was hardly very British. Next came the route. London to Sydney seemed as good as any; none of us had been to Australia and we fancied seeing some kangaroos. As we started looking at the map and sketching out a roughly direct route to Sydney, some bright spark pointed out that a true black cab driver would take the longest route possible to 'rack up the meter'.

Before long, a marker pen had carved a line across the map passing through Europe, Russia, Africa, the Middle East, India, China, South East Asia and Australia, with a beer spill smudging the line somewhere over Cambodia.

This idea was faultless, perfect and, most importantly, hilarious.

Well, it was at the time at least. And the more we thought about it (which was directly proportionate to the amount we drank) the funnier it got, and, as the owner of a big camera (the basic requirements for the job), we had even persuaded Johno to come as the official expedition photographer. Leigh was the mechanic and I, being the holder of no actual skills of note (or a big camera), would deal with borders.

What could go wrong?

Now that Paul and Leigh had mentioned the journey more than a few times I started to realise, with both horror and excitement, that it might actually happen. My enthusiasm for the idea started to grow. Before long, I had told anyone and everyone who would listen about our planned post-graduation journey. However, when bemused friends and family and incredulous workmates greeted the plan with a sea of rolled eyes and smirks, we quickly decided that we needed to give our idea some kind of collateral. We needed to buy ourselves a taxi.

After scouring the Internet and classified papers we eventually found what seemed to be the perfect model. The LTI FX4 is the iconic London black cab, famous throughout the world, and

Leigh had managed to find a 1992 model going for the bargain price of £1,350 on eBay, hidden amongst the knock-off iPods, old CDs and pieces of toast with the image of Jesus burnt into them. Leigh thought that the 1990s workhorse was a good deal but unfortunately he couldn't make it down to London to check it out in person. This left Paul and I, meticulously briefed, to go along with £450 from each of our student loans in our pockets, to inspect the car.

So that's how we found ourselves on the outskirts of London, mugs of tea in hand, strolling round a vehicle we had both ridden in many times but never properly looked at, kicking the wheels and trying to give the impression that we knew what we were talking about.

'Hmm, it says it has done ninety-nine thousand nine hundred and ninety-nine miles here,' I commented, looking at the ancient odometer, 'that seems like quite a lot?'

'Oh, don't pay no notice to that,' replied the cockney salesman, 'the mile reading is stuck.'

'So how many miles *has* it done?'

He furrowed his brow. 'Probably about three-hundred thou.'

Paul and I looked at each other and shrugged – how bad could it be?

'We'll take it.'

CHAPTER 2

HARD HEARTED HANNAH

I watched impatiently as the signal on my phone flashed 'Searching'. I had just finished my final exam at university, and quite possibly my final exam ever – marking a triumphant finale to my overwhelmingly average academic career.

In theory, I had been working up to this moment since I was five years old. Had I not been so laser-focused on finding signal so I could track down my friends and have a mammoth celebration, the reality of graduate jobs, real life, growing up, marriage, kids, pets, retirement and death would have been crushing.

I watched as 'Searching' suddenly turned to a bar of signal, then two, and then the phone started to ring and a London number showed on the screen.

Oh God, please tell me they haven't travelled to London to celebrate? I'm still stuck in bloody Birmingham!

'Hello?'

'Hi Paul, it's Matt,' said a man with a strong Essex voice. Matt... Matt... None of my friends are called Matt? I had no idea who this was.

'Matt! Mate! How's it going?' I replied searchingly, hoping for something that would help me identify this Essex man called Matt who was calling me immediately after my final exam.

'Good mate, you?'

Not helping, *Matt*.

'Yeah, great actually, just walked out of my final exam, I'm finished!'

'Fantastic, mate, congratulations.'

Still not helping, *Matt*.

'Yeah, thanks.'

His chirpy tone suddenly turned serious, almost sombre.

'Right, Paul, we've come to a decision.'

'Great… on what?'

'On the Non Standard Awards, of course.'

Ooooh, *that* Matt!

The taxi dream had fallen somewhat by the wayside, forgotten amongst finals and the realisation that, even though we had bought the cab, we couldn't afford the trip. In a last-ditch attempt, we had applied for the Performance Direct Non Standard Awards, a competition that awards cash to people doing non-standard and generally stupid things with cars. We had got through the preliminary stages and had gone to their office a few months previously to give a presentation on our expedition idea.

It had been a stab in the dark, but we figured we would give it our all. We had the local printer make us some smart polo shirts with 'It's on the Meter' stamped on the front, took our slightly beer stained map, redrew the line over Cambodia and bought a miniature model of a London taxi.

Our presentation plan had been simple: lay the map on the table, tell them that we were going to drive a taxi to Australia, then, in case that wasn't clear, we'd push the little taxi along the route making car noises. We'd then show them a picture of the real taxi to prove that we were serious, show them a picture of a kangaroo to illustrate the typical wildlife we would encounter along the way, grab a muffin from the pile in the centre of the table, and kick back and wait for the praise and money to flow in.

Unfortunately it wasn't quite so straightforward. Johno's car noises sounded like a race car, which was clearly inaccurate, they'd eaten all the muffins by the time we arrived and, instead of praise and money, complicated questions started to flow.

We were pretty well prepared to answer these after nearly two years of research and Leigh could answer most of the technical questions, but when the overlanding expert looked at our idea to assess the feasibility of the hare-brained scheme, he didn't seem too impressed.

'Are you definitely going through Pakistan? You'll die if you try to drive through Pakistan in a black cab. In fact you'll probably die if you drive through it in anything.'

We had left the meeting feeling rather sceptical. As time passed with no contact, we had given up any hope of acquiring the sponsorship, and now here he was calling me to break the bad news.

The tone of Matt's voice confirmed what I had feared.

'So, we've decided…'

Here it comes. I was ready with my gracious defeat speech.

'… to give you the Non Standard Award.'

We had won! This group of idiots (sorry, Matt and co) had faith that the three of us and our 20-year-old black cab would make it to Sydney. So much faith that they actually wrote us a cheque. This news was incredible: the expedition was going to happen.

Although we would be putting everything we owned into this expedition, it would still be very, very expensive. Winning the Non Standard Award would cover our fuel and a couple of visas; the money we had accumulated from years of saving and working non-stop for a year, plus an overdraft or two each, would pay for the rest of the trip, but we would need more.

We realised quite early on that the black cab and the preposterous nature of the trip, coupled with a potential world record for the longest ever journey by taxi, made the expedition quite unique; there would be amazing stories and photos along the trip which meant we would be able to garner some media attention. Performance Direct's conditions of us winning the award were that we would maximise the exposure of the expedition and cover the cab in their stickers. If they would give us a load of cash to do this in return for the media coverage their brand would get, why wouldn't other companies? We started working on getting more sponsors.

Then there was the cab itself. What do you do to a decrepit old rust bucket of a taxi to prepare it for an around the world expedition?

The preparations to make the taxi roadworthy seemed never-ending, but thank God for the power of sponsorship: if you ask companies for money, you'll almost always get a no, but if you ask for a product they'll give you two. Winter tyres arrived from MaxSport in Ireland, cameras came from Korea, and a race-spec alternator and starter engine were customised to fit the taxi by the lovely folks at WOSP Racing. Samco donated a set of custom silicone hoses for every hose in the engine and a giant Kamei roof box arrived from the Roof Box Company.

The cab's suspension was never going to cope with the mileage, so Paul acquired some double-strength leaf springs from a tractor yard in Staffordshire and front springs from a truck suspension maker in Sheffield. We found an old Land Rover roof rack for sale in Kidderminster and welded it on for storage. All the while a load of personal equipment, bags, cameras, sunglasses and clothes started arriving in the post.

Leigh had been ordering the car parts, and a pile of cardboard boxes in various shapes and sizes sat next to the taxi. One particularly heavy and awkward one begged the question: 'What is this?'

'It's the winch bar.'

'The what? I thought we agreed not to get a winch?' I ventured.

'No, we said we would.'

'We definitely didn't,' Paul cut in.

'How much was it?'

'Five hundred.'

'Bloody hell mate, we've got to send that back, we don't need it, nor can we afford it – that's a person's living allowance in Asia for two months.'

'Can't,' Leigh replied. 'It's custom built for us.'

'So we can't return it?'

'Nope.'

'Balls. Tenner says we never have to use it. But it's custom built for a London black cab? So it will just slide on easily, right?'

'Yup.'

Two and a half weeks of drilling, welding, bolting, a few fires and lots of swearing (especially from Leigh's girlfriend) later, the winch was finally attached. This put us two weeks behind schedule, which meant we had just a fortnight to do everything else.

The months leading up to our journey were spent snatching a few hours' sleep a night on a friend's floor near our makeshift workshop in the basement of Aston University, as Leigh and I struggled to bring the car up to a driveable standard. Paul finalised all the sponsorship and press preparations during the day and joined us on the car each night. Our tempers and friendships grew increasingly strained as we put in marathon work hours; at one point Leigh and I worked on the car for over 50 hours without sleeping. We decided to have a rest after I had jolted awake to find myself holding a still-running heavy-duty power drill inside the stripped-out taxi frame.

Late one evening when we were working on the stripped-out cab, our sound system arrived. We obviously knew that in the grand scheme of things, we needed to have wheels and seats before a sound system. However, we were three young lads, and when

JBL says it'll give you a free sound system, you say yes – but we did add that it needed to be one of their compact versions as we were very limited on space already. However, the box that arrived was anything but compact. We had been delivered a 1,000-watt subwoofer, two huge amplifiers, an iPod-ready head unit and speakers to match.

Pete, one of the awesome people who rolled up their sleeves to help us with the final push to get everything done in the workshop, said that it would be impossible to fit in – we just didn't have the space due to all the tools and spare parts, and he was right. The three of us looked at each other and asked the silent question: 'Would we be the lads who got stuck in the desert because we chucked out a spare part to fit in a humongous sound system?'

Without speaking, the three of us started removing tools from the car, while scrolling through our iPods to find the bassiest tracks we had to test out our brand new system.

It set the precedent for the trip. We were going to be 'those guys'.

Our cab was becoming quite unique, but we still didn't have a name for her. I had recently heard the classic 1920s song 'Hard Hearted Hannah (the Vamp of Savannah)', about a famous femme fatale in Georgia who hated men and relished watching them suffer. At the time, 'Hannah' seemed like the perfect name for our little cab. Little did we know that she would live up to her moniker, time and time (and time!) again.

CHAPTER 3

NO U-TURNS

Our trip officially began outside the London Transport Museum in Covent Garden on 17 February 2011. The custom-built taximeter was ceremoniously switched on and the press were there, gaining us more valuable coverage for the Red Cross, who we were fundraising for.

We were waved off by tearful and jubilant friends and family, as we drove across Tower Bridge, trailed by a parade of vintage pre-war taxis, before heading out of London and south towards Dover – and Hannah the taxi's first foreign country. It all seemed to go so well and nobody seemed to notice that we had no idea what on earth we were doing.

The stress of the months of hard work and uncertainties, of lost tempers and strained friendships, of undelivered promises and endless problems, evaporated the second we drove on to the ferry and set sail for France. That single moment made everything worthwhile and in an instant all the petty arguments of the previous months were forgotten. We were the best of friends again; this was it, we were finally living our dream.

Of course in reality those problems still existed: due to a lack of funds and, more critically, time, we were barely even roadworthy. The brakes were so spongy and ineffective that they bordered on dangerous, the indicators only worked occasionally and the driver's seatbelt constantly jammed leaving the driver locked back in his seat, unable to turn to see his blind spot.

We also had no working fog lights and no heating, the importance of which quickly became apparent as we raced into smoke-like fog banks on the gloomy French autoroutes on the way down to Paris. I was constantly bracing myself for a rear-end collision with a French 18-wheeler as I sat, shivering, in the back seat, while Paul and Leigh peered out of gaps wiped in the steamed-up windscreen.

My fears were unfounded and after what seemed like far too short a drive, Leigh faithfully followed the satnav directions off the autoroute, away from the junctions clearly marked 'Paris' and on to mist-shrouded country lanes. As we passed increasingly tiny French towns and villages, their streets paved with cobblestones and lined with pretty little patisseries, we all realised something was amiss. As pretty as *les hamlets* were, this didn't feel like the right way to get to Paris.

We jerked to a halt at a camouflaged traffic light and tried to find the problem. An ancient French lady shuffled past the idling, steamed-up taxi with a bemused look on her face as we fiddled around with the settings buried deep in the guts of the satnav.

'No wonder we thought this thing was crap!' I cried. 'The bloody thing is on No U-turns!'

Despite this hiccup, at least we were on our way, and now we were nearly at our first destination. We had actually managed to agree upon a specific route quite early on in the planning. Australia was the goal but there was more than one way of reaching it. Apart from detours to see other countries, there were three main routes to choose from (avoiding Afghanistan at least).

The northern route, through Europe, Siberia and Kazakhstan before heading south into China, looked quite good, but we'd heard the roads were atrocious almost the entire way – if you could call them roads at all. The central route wound through Turkey, Turkmenistan and the rest of the 'Stans', and had pretty bad roads and a raft of challenging entry visas to secure. Finally, the southern route, crossing Iran, Pakistan, India, Nepal and Tibet, was the most dangerous, but it involved going through some incredibly interesting and diverse countries, plus a crossing of the Himalayas. More importantly than that, the route was, in theory, entirely paved, and when driving a two-wheel-drive taxi designed for the inner streets of London, this was the obvious one to take.

After one drawn-out day at university spent with Google Maps and a laptop, we had come up with a first draft that was acceptable to everyone, but further research and tweaking had continued to take place as new information came to light. We would have to deal with closed African land borders, border-crossing difficulties in Israel and the neighbouring Arab states, and we realised what an expensive, impractical and difficult detour Mongolia would make. However, the route remained essentially the same as it had started out in spirit: an overly meandering path from London to Sydney through some of the most varied and extreme terrain in the world, from the frozen Arctic to some of the hottest deserts.

After driving down to Paris, we would turn north to Scandinavia and the Arctic Circle, then down through Russia. We'd then swing back west through Eastern and Central Europe before driving through the Middle East to join the ancient Silk Road through Iran and Pakistan and into India.

The plan was to then head north through Nepal and China, before cutting through the middle of China down to South East Asia and shipping the taxi to Australia from Singapore. The drive down the east coast of Australia would make up the final leg. We'd hopefully cross the Sydney Harbour Bridge about nine months and 30,000 miles after we'd left England, easily breaking the current record of 21,691 miles, set in 1994 by three bankers who drove from London to Cape Town and back.

So why was our first stop Paris? We weren't exactly sure, but my aunt lives there and had promised us champagne on arrival, and apparently that's all it takes for us to make a 250-mile detour. Plus the photo opportunities seemed too good to miss.

CHAPTER 4

- - - - - - - -

THE HORNY DUTCH CAT

Touring the outskirts of Paris and crawling through the fog, we eventually arrived, after seven hours of driving, at my aunt's house at 4 a.m. Exhausted, we slept for the first full night in weeks, and in the morning we ate croissants and baguettes and finally packed the car properly. Despite the roomy taxi interior, space was at a premium as we had been joined on the London to Berlin leg by our good friend Chops, further adding to the mountain of bags and spare parts we were carrying.

The next day we headed off before dawn to get the first landmark picture of Hannah's travels: we imagined her parked proudly in front of the famous Eiffel Tower, which would be all lit up and looking majestic. It would be all we'd have time to see in Paris, but we had to keep moving, and we thought it would make a nice memento of our short time in the City of Light. However, when we got there the tower's lights were out and it was shrouded in fog. Not the types to be so easily defeated, after checking there was no security around (it was 4.30 a.m.), we unclipped a fence that said *'Piétons seulement'*, 'Pedestrians only', drove down the Champs de Mars, got the best picture possible, considering the dark, and got on our way.

One of the many things on our biblical to-do list that had slipped during the manic final week before leaving was to book accommodation at our next stop: Amsterdam, European capital of prostitutes, weed and stag parties. After one of the most stressful and hectic months of our lives, we were ready to pull on our party boots and were expecting big things. However, a last-minute Internet search just before we left Paris had horrified us as we saw the extortionate hostel prices, particularly at the weekend. The thought of paying over €100 for one night in a grotty hostel filled with British 'lads on tour' forced the others to take my suggestion of Couchsurfing seriously.

I had been Couchsurfing for a few years and singing its praises to unconvinced friends for nearly as long. The idea of finding a host who is willing to let you stay in their home for free, in a reciprocal-karma-community kind of way, appealed to me. The search for a like-minded host can be narrowed down by any number of factors from age and gender, to music interests or life philosophy, and a feedback system keeps the whole process pretty safe.

I originally started using Couchsurfing as a way to save money on a previous trip to pricey Helsinki, but soon found that the hosts were almost universally interesting and friendly people who delighted in showing surfers a side of their cities not usually seen by guidebook-clutching tourists. Far from being awkward or uncomfortable I had found that staying in the home of a total stranger was a great way of travelling and I had since used the site for trips all over Europe.

We had just entered Belgium when my phone vibrated with a message from a Dutch Couchsurfer named Jasper, inviting us to stay and giving a postcode for our satnav. With my previous Couchsurfing I had always searched and chosen specific hosts based on similar interests, but due to the eleventh-hour nature of this request I had posted our situation in a last-minute group, basically asking the whole of the Amsterdam community if any of them would host us.

Meeting new Couchsurfers is always a bit of a nerve-wracking experience, but as we sped ever north towards the city, not knowing anything about Jasper other than his name, address and telephone number, and with three sceptical friends in tow, it seemed especially ominous. When the satnav took us to what appeared to be a derelict industrial estate on the outskirts of Amsterdam, the derisive voices began:

'Are you sure this is the right place, Johno?'

'There's nothing here.'

They were right. All we could see were low industrial buildings with roller-shutters long since pulled down, and the occasional vacant two-storey office building with flaking white paint and overgrown parking spaces. It seemed almost as if someone had played a trick at our expense.

The idea of just inviting yourself round to someone's house and sleeping on their sofa is just plain weird. No matter how much Johno tried to persuade Leigh and me, I just thought it was one of his strange Johnoisms. He's northern and also a fan of freeganism (he claims it's good for the environment or something), but being so tight you'll hunt in supermarket bins for free food is a step too far for me, no matter how skint I am.

I was worried that kipping on a stranger's sofa could be another such experience.

However, having now developed a healthy disregard for the satnav's ability, we had little faith that the empty industrial estate we finally rocked up at was the right place.

'You have reached your destination.'

'This is not our fucking destination, this is a derelict office block,' Leigh correctly informed the inanimate object. Just then a man with floppy hair, who looked inherently Dutch, stuck his head out of a window and started waving.

'Hi, I'm Jasper, this is my house,' he announced as he led us into his huge living room. 'I don't pay very much rent because I prevent people squatting here.'

Vintage electric organs lined every inch of wall space that wasn't occupied by threadbare sofas. We threw our bags down in a pile in the middle of the room and made ourselves comfortable. Introductions were made, cups of tea were produced and Jasper asked, 'So, what do you want to do in Amsterdam?'

We had all decided on the drive to throw ourselves into the Dutch culture with vigour, and Leigh, in what was probably an attempt to endear himself to the stereotypical Dutch man, announced, 'We want to get really, really stoned.'

'Oh yes? Well, here's one I rolled earlier,' Jasper replied, pulling out a humongous joint.

We spent the next hour transfixed as Jasper jammed on the organ, occasionally pausing to comment philosophically on life in general, and to let us know why his cat was humping Chops' bag.

'She's on heat, so she wants to go out and have sex with lots of tomcats... but she has to stay indoors no matter what, so she tries to have sex with your bag, no?'

He carried on jamming for a bit before stopping to watch the cat again. She was obviously exceptionally hot and bothered, stretching out and rubbing herself against Johno's leg.

'Can you imagine being that horny? She's just so horny she can't function.'

We giggled in a moronic manner, then after an unidentifiable period of time we realised that we were all really rather stoned and that we hadn't spoken for an extremely long while. We thought that we were obviously too amateur to smoke in Holland and decided to head into town for something we had a bit more experience with: beer.

As the alcohol flowed and we slowly regained our power of speech, our group of five had become ten, then 15; some of them Jasper's friends, others just random pub-goers or friends of friends. Eventually it was decided that we would all pick up some booze and head to one of their houses, which turned out to be a large, open-plan, beautifully furnished top-floor flat. Everybody crammed in, guitars appeared and joints were washed down with cheap wine and bad songs.

I told the owner how lovely her house was and she thanked me, swigging red from the bottle.

'It's actually used for filming a lot.'

'Really? Amazing! For TV and stuff?' I asked, impressed.

'No... not for TV – for porn. In fact they were doing a movie in here just yesterday,' she said, perfectly casually. 'We had two girls over there on the table and, actually, a boy–girl scene just where you're sitting right now...'

'Oh, how, err, lovely.'

I suddenly felt incredibly English as I leant forward from the sofa I was sat on, now somewhat unsure of where to safely rest my hands.

The thing I remember most vividly about that night was the intense look in Paul's eyes. During the five years I had known him I had never seen him looking as afraid as he did at that moment, sitting across the room from me mouthing, 'We have to leave here, right now!'

I was sat on a bright-red leather sofa, sandwiched in between a well-groomed and immaculately dressed guy in his 20s and his much older female partner, who presumably owned the luxurious flat. Each of them had a hand resting suggestively on my thigh and I had spent the past 20 minutes trying to figure out whether they were hitting on me or whether the evening's immersion in Dutch coffee-shop culture had left me too paranoid for my own good.

They had forgotten me for a moment though; distracted by a brewing argument between one of their party guests and our new friend and host, Jasper.

With the couple's attention elsewhere Paul hissed at me in a low tone, 'Dude! We have to get out of here, that guy just actually threatened to kill me.'

I summoned some mental clarity and thought over the past few minutes. From what I could tell, the troublemaker party guest had suddenly ripped off his shirt and pulled down his trousers before grabbing the quintessential Dutch flower, a tulip, from a vase on the glass coffee table. He then proceeded to shove the tulip where no tulip should go and dance around, completely naked, trying to whack other guests in the face with the pretty end.

Paul and Leigh were eager to record some of our experiences throughout the trip, so they pulled out our sponsor-provided pocket video cameras and slyly started filming the whole affair from opposite sides of the room. Unfortunately, Paul was not so sly.

The next thing we knew, an inexplicably topless Jasper was doing his hardest to calm the increasingly irate Mr Tulip, promising that Leigh and the now heavily sweating Paul would delete the videos.

Snapping out of my meditations, I slapped away the hands from my thighs and said decisively, 'OK guys, I think it's about time for us to get going, thanks for having us.'

I was pretty gutted they made me delete the video: I knew that if I told someone we went to Amsterdam where we partied on a porn set and a Dutch guy stripped naked and shoved a tulip up his arse, they simply wouldn't believe me.

Jasper had found his top and hopped out of the house behind us.

'Fuck them, I stole some of their wine, too!' he shouted, laughing as he cracked open a bottle.

We hadn't gone more than a few metres before two police officers pulled up behind us on their bicycles and informed us that street drinking was illegal in this area and we must throw away the wine immediately. Jasper got rowdy and started to kick off about something in Dutch, all the while cheekily swigging the wine. The police told him if he kept on drinking, they would arrest him.

'OK, OK, OK,' Jasper replied as he casually walked over to a bin. Just as he was about to put the wine in the bin, he looked up, caught the policeman's eye and took a heroic swig before smashing the bottle into the bin.

Out came the cuffs and a van was soon on the scene to cart Jasper away. We stood around awkwardly, unsure of what to do. As Jasper was manhandled off, he somehow managed to fling a set of keys at us, along with a strained, 'I'll seeee you back at the flaaat.'

Thanks to the hordes of mainly British and American rowdy tourists, the Amsterdam police are remarkably experienced and efficient at dealing with 'antisocial behaviour', and we were relieved to get a text message soon after from the angry Jasper, saying that he was now on his way home with nothing more than a €70 fine and a bruised ego.

As soon as he got in he cracked open the bottle of French wine we had brought from Paris as a thank you gift and told us that apparently the main problem hadn't been that he was drinking, but that he refused to show the police his identification – something he furiously disagreed with on principle.

As the level of wine in the bottle dropped, Jasper grew calmer and calmer until he suddenly sat bolt upright.

'Guys!' he yelled, startled, '… where is the cat?'

CHAPTER 5

DUDE, WHERE'S MY CAB?

It took the best part of 13 hours of straight driving to get to Berlin, with the most exciting moment coming when our meter successfully went over its first £1,000 without any millennium bug-style disasters. The German countryside passed by in a hungover blur; little villages and green fields that we half-heartedly watched as the day drew on. We had arranged to stay at one of my brother's friend's houses – her name was Anne, and she lived in Berlin, so she was rapidly dubbed 'Anne Berlin', much to her puzzlement – but unfortunately by the time we arrived it was 1 a.m.

Buzzing from the fact that after three years we were finally on the road, we were ready to go out again. But we assumed that nothing would be open, especially on a Sunday and at this time of night.

Anne tutted at our ignorance. 'My God, guys, this is Berlin, anything goes. The clubs stay open all night.'

'Even the filthy rave clubs?'

'Yes Paul, even the "filthy rave clubs",' she impatiently scolded.

'Do we need to dress up, wear shoes?'

'You really don't understand Berlin,' she said, 'we'll just turn up like this.'

Apparently Anne didn't understand Berlin either. After being turned away from three different clubs for not being 'hip' enough, we eventually found ourselves in the only place that would take us, a German reggae bar complete with a man-made beach in the car park. After sampling some traditional German beverages, the conversation had turned to tattoos. The combination of peer pressure and alcohol somehow managed to persuade Chops that it would be a good idea to get a tattoo of the taxi, and with filmed footage of him agreeing to this we retired from the bar with a mission for the following day set in our heads.

When we came to, in a sprawl of sleeping bags and the scent of stale alcohol, lunchtime had been and gone, unnoticed by the five comatose people squeezed into the one-room apartment. Chops groaned with despair as soon as he was reminded of his promise and Leigh groaned even louder when he looked in a mirror and saw that after passing out upon our return someone had given him a new, very unflattering, haircut.

It was mid-afternoon by the time everyone was dressed and out the door, ready to jump in the taxi, see the sights and find a tattooist.

Paul reached the corner of the road first and turned to us all with a grin. 'Guys... where's the taxi?'

'Ha ha, very bloody funny!' snapped Leigh, who was not really in the mood for joking around after his unexpected haircut.

'No, really; the taxi is gone.'

'Why are you bloody laughing then?' asked Leigh.

'I'm not, I mean, I just don't know what else to do,' he said, suddenly serious, 'I swear I haven't moved it.'

The colour drained from all of our faces and a sense of dread settled deep in our stomachs as we looked at the empty space where we had parked the car the night before. How could we have lost the car on only the fifth day of the expedition, and who would steal such a conspicuous car? Could things really be over before they had even really begun?

When we got to the police station they informed us that the car had actually been towed, due to illegal parking, and not stolen. They made us pay them €150 to tell us where it was; all of the money, and more, that we had pooled for Chops' tattoo. Slightly depressed and rather concerned that we had already managed to misplace the car and had yet to leave Western Europe, we headed to the airport to drop off Chops. His part in our adventure was over; he went home tattooless, leaving the three of us to carry on to our next stop: Copenhagen.

It was cold. Bloody cold. And as we headed further and further north, past fields of whirring wind turbines, unsurprisingly, it got colder. We started to regret not fixing the heating system in the back when we were in more civilised climes. Wrapped up in skiwear and in a sleeping bag, with only his eyes and his woolly hat poking out, Leigh got a text from our planned Couchsurfing host for the night telling us that something had come up and we couldn't stay. So we put up another 'emergency' Couchsurfing message. Within 20 minutes a text came through:

> Hi, we have space for you, two spare rooms and we're having pizza tonight. This is our address, see you soon.

Amazing, this was perfect. Then another text followed soon after:

By the way, we are a same-sex couple and we're ordering a Hawaiian, we hope that is OK?

This was a bit awkward and not really that OK with one of our party: Leigh doesn't like pineapple and we didn't want to offend before we even arrived.

We arrived at Lars and Kian's very Scandinavian home soon after and, sure enough, found it was pizza night – which was made all the more awesome when we discovered that a ham pizza in Denmark has as much ham on it as cheese. Leigh picked out the pineapple and retired to the bathroom with some clippers to try to straighten out his hair.

We spent a delightful day in Copenhagen, and Lars and Kian were kind enough to give us a tour of the sights: the royal palace, the Guinness Book of Records Museum (it was closed, but we still posed for a picture outside) and the famous statue of the Little Mermaid sat on a mini island poking up out of the sea, which Leigh imitated for the camera. However, soon we had to be back on the road.

Shivering violently, having just scraped a thick layer of snow from the cab, I climbed in to find it was actually colder inside it than outside. Enough was enough; we were going to fix the heating.

The 1992 LTI FX4 has a very unique heating and cooling system. It is supposed to pump water around the engine to cool it and then the engine-heated water travels through a system of pipes to heat the car. At some point when we rebuilt the car, these pipes were removed, but never replaced: the area where the heat exchanger should go was where we had built a wooden storage compartment that had been christened 'The Bar' due to the 15 bottles of French wine we had filled it with to be used as bribes for police and gifts for Couchsurfing hosts.

After three hours in the car park of a DIY store, hacksawing, swearing and lying under the car in the snow trying not to get covered in antifreeze, we finished our haphazard fix. Two metal pipes protruded from the centre of the dashboard, around the handbrake and into the blower, which had been attached to the top of The Bar's lid, and wired into the electrics to successfully blow blissfully hot air into the face of the passenger in the back.

We could now go onwards to Sweden without freezing to death.

CHAPTER 6

- - - - - - - -

HERBS AND HIPPIES

You could tell immediately that Anders was in a band. It wasn't the recording studio or the guitar slung around his neck that gave it away, it was just the way he oozed cool. The long blonde hair, velvet shirt and gold medallion somehow combined to suit him perfectly.

Our new host welcomed us into the toasty studio and immediately presented a carton of red wine.

'And what do you play?' I asked to break the silence.

'I play the bass most of the time in the band, but my real love is the sitar.'

I should have guessed.

The rest of the band was similarly hip and undoubtedly would have had no problems getting into *filthy rave clubs*. One of them brought out a small pouch full of what looked suspiciously like rabbit droppings.

'This is Swedish *snus*, you have to try it.'

Against our better judgement we each placed a little brown pouch between our lips and gums as instructed, and waited for the tingling nicotine hit, which is apparently equivalent to smoking three cigarettes.

After a short jam we left the rest of the band to finish up their recording and drove out to the farm that Anders and his friends called home.

We pulled up to a small wooden cottage in the middle of a forest, around 45 minutes outside of Gothenburg.

In the kitchen stood a late 1960s John Lennon incarnate, his train driver's hat at a jaunty angle over his purple haze circular glasses, hands deep in a pile of dough.

'I fucking love making bread when I'm stoned,' he announced by way of introduction.

A previous batch of buns hot from the oven was presented to us with freshly churned butter and we dug in.

Anders walked in from the car, his shirt open to his navel, the medallion dangling amongst his long loose blonde locks and his flares dragging against the ground. It dawned on me that this man actually might be a cartoon character, and I was stuck in some sort of real-life *Roger Rabbit* mash-up where he conversed with John Lennon, the baker.

'Hey man, this herb bread will fuck you up,' said Lennon, staring at us from over his 'Imagine' glasses.

Herb bread. That would explain why everything suddenly felt very surreal.

Anders took us through to the living room where we were introduced to a group of girls dressed in odd spun-wool outfits – who turned out to be a travelling Lithuanian folk band – and the rest of Anders' crew of Summer of Love enthusiasts. The walls had fabric and tapestries of sorts hanging from them, as well as about ten guitars, and in the corner sat an old record player. We made ourselves comfortable on the deep sofas covered with throws.

'Tonight, we will only be listening to The Doors,' he announced to the audience of guests, nudging the needle over to start Jim Morrison's soulful warbling. We'd inadvertently walked into a time warp.

Jim's record spun out and gave way to a guitar, then a mandolin. I found a guitar in my hands and started to jam along. Someone else started hitting a bongo, and Lennon produced a flute from somewhere and proceeded to prove that he didn't know how to play it. The Lithuanians added a strange guttural drone with their singing, but Lennon was evidently bored and started to roll a joint. Once lit, he passed it over to me.

'I'm good mate, that "herb bread" was enough for me.' I was feeling rather spaced out.

'You liked my rosemary bread? It fucks you up, man, you just can't stop eating it, man, and it's so tasty. But do you want to get high?'

Ah.

Having learned my lesson in Amsterdam I respectfully declined and stuck to my carton of wine and watched the people at the party with a pseudo-scientific anthropological eye.

A smoky haze filled the entire house and now almost everyone was playing an instrument, including Leigh, and he doesn't know how to play anything for the life of him. The Lithuanians were sat on the floor chanting, cross-legged with closed eyes. After ten minutes they stopped their song and painstakingly explained the lyrics in English for our benefit. The overriding themes seemed to about virgin fairies riding bareback on horses through mystical lands.

Anders sat seemingly transfixed, listening intently to a strikingly pretty girl with long braided hair. He caught me looking over at the unlikely exchange and fired me a sly wink. It took all of my effort not to crack up at the entire situation but the tension was broken by one of the housemates.

'Come on guys!' he shouted, jumping up and surveying the room. 'Get your jackets on; it's time for the creepy midnight forest walk.'

Anders excused himself and his new lady-friend from the outing, and the rest of us tried our best to remain upright as we were taken out into the pitch-black pine forest along a frozen-over stream.

In the silent, freezing air we were told stories of the trolls that come over the border from Norway, who hate the electric lights of the city and hoard their mounds of gold up in the mountains or under bridges, ready to spirit away any beautiful maidens who pass by.

We made it to bed sometime in the early hours, the sounds of rock 'n' roll still reverberating from the nearby barn.

Stepping out of the warm, dark house and into the silent bright snow the next morning was almost like being in a dream. We were back on the road before most of the revellers had surfaced, heading to Stockholm, our next destination, on the long road north to the Arctic Circle.

As we followed the satnav back towards the main road, I got a new message. It was from Jasper:

> Hi guys, just to let you know that Cat came back today and she had a big smile on her face.

CHAPTER 7

- - - - - - - - -

THE HIPSTER ELVES

Arriving in Stockholm, we entered the address we had been given into the satnav:

Lönnvägen, Stockholm. Apparently, Lönnvägen means Maple Road, and it's a very common street name in Sweden – with four Lönnvägens in central Stockholm alone. After an old lady told us we had the wrong address (and that we had woken her up – or so we guessed from her nightgown and angry Swedish tones), we deduced that this address was not the right one. We headed off to the next Lönnvägen, on the other side of the city, to find this, too, was the wrong street.

On we trudged to Lönnvägen number three, faithfully following our satnav up a very steep hill. It was late February and over the past few days we had travelled far enough north through Europe to reach snow. It was about three feet deep over the whole city, but Hannah managed to make it up the hill, only to discover at the top that it was a dead end. We would have to go back down the snow-covered slope.

The Red Cross had promised to put us through an off-road driving skills course before we left, but it had turned out their instructor was in Sudan at the time, saving lives (and probably driving off-road in a skilful manner). Untutored, I turned the cab around and used my rudimentary knowledge of off-road driving, from the 20-second lesson Leigh taught me at the top of the hill, to work out how to get the two-tonne car without ABS braking, snow chains or spiked tyres down a 1-in-3 snow-covered incline. Cars were parked on both sides and at the bottom there was a T-junction. A wooden house stood at the foot of the hill, perfectly lined up to stop any out-of-control taxis careering down the slope. Through the window I could just make out a family about to start their evening meal as I edged the cab to the start of the drop, put it in first gear and took both feet off the pedals to allow the engine to slow it and prevent any skidding.

The engine started to idle high as we picked up speed, slowing us just enough. But at that moment, the gearbox made a huge THUNK and kicked itself out of gear into neutral. Unable to touch the brakes for fear of a collision into one of the Volvos on either side of the road, the cab started to bear down on the family's dinner at full speed. Leigh began repeating the same words faster and louder: 'Paul; gear', 'Paul; gear', 'GEAR!' While desperately trying to throw the stick back into gear, Hannah kept gaining speed and I could almost make out what was on their plates.

First gear had gone, and now we were already too fast for second. I jammed into third and with a roar of our strained engine we started to slow, just in time to hit the bottom of the hill. Turning hard right, the whole cab veered hard on its side and started to slide. Fortunately the loose snow stopped the top-heavy cab from flipping as she slid round, instead settling to a stop just around the corner, leaving us to check our heartbeats and observe the family dig in, oblivious to their near demise.

We found Johan's house at last; a small mansion he was house-sitting, complete with sauna and frozen garden. He welcomed us in and we told him of our near-death experience over a nice relaxing dinner.

Staying with Couchsurfers was brilliant for two reasons: firstly they often cooked their local speciality meals for us and secondly they showed us cool places in their city that we would never have found by ourselves. Johan did both of these things and after a good night's sleep, we found ourselves strapped into ice skates on a humongous frozen lake.

The entire circuit was ten miles long; no problem we thought as we raced off confidently. Two and a half miles and many slips later I fell by the wayside, and after five miles Leigh came and joined me in the outdoor cafe on the edge of the lake, laughing that I looked like 'Forrest Gump on Ice'.

We sat there eating the ubiquitous Swedish hot dogs and waited to be joined by a sweaty but triumphant Paul, who had finished the whole circuit.

After an evening of drinking and dancing to Abba songs at a university party that Johan took us to, we staggered out to the sauna – perhaps not advisable after the evening's dehydrating exertions. If we thought the heat of the sauna was a bad idea the previous night, we knew for certain that it was in the morning as we groaned and peeled ourselves out of bed for the 700-mile journey towards Finland and the Arctic Circle.

When people first started asking us why we were taking such a long route, why we were driving up to the Arctic Circle before heading out into Russia then down through North Africa, the Middle East, India, China and South East Asia, rather than just zipping down to Australia in a straight line, we thought it was funny to tell them that no true taxi driver ever takes you the shortest way. However, after explaining this time and time again – and particularly after hours of driving through the vast icy pine forests of northern Scandinavia – we didn't find our smart answer quite so funny.

During the days we exhausted our iPod music collections and chatted about every topic under the sun. We were sustained by the 'road sandwiches' that had become our staple diet. They were filled with various pastes of dubious origin that came from the rows of *ost* – squeezable tubes that filled the chilled section of every Scandinavian shop and whose contents ranged from reindeer to shrimp. After a few meals-worth of experimentation, our favourite turned out to be *BaconOst.*

After struggling up over the horizon at 9 a.m. the sun dipped back below it again at 4 p.m., which inevitably meant we had to drive in the dark. This night driving consisted of long solitary stretches of darkness punctuated by the sudden interruptions of the dazzling spotlights of giant oncoming wagons. Their explosively powerful lights could be seen from hundreds of metres away, to give the best possible chance of missing the moose, deer or any of the other dangerously large forest animals most likely to become roadkill.

Thankfully, the moment we crossed the border into Finland, at about 65 degrees north, the roads immediately became smoother and wider. We were now on the last stretch to Rovaniemi, capital of Lapland and best known for being the home of Santa Claus.

By now, we had got the hang of this Couchsurfing lark. It was cheap and easy and we had loads of fun. When we arrived in Rovaniemi, our host, Taina, and her family were incredibly welcoming. We became just three more of her large brood, digging into the vast pile of lovely food she set out and playing with Lego with her toddlers. On the way to their house we had seen two snowmobiles speeding along the banks of the river and over dinner Leigh mentioned that he would like to go for a ride on one of the giant jet-ski-like contraptions. We asked our hosts how we should go about hiring them but Taina and her husband, Tony, exchanged a look and said they didn't have a clue.

After the meal we went back to the Lego with the kids but outside the window there was the unmistakable 'rum… rum… rum… rumbababababababab' of a two-stroke engine starting up. I looked out and saw Tony on a huge snowmobile.

'You can go and have a ride if you want,' Taina said, beaming.

She didn't have to offer twice; I was already dressing in my snow boots, ski jacket and hat and running out the door. The controls were simple: push a little lever to go and pull another one to stop. I rode around in a little circle grinning like a schoolgirl on a pony.

'If you want, just follow that track, it goes to a meadow. Put these goggles on though,' Tony said, laughing at my enthusiasm.

My headlights showed a path in the snow heading into the dark forest, with barely enough room for me to squeeze between, let alone the snowmobile. Gingerly, I edged forward in short lurches as I got the feel for the throttle. Nothing was in front of me but trees and darkness. However, they soon disappeared, revealing a narrow meadow. Tentatively I started to build up speed as the wind whipped at my jacket and hat and snow beat against my goggles. Nothing was in front of me, so I went faster, and then faster still. Getting to the end, I spun round and floored it. The acceleration almost pulled my arms off and within a few seconds I was doing 35 mph, in the dark on a machine I'd never used before. Bringing it back to the house, I ran to the lads.

'You have GOT to come and play on this.'

Leigh sprung up and ran outside. By then a second snowmobile had appeared, so I sped off into the darkness, leaving Leigh lurching his way forward just as I had been.

After about 20 minutes of the most incredible fun, we went back and tried to get Johno.

'Maaaate, seriously, come and play. SERIOUSLY.'

'But it's freezing,' he replied, '... and I'm busy playing Lego.'

Since we'd been gone he'd built a rather impressive car-ship-house, which the three year old was attacking with his own house-car-ship. After a bit of gentle persuasion he was soon convinced and by that evening he was as hooked as we were.

The thick forests around Taina and Tony's house were zigzagged with snowmobile tracks. Their eldest daughter, Santra, and her friend had taken on the role of our guides and we spent the evening zooming around almost as fast as Hannah once we got to know how to use the machines.

It felt like we were in a computer game as the dim headlights illuminated the snow-covered boughs and the troll-like lumps of snow emerged out of the deep blackness. By the time we collapsed into bed that evening we had already planned another full day of snowmobiling; our planned departure down to Helsinki was now delayed with the minimum amount of persuasion.

The next morning our plan to drive all the way to Rovaniemi along the trails was foiled within a few hundred metres of the barn, as we sank the heavy machines into a deep snowdrift of soft powder reaching up to our chests. We had been cautioned to stay off the roads but the trails next to them were seldom used and covered with a heavy coating of fresh snow. Over the next two hours, we heaved the snowmobiles towards the more established tracks less than a half a mile away.

All the exertions were worth it though and by the afternoon the three of us were racing along at 40 mph on the two snowmobiles, swapping every so often to give everyone a turn at driving. It was the perfect way to blow off steam after weeks of being cooped up in our taxi. That was until Paul and I came around a corner and saw Leigh's snowmobile on its side next to a fallen tree, far ahead. About four metres in front of it, Leigh was lying on his back in the snow. He wasn't moving.

As we skidded to a halt, I noticed that we were in a massive open expanse and the tree that Leigh had hit was one of only a handful for hundreds of metres. He had managed to drive full-pelt into one of the solitary trees, catapult himself over the handlebars and fell the tree in the process.

'Quick, take a picture!' howled Paul, as Leigh came around and struggled to pick himself up out of the snow.

'Guys, the worst thing was...' Leigh giggled, once we had confirmed that both he and the snowmobile were unharmed, 'the last thing I remember is that I was humming the James Bond theme tune.'

Overjoyed from our day of snowmobiling, we relaxed in a sauna before being treated to the most incredible Northern Lights show from the roof of the barn. It was more spectacular than it is possible to describe, and nothing could have prepared us for how beautiful the display of colour was. We weren't missing the long days in the bowels of Aston engineering department's basement now.

The next day we visited the 'real' Santa Claus in Christmas Village, who signed our world record evidence book. Unfortunately, his elves – who were disappointingly full-sized humans with skinny jeans and hipster haircuts – wouldn't allow him to come and sit in the taxi for a picture.

Taina had one more surprise up her sleeve – Santra was home with her team of huskies, who needed running, so she took us husky sledding around the forest. It was the perfect way to end our time in Rovaniemi, and Taina and her family had made us so welcome that we almost didn't want to leave. Our few days here at the top of the world had quickly become a highlight of our trip.

We had planned to drive most of the length of Finland down to Helsinki over two days, but the extra hours snowmobiling and husky-sledding meant we now had a day to catch up on. Luckily the roads and weather were relatively calm for most of the way until we were a few hours north of the city, when a heavy snowstorm struck and our tiny windscreen wipers decided to quit.

One of the blades had pinged loose and was flapping around on the end of the wiper-arm, in danger of flying off into the slush, so we pulled over on the hard shoulder to attempt a quick fix. Standing there in the biting wind with 18-wheelers roaring past, I tried to snap the blade back into place with numb fingers. Suddenly the spring-loaded wiper arm slipped out of my hand and thwacked into the windscreen, sending cracks spiderwebbing across the glass.

I looked in horror at the guys through the windscreen for a painfully long few seconds before we all burst out laughing.

Barely a month earlier Leigh would have probably punched me in the face, but now he just chuckled at my clumsiness.

Thankfully the fractures hadn't reached all the way through the glass but we spent the rest of the drive trying to figure out where and how we would get a London taxi's windscreen replaced in Finland.

CHAPTER 8

TO THE EAST

After another party and another night of Couchsurfing, we were up and back on the road and heading to the Russian border. Leigh and I were sweating out the evening's booze thanks to the new heating system. We had spent the night at a gig watching a Finnish folk-punk duo called Jaakko & Jay. They had toured all over the world with some of my favourite bands and I felt a bit star-struck as we chatted with them in the club afterwards about life on the road. I felt a certain affinity between their touring lifestyle and our first three weeks on the road around Europe. We all just seemed to drive during the day then get drunk with strangers in the night, every day bringing a new city and new friends.

We had been acutely aware that every accidental hungover lie-in was a missed opportunity to explore the cultural richness of Europe but in reality we were also having a great time. After all, we were three 20-something lads who had been dreaming about this trip for years. It was natural that we wanted to let off a bit of steam and we knew that there would be plenty of great cultural sights to come, but for now we were content just to get our partying out of the way and see how the Europeans kept themselves entertained.

TO THE EAST

We drove along smooth roads through the snow-white landscape, drenched in the blindingly bright sunlight that can only be found in the early morning of the Scandinavian spring. It felt strange to be leaving Finland, where we had found an almost overly civilised society of some of the nicest people in the world. It was even stranger to think we were now about to enter Russia, the first really alien country and one that has always felt a lifetime away from my life in England.

This was our first real border – country number nine – and the first crossing where we had to have our documents checked. Our passports were seen by a gruff looking border guard in a woollen hat and a trench coat. He had the look of an extra from *Goldeneye* and we were all very excited as we realised we were entering real ex-Soviet land. Having budgeted for spending the day at the border, we were pleasantly surprised to be waved on and drove straight past the queues of lorries trying to go the other way.

'Well, that was an easy border crossing,' I chirped, as we were given back our passports and trundled down the heavily potholed road that lay between rows of grey-green pine trees. 'Let's stop here and see if we can get Russian car insurance.'

It was a windowless shack. Inside, there were rows and rows of cheap cigarettes and bottles of vodka of all shapes and sizes, but our requests for *machina insurance* were met with blank looks. A passing English speaker overheard our predicament and casually informed us that we were actually at an inter-border duty-free shop, not in the mighty motherland herself.

'This not Russia. This no-man's-land,' he graciously informed us, 'Russia: two kilometres!'

Paul and Leigh cursed me for speaking too soon.

'Johno! Why'd you have to go and jinx us. Now they're probably going to strip search us all,' moaned Leigh.

The road wound through a forest and a line of lorries materialised on the road ahead. We queued, our passports were looked at, our visas scrutinised, and we were presented with a form. I took the lead as the car and all the paperwork was in my name, and, besides, being the holder of no skills of note or a big camera, I was in charge of borders.

My English is OK, my French terrible and my Russian is limited to the word 'cheers' – and the only reason I knew this was because a barman once told me (he was from Bristol and had never been to Russia, so I wasn't even confident that was correct). Even worse than my Russian is my knowledge of the Cyrillic alphabet, which was all that was on the form. We laughed about the ludicrous situation, still elated by the excitement of our first border in an exciting country, but the problem started to seem insurmountable the more I analysed the form. The guard looked at me and shrugged in a fabulously Gallic manner when I asked for help. Eventually I was shown, by a helpful old woman who got out of her beaten-up Lada, to an old form taped to a window that had been completed in the Latin alphabet (but was still in Russian). Reverse-engineering the form against our V5 vehicle registration document, I eventually got to the end and presented it to the border guard with a flourish, grinning at my triumph.

He withdrew a red pen from the depths of his trench coat, crossing out, scribbling and circling all over my document, and handed it back to me. I looked at him blankly. Only when he took a new form from the stack and shoved it to my chest with a grunt did I realise he wanted me to redo the form. Unsure of what had to be done, I tried again, writing more clearly. The same thing happened, but he circled other sections in red this time. I filled in the form for the third time, made a mistake (biros and fingers don't work well in sub-zero temperatures) crossed it out, corrected it, then handed it in.

No mistakes allowed, do it again.

This process was repeated seven or eight times before the guard accepted the form and eventually allowed us through the border. We watched people in the queue of traffic ahead as they stopped at one last checkpoint and then sped off into the distance. We could almost taste the success of our first major border crossing.

After being channelled away from the main queue and into a warehouse, our eyes lit up as the first guard entered: she was the spitting image of Tatiana Romanova, the femme fatale from *From Russia With Love*. However, the second guard, who was clearly the dominant one, dragged us back down to reality, looking like a 1980s Bond villain who bench pressed Aston Martins with one arm. She was closely followed by a sniffer dog, its handler and more guards.

The guard barked something in Russian, which we assumed was something along the lines of: 'You have been specially selected for a customs inspection due to your good looks and charming personality.' Turns out it wasn't a compliment, as they thoroughly searched the cab, which we had left in a characteristic shit-tip. Every box was taken down and a sniffer dog gave it the once over. Panels were banged with fists and every nook and cranny had a nose shoved into it. We weren't sure what they were looking for and even more puzzled why anyone in Finland would be trying to transport illicit items *into* Russia anyway. Perhaps they were so confused to see a black cab at their border that they just had to see what was inside.

We were given the all clear – it was reassuring to know my two travel companions weren't secretly drug smugglers – until one of the guards found our first aid kit, built by Leigh's parents who worked for the NHS.

The guard began cross-checking every single item against a little book of 'Drugs legal to import into Russia'. It dawned on us that although the drugs in the box were all legal in the UK, it didn't mean they were legal in Russia. This was it: we were going to a Russian jail for importing illegal drugs. She held out the offending item, giving us one redeeming chance. It could have been the syringes, the amoxicillin, or the dextropropoxyphene, whatever the hell that was. But it wasn't. In her hand was an unassuming box of Tesco Everyday Value antihistamines.

After giving up on the Russian translation, Leigh tried to act out what the antihistamines were for: theatrical sneezes, a wipe of a runny nose, a rub of the eyes. Johno and I burst into hysterical laughter at the display and, despite the angry looks from the guards, after six hours of having our feet frozen in the snow they eventually set us free.

We were on the road to St Petersburg, hoping the next borders would be easier.

CHAPTER 9

- - - - - - - -

'RUSSIAN TRADITION!'

As we inched through the stacked banks of dirty, shovelled snow and into the inner suburbs of St Petersburg all we could see through the dirty, fogged-up windows of the car were the ubiquitous squat, concrete tower blocks lined up in rows. Since we left Finland we had put our trust completely into the satnav. Every so often a text message would arrive from our next host. The latest one said:

> Hurry up guys, it's Mardi Gras so you can't get here too late.

This new titbit of information spurred us along through the traffic-clogged roads as visions of bikini-clad girls with sequinned masks and strings of beads around their necks flooded our minds.

'Yeah, I'm gonna get me some beads, I'm gonna have a good time!' whooped Leigh.

'But, how can it be Mardi Gras?' asked Paul. 'It's about minus ten outside.'

Leigh and I ignored him, happy in our fantasies about the parade that awaited us.

Climbing out of the warm cocoon of the car and into the crisp evening air, I stamped my feet briskly while I searched for the correct apartment number on the peeling metal panel. As we stared up at the snow falling thickly around the huge tower blocks an industrial-sounding buzzer echoed and the heavy door jumped ajar, almost like something from a fallout shelter. I tugged it open with a mighty heave and we stepped into the damp and dimly lit lobby.

A musty smell filled my nostrils as we warily climbed into the creaking lift and pushed the chunky Formica button to take us up to floor 11. I studied the graffiti-covered walls as the cables groaned and breathed a sigh of relief when the doors parted and we were met by our smiling host.

Like many of our Couchsurfing hosts, Sasha came from a relatively well-off middle-class family and any preconceptions I had about her place were washed away as soon as we stepped through the two security doors and into a bright and warm apartment. The place was stuffed with the kind of trinkets families collect over the years and Sasha explained that the place was her parents' but these days they spent most of their time at their summer *dacha* in the countryside leaving this city apartment to her.

Soon afterwards we were sitting in Sasha's kitchen as she whisked up some eggs and flour in a bowl.

'So do they have a parade in the city for Mardi Gras?' Leigh asked, the visions of the beaded-girls clearly still on his mind.

'For Mardi Gras? No, normally we just make pancakes... you know, to mark the start of Lent,' she replied, motioning at the mixture.

Chuckles burst out all round as we realised our mistake. Mardi Gras was Shrove Tuesday in Russia; very different to the parade held in New Orleans every year. Our parade dreams vanished into thin air.

We quickly found out that Sasha and her friends were total Anglophiles; they loved the British comedy shows we showed them on YouTube and were in awe of Hannah. Before long they decided to repay the favour and educate us in their Russian culture.

We found ourselves in a vodka bar where the last five minutes of every hour were deemed 'Very Happy Five Minutes', with all vodkas half price. It didn't take long for us to feel like we were fully versed in 'Russian culture'. The next thing we knew we were all hopping out of unlicensed cabs back at Sasha's apartment, but Paul was nowhere to be seen.

'I thought he was in your cab?' I asked Leigh.

'I thought he was in yours?'

Although we had only just arrived in Russia and were already a man down, I wasn't too worried as I knew Paul was an incredibly resourceful guy. Whenever we pitched up in a new city it was always Paul who almost automatically figured out his bearings, leaving Leigh and me tagging along like two toddlers on a walk to the park. If anyone could find his way home it was Paul. Besides, after braving the new and challenging Russian roads for eight hours and then drinking a small distillery's worth of vodka, after our much-feared crossing of the Russian border and spending the previous night partying, all I could think of was sleep.

I wandered out of the loo and failed to find Johno and Leigh, so I did what all self-respecting males do when they lose their friends – I went to the bar. A beer later and they still hadn't turned up, there was no answer on their phones, the club was kicking out and I didn't have Sasha's address to give to a taxi driver. I knew how to get there from the Metro station, but the trains had stopped, and although I would recognise the Cyrillic of the stop on a map, I was unable to ask for a taxi there in Russian. So, with few other options, I wandered around a bit, found the cheapest hotel I could, checked in and went to sleep.

When the Russian living room stirred through my blurry eyes the next morning and it became clear that Paul still wasn't back, I immediately felt terrible. How could he still not be home? It was now almost noon with no word from him. While we had been tucked up in our toasty flat with its furnace-like heating, the outside temperature had been way below freezing.

Leigh remained unconcerned, mainly because he hadn't yet awoken from the comatose state he had immediately fallen into upon our return. In the night Sasha must have positioned the huge teddy bear that he was now cuddling up to next to him. The only sign of life from him was his occasional nuzzling into the furry chest and his murmuring of pleasant-sounding sweet nothings to the huge stuffed toy.

I had a minor panic when I realised my phone battery was dead, and I rooted frantically through my bag to dig out my phone charger. Luckily Sasha was way ahead of me; although she couldn't get through to Paul, she had texted him her details and she was confident that he would be able to decipher the Cyrillic address and make his way home.

I woke to find a text message from a considerably-more-concerned-than-my-so-called-friends Sasha, so I found the nearest Metro and went to the station by her place. Hopping out, I got on the bus from the stop we had taken the day before and absorbed the bright Arctic sunshine through the muddy windows of the trolleybus in an attempt to burn away some of the cranberry shots from the night before. I was pretty sure I would be able to recognise Sasha's place – it was the concrete prefab tower block by the red and white smoke stacks...

After the fifth almost identical red tower block, I realised I had no idea where to get off. I asked an old lady by showing her the text message and smiling. She looked at me gravely and pointed back the way I had come. I hopped off the bus and asked a passing gentleman the same thing. He started chatting away at me in excited Russian. I stopped him short with my new Russian phrase: '*Nay Par Ruski*.'

'*Americanski?* he enquired.

'No, no, no, English.'

'English? *Anglaiski?* LONDON! LONDON!'

He started hopping from foot to foot before pointing at his chest. 'St Petersburg,' he grinned.

I gave him a little cheer and he gave me a hug. He smelt of vodka, but then again, so did I.

He pointed at me, smiling.

'LONDON!' I could see how this game worked now, so I pointed at him.

'ST PETERSBURG!' He cheered, I cheered and we hugged again, both proud to have created and mastered the game of naming cities. However, it didn't cover the fact that I was still truly lost in a very large city. I showed him the address again and he smiled, turned on his heels and walked directly into the oncoming traffic with his hands outstretched.

I let out a little scream.

Fortunately, the oncoming Lada stopped and my city-naming friend spoke to the driver and hopped in, leaving me on the pavement looking very puzzled. The passenger door opened and he beckoned me in.

My mother told me as a child that I should never get into strangers' cars. She didn't, however, say anything about adults getting into strangers' cars in foreign cities, flagged down by other strangers you've just met in the street and with whom you've invented a new game. And then hugged. Twice.

Figuring that all the strangers and cars and hugs and games probably cancelled each other out, I hopped into the Lada. We started driving and my now friend-cum-kidnapper started gesticulating towards my phone for the address. I gave it to him and he read the address, but firmly held on to the phone. I started to scrutinise my kidnapper a bit more closely now I was out of the dazzling morning sunlight. He was covered in tattoos from his neck to his knuckles, he was wearing a tracksuit and he had my phone.

'Oh God. You're being robbed, you silly tit,' my hungover brain rationalised with me.

In fact, I was being robbed *and* kidnapped. And I had got into this car willingly.

What an idiot. Who actually willingly gets into their own kidnapper's car?

We were driving pretty far as well. I started to look panicked and pointed at the address. My kidnapper spoke to his getaway driver; they both laughed.

'RUSSIAN TRADITIYYY-SHON.'

Kidnapping is a Russian Tradition? I *knew* I should have read the Russian *Lonely Planet*.

'ST PETERSBURG!' Tracky-tat-kidnapper cried, smacking his chest.

'London!' I played back, weakly.

I tried to smile – endearing myself to my kidnappers would minimise, or at least soften, the inevitable beatings.

'RUSSIAN TRADITIYYY-SHON.'

We kept on driving. Faceless tower block after tower block, red-and-white smokestack after red-and-white smokestack passed. I remembered reading somewhere that you should memorise the route the kidnappers take so you can backtrack your way if you ever escape. But backtrack to where? The red-and-white smokestack? I was bloody lost in the first place!

We drove for about 20 minutes, further and further away from my last known whereabouts; but a few more rounds of the 'cities' game made it an amiable and rather enjoyable kidnap. The Lada stopped in a grubby car park next to a stairwell and my kidnapper gave the driver 100 roubles, about £2, and got out, still holding my phone. I could have run, but he had my phone and on my phone was my only way of finding my way home, so I wandered along with my kidnapper.

The stairwell was dank and smelt like piss, much like the majority of stairwells the world over – being mistaken for a urinal appears to be a global stairwell problem.

We stopped at some heavy steel doors at the top. There was nobody around.

'Russian TRADITION!' he shouted again, and with a flourish, he pushed me through the doors.

It was dark inside. I could hear Russian voices and it smelt like vodka (although that could easily have been me... or him). As my eyes grew accustomed to the darkness, I made out a snooker table, then another five.

And a bar.

My kidnapper pushed past me, went to the barman and patted the stool next to him, proffering a small glass of clear, triple-filtered 'Russian tradition'.

'VOD-KAHHH!'

He wasn't kidnapping me – he was taking me for a drink.

It was 9 a.m.

Feeling relieved and not wanting to be rude, I drank. Then another was poured, and being English and polite, I drank again. Another was poured, so I took out my phone and pointed at the address. He fired Russian at the pretty waitress who appeared and she translated it into English.

'Yes, he will take, but first you drink, it is Russian tradition you see?'

I saw, and then I saw off my shot.

We drank another shot; he slapped her on the bum and winked at me. I nodded my approval, as that seemed to be what he was looking for and we drank another shot.

'No more, I must go,' pointing at my phone.

'NO. Russian tradition,' he looked hurt as he poured another shot. Not wanting to offend his heritage, I felt obliged to drink it. Pointing at his chest he said, 'ST PETERSBURG.'

'London!'

Turns out the cities game was even *more* fun with vodka.

By 10 a.m., I was smashed.

At 10.30 a.m. I told him I *had* to go, so my new best friend – and definitely not my kidnapper – walked me down the stairs and around the nearest tower block. Parked in front of me was a 1992 London black cab. The bar was around the back of Sasha's flat.

We hugged our goodbyes, with my new friend looking very sad. He asked to come up, but I told him no (he was, after all, a stranger from the street, covered in tattoos and in a tracksuit – even if we had invented a game together and had a relationship that involved a hug every couple of minutes) and watched as he stumbled off into the street to get another unsuspecting lost tourist drunk. *Well, Russia is different*, I thought as I headed upstairs and attempted to sleep off my unexpected morning inebriation.

Sasha and her friend Anna were so taken with the idea of the taxi that when the time came for us to leave they caught a lift to the next large city with us. At the time I couldn't really understand why they'd want to drive for four hours south crammed into a bumpy and smelly car just to get a bus straight home again. However, they looked so happy when we dropped them off at the bus station in Novgorod that it all made sense to me. The ride for them, as it was for us in theory, was so much more about the journey than the destination. The drive in a London black cab through northern Russia was the perfect experience for a girl who loved England so much she had an English fiancé, studied English at university and now worked as an English translator. It was also our way of expressing a tiny bit of gratitude for the great hospitality they had shown us.

The journey itself had been as we'd promised: bone-shatteringly bumpy. After driving through Sweden, one of the richest countries in the world, and seeing the havoc that the winter conditions wreaked upon their roads, we hadn't held high hopes for the state of Russia's road surfaces. Frequent and deep potholes littered the surface, forcing us to quickly adopt what we called the 'Russian driving technique'. The main feature of the RDT was a constant, sharp weaving from side to side as the driver tried their best to pick the least bumpy path around the scattered craters while keeping up the maximum possible speed so as not to lose the road position to one of the many Ladas. All lane discipline went out of the window as the fast lane, the hard shoulder, the other side of the road and even the opposite hard shoulder all became fair game for overtaking.

Once the girls' bus pulled away we realised that for the first time we were stuck in a strange city after dark without an inkling of where we could rest our heads. We had been surprised to discover that this city of 200,000 people had no emergency Couchsurfers we could call on, but it was a small blessing in disguise: after nearly a month of nights spent on strangers' sofas, a real hotel gave us the chance to officially register our Russian visas and catch up on admin. It was also a chance to have a decent night's sleep without any guilt – we loved staying with Couchsurfers and were extremely grateful for all they had done for us but it was sometimes hard to muster up the energy to face a new inquisition by friendly hosts asking us where we dreamed up the idea for the trip or what we studied at university. Sometimes, the greatest luxury is just to sleep.

CHAPTER 10

- - - - - - - -

'TO INTERNATIONAL FRIENDSHIP'

Moscow: home to the Kremlin, Red Square, St Basil's Cathedral, the Bolshoi Theatre and people in funny fur hats, not to mention Dostoyevsky, Kandinsky and Anna Kournikova. One of the greatest cities in the world.

However, it was also home to a *lot* of concrete Soviet tower blocks and one of these was to be our home for the night, as we were once again Couchsurfing – this time in a commune just outside the city limits. We envisioned another open-door community with Beatles lookalikes baking bread for us upon arrival, but when we stepped through the main door to the building we were met with a dimly lit hallway that reeked of urine and was filled with empty vodka and super-strength beer bottles.

When we reached the top-floor flat, we were greeted warmly by a grubby toddler and our host, her father, who gave us the grand tour of two rooms and a kitchen crammed within dimensions not much bigger than our taxi. A hole in the brickwork revealed a miniature shower.

'No fucking in shower,' our new host announced with a big grin on his face and an air that showed he had been practising this phrase. From the way it was said, I presumed an industrious duo had succeeded before.

It transpired that this was home to Sasha, his wife Dina, their daughter, and four other guests, as well as ourselves. They were all part of a 'hitchhiking community' with a penchant for super-cheap travel and an aversion to furniture; they had nothing other than camping mats covering every inch of the floor. They pointed out that one was the three-piece suite, another was the chaise longue and another the table. Chuckling at their joke, we stepped in and were quickly reprimanded for stepping on the table. Apparently they weren't joking.

Although we were massively grateful to have been invited into Sasha's home, we were exhausted after a 14-hour drive, which made the hours until it was acceptable to go to bed tick by frustratingly slowly.

If Dina and Sasha's place lacked anything in space, furniture and creature comforts, they certainly made up for it with their warmth and kindness. Just after we were settled in and were making exaggerated yawning noises, while wondering where exactly we were all going to sleep, three more people appeared at the door and shoehorned themselves into the living room. One was cradling a rather large bottle of vodka and this was soon doled out into all manner of cups and containers as we sat cross-legged on the camping mats. A bottle of vodka between 12 people doesn't last too long in Russia and I was secretly relieved when the bearer told us that it was now illegal to buy hard liquor in Russia after ten at night – it was now nearing 11 p.m.

'It's OK though,' he grinned, 'I know shopkeeper!'

Slightly reluctant, we whipped out our wallets as an offering and he returned with a couple more bottles that were soon cracked open for toasts to the Queen and 'international friendship'.

The vodka was chased down with nothing more than raw pickles from a head-sized jar and as it disappeared so did the language barrier we had so awkwardly felt upon our arrival. Thankfully, the quantity and the strength of the alcohol we drank ensured the cramped conditions were not a problem and we slept like logs.

We had found a Couchsurfer in central Moscow who was keen to have three smelly lads to stay, so we made our way into the centre of the city. Moscow has some of the worst traffic in the world. Crawling the final miles took hours and wasn't helped by our first run-in with the local constabulary.

A policeman flagged us over with a baton – the kind ground crew use to guide approaching planes – and walked to the taxi's passenger window. After a moment of confusion before he realised that the person he was interrogating didn't have a steering wheel in front of him, he trudged to the other window. It didn't look like he had seen the funny side of the situation.

'*Machina passport*?' he asked, his breath stale with vodka – possibly explaining his slow reactions to finding a right-hand-drive car.

I handed over the V5 ownership document with the rest of the paperwork, along with our passports, and waited as the officer took them back to his car to scrutinise everything. He eventually returned and started to speak to me in Russian. I smiled and looked at him blankly, raising my hands in an apologetic way and brought out my trusty phrase.

'*Nay par Roooski*.'

More document analysis followed as he strived to find the slightest error in our paperwork that would presumably result in a fine. Having apparently failed to find anything, it was time to try plan B. The officer looked at me, then did a chopping motion with the flat of his hand against his neck. As far as I was aware, the only meaning for that was chopping someone's head off. More puzzled than concerned, I looked at him blankly and he did it again. Was this policeman threatening to decapitate us? Our paperwork couldn't be *that* bad? The officer then started to flick his throat with his middle finger.

Again he got a similar puzzled response.

'Vod-ka?' he asked, again chopping his neck.

It appeared that in Russia, chopping your throat means 'Have you been drinking?' It was one in the afternoon and the effects of the previous evening had long worn off.

'*Nyet, nyet!* I stressed.

However, the officer wasn't going to give up that easily. He started miming a breathalyser and threatening that he would take us to the station (which was ironic, given the smell on his breath). Unless of course… he trailed off in that inimitable way corrupt officials do when hinting that an arrangement could be found.

He clearly thought I was trying to call his bluff and tried to reaffirm that he actually would breathalyse me, as though to say, 'Of course you're drink-driving – everybody's been drinking. The difference is, I'll actually bust you for it unless you bribe me…'

Knowing full well I would pass a breathalyser test, and refusing to bribe him, we were at a stalemate. After 45 minutes the thought of doing actual paperwork finally got too much for him and we were released on our way.

Four thousand miles through the harsh northern climes of Scandinavia in less than four weeks had battered Hannah's already-shaky electrical system and now each morning brought a lottery about which part would fail next.

Every time one problem was fixed, another seemed to pop up somewhere else, just like those fairground moles. The one snag that had been consistent was the lack of indicators. Apart from a short time where Leigh had temporarily patched up the wiring, we had been without a left indicator ever since we left London and as something of an indicator pedant this massively annoyed me. Back in the UK I would use my indicator for even the tiniest manoeuvres, so driving through France, Belgium and the Netherlands without the little flashing orange light really got on my nerves. But as we hit Germany and Denmark I had started to get used to the idea and by the time we reached the Arctic Circle I had even started to think that it might be funny to drive all the way to Australia without them. Whenever Leigh mentioned fixing them I would subtly steer the subject on to something else, to Paul's increasing annoyance.

However, the moment we hit the central Moscow traffic I immediately changed my mind. The dirty grey slush on the road mixed with the grime from car and truck exhausts had formed a filthy layer on all of our windows, and our tiny ineffectual wipers only cut a narrow swathe to peer through. With vehicles merging from multiple directions into lanes of their own making, I decided too late that the indicators were actually a necessity and not a luxury, even if the Russian drivers would ignore them anyway.

We were left with just our arms to indicate a turn, making driving through the dense fast-moving traffic a half-blind, terrifying ordeal, punctuated by cries of 'stick your arm out!'

The horrifically bad traffic and a number of lengthy police stops meant that we were characteristically late to meet our next host: a student called Anna. This wasn't a huge problem as we were planning a quiet night anyway – our daily budget and our livers had been utterly obliterated over the past few weeks.

Naturally we blamed our tardiness on our various run-ins with the law and Anna reassured us that she, and pretty much everyone else in Moscow, hated the notoriously corrupt police. She invited us to sit down and made us feel at home.

'So', she said, 'have you got any good stories about your journey so far?'

CHAPTER 11

MOSCOW PRISON BLUES

The doors slammed behind us. My knees were by my chin, interlocking with Leigh's, whose now ghostly white face was inches away from mine. Judging by the wire mesh and the pervading smell of shit, we were in the dog cages.

The dog cages in the back of a Russian police van.

On our way to jail.

To make sense of our new confined surroundings we need to rewind a few hours. Soon after meeting Anna and telling her about our quickly emptying pockets, she had told us to get ready for her friend's birthday party that evening, reassuring us en route that she had a plan to save us some roubles.

Anna's idea was to pick up some cheap bottles of vodka and cognac and swill them down in Red Square in front of the Kremlin, one of Moscow's biggest tourist attractions and Russia's centre of government, before heading to the party. It was a sort of two-for-one, time and money-saving measure.

'Are you sure we're allowed to do this?' we asked as we looked around the garishly lit Kremlin, decorated like a Poundland store at Christmas.

'Yes, yes, of course, "Russian tradition!"' she scoffed sarcastically.

We weren't fully convinced. This was one of the most famous landmarks in Russia and Anna was quite obviously hiding the bottle. A few drinks later, though, we no longer really cared. We had even made up a stupid little song that we sang quietly, giggling, 'We're the kings of the Kremlin, you're a dirty gremlin!'

With the bottles about half-empty we moved out past the brightly coloured onion domes of St Basil's Cathedral and made one final toast to being the 'kings of the Kremlin', when the police car screeched up and we were caught looking like guilty schoolchildren.

Anna turned around and her expression had changed, 'This is bad, do what they say and I'll try and fix it.'

We were not giggling anymore.

Contrary to everything that was going on, strangely, I didn't feel scared or nervous. I had a dangerous feeling of invincibility – maybe I was blinded by the arrogance of being a Westerner with a British passport, or (more likely) the fact that there wasn't much vodka remaining in the bottle – but something in my gut told me we would be able to get out of this situation.

'What could they do?' I foolishly reasoned with myself.

At that moment a phrase that Dutch Jasper had told us in the depths of the Amsterdam haze sprung to mind – a moment of clarity from this stoned sage, issuing words of wisdom from a porn set surrounded by swingers and nutjobs: *You never get any good stories when everything goes to plan...*

It was true; it's always the things that go wrong that you tell people about. For better or for worse, I thought that maybe I'd be telling people about 'that time I got arrested for drinking vodka in front of the Kremlin' for years.

Unfortunately it looked like Leigh did not feel the same as his face developed a pronounced shade of white.

'Mate, this is going to be such a good story!' I grinned.

He didn't.

'I've still got the vodka in my jacket pocket,' he squeaked, tapping the lump in his ski jacket. He looked more like he was about to get busted for sailing a yacht full of cocaine and guns (or even antihistamines) into the country than having a bottle of the national tipple in his pocket. Judging from our previous run-ins with Moscow's boys in blue, the officers driving our van probably had one of their own. However, it's easy to be flippant when you're not the one carrying the incriminating evidence.

At the station we were led past the open Wild-West-style cells housing Moscow's criminals. They reached out through the bars for cigarettes, making me feel like I was in a bad prison film. I think we were all thankful when we were taken to a separate interview room and the four of us were told to sit on the hard two-man bench.

Two serious-looking police officers, both resembling their great leader, Vladimir Putin, entered the room and began the interview.

Anna translated for us, telling us that we would now be searched. We had heard of a well-known scam where the Russian police take foreigners' passports and don't return them until a substantial bribe is paid, but luckily we had left our passports behind at Anna's. I went first, depositing my wallet and phone on the desk before being loosely frisked. Johno went next, removing the four hoodies he was wearing against the cold in lieu of a proper jacket he was too tight to buy before we left. From numerous pockets came his wallet, phone, various scraps of paper and... a toothbrush? Even the police laughed at his optimism for the direction of the evening.

Anna followed suit and then it was Leigh's turn. He had, if it was possible, turned even whiter, and silence descended on the room. He rose to his feet with a stance that couldn't have looked guiltier if he had tried. For a moment we thought he was going to refuse to unzip his jacket, but at the policeman's fierce look he gave in and haltingly pulled out the almost-empty bottle of vodka. He let out a very guilty sigh.

'Oooooohhhhhhhhhh,' said the older officer. Both police officers tried their best to look disapproving of Leigh's major crime, while the rest of us tried to stifle our half-drunk giggles.

What followed was the least effective, most absurd good cop, bad cop routine I've ever seen. I have never been required to actually carry one out myself, but I've watched enough episodes of *The Wire* and *Police Academy* to have a pretty good understanding of how it should be done.

Anna translated.

'This is a very serious crime,' said the younger officer. The other nodded gravely. 'We cannot leave it unpunished. My colleague will take some of your details now.'

The older officer upped and left, locking the cell-office behind him, and the younger one put on a big smile and asked us what football teams we supported.

Much to my father's constant disappointment, my interest in football is so negligible that I would rather watch an episode of *Loose Women* than the FA Cup. However, when travelling, football can be a fantastic talking point when you only share a handful of words in each language, and which team you support is often the first thing asked when somebody finds out you're from England. The concept that you don't actually support a football team is often met with dismay and general confusion, so I usually just say Manchester United, which provokes a look of satisfied glee because the person you're talking to has actually heard of the team. (My local team, Swindon Town, doesn't have the same reaction – I've tried.)

The other lads' feelings towards the sport are similar, so we plumbed for the nearest geographical locations to our homes; Johno opted for Manchester United, Leigh for Aston Villa and myself, knowing only one other team name, Chelsea.

Our teams were greeted with a satisfied nod, before the younger officer launched into a long diatribe about how poor he was, how poorly paid police in Moscow are and how expensive it is to live.

'This is true,' Anna embellished as she translated, 'but they make so much money in bribes that they make more money than most – and certainly more money than me.'

He then went on to say how the other officer wanted to write up our crimes, pointing at a form on his desk, but that he liked us so he just wanted to let us go.

Right on cue, the older officer came in with his best stern face and started to write up our 'crimes'.

'Name?' he demanded.

His partner jumped in and said something that made him huff and puff, and then leave. The same pleas followed.

The farce repeated itself a couple of times and started to get quite boring. It didn't look like there'd be any other way out of this without spending a night in one of Moscow's finest jail cells, so we started dropping hints back.

'I wonder,' Anna translated for us. 'Is there possibly a way we could just… make this go away?'

We don't pay bribes generally. No matter how difficult people make our lives, if we haven't done anything wrong, we're not going to bribe a corrupt official. However, when you're caught in front of the national government office with two bottles of spirits, singing poorly formed nursery rhymes and you have an important party to get to, sometimes one needs to hurry things along.

The three of us were sent out and Anna was kept back. Ten minutes later she emerged saying that we were being fined 500 roubles each (£10), but 'so we wouldn't have a record' our names wouldn't be put on the forms and the forms wouldn't be filled out. Wishing they had just asked for the bribe an hour and a half earlier, we paid up and were greeted by an instant change in our captors, who both became very jovial as soon as they had each doubled their salary for the day. As we waved *do svidánija* to the older officer at the door, he called me back. I walked back over and he produced our half-full bottle of vodka. Thinking this was a gaff, I joked, 'For me?'

'*Da*!' he said.

I reached out, took it and mimed walking off – expecting him to take it back with a cheeky chuckle. But he just nodded, turned and strolled off, leaving me, vodka in hand, to hail a cab with the others and head to the bar.

CHAPTER 12

- - - - - - - - -

THE CITY OF RUIN

I unpeeled my face from the leather Ford Cortina seat – rubbed raw by 30 years of arses – that we had bolted in for extra passengers, and rose to the sound of a large truck revving next to us. I woke up the lads from their equally uncomfortable sleeping positions in the back and we began the drive onwards to Minsk. We had stopped at the side of the road after a late-night dash through the border out of Russia; no hotels in the area would accept our visas, so we were forced to use Hannah as our accommodation for the night.

I've never known a thing about Minsk. I had always incorrectly presumed it to be a virtually uninhabitable city in the farthest reaches of Siberia, basing this assumption (and I would guess I am not alone in this) on an episode of *Friends*.

It is in fact the capital of Belarus.

Directly translated as 'White Russia', Belarus is a dictatorship situated on the European side of Russia, just north of Ukraine. Minsk was rebuilt in the 1950s by Stalin as a show city to display what the USSR had the potential to produce. It is still a show city, albeit a slightly eerie one, run by the only totalitarian regime in mainland Europe and one which is desperately trying to prove that it can hold its own on an international level.

Our decision to go to there was a simple one: nobody in the team had ever known anyone who had been and it sounded like an adventure. We stayed with a Couchsurfer host called Tania, who was attempting to study Art and Business in a country where, like everything else, both of those things are highly influenced by the state.

The sun was out and Leigh finally fixed the indicators on the car before we toured the city. We each went our separate ways to explore the collections of Stalinist monuments, show lakes and functional tower blocks, forming a bizarre combination of Western-facing show city and run-down ex-Soviet dive.

When it was time to go, after giving Tania our final bottle of French Couchsurfing-host wine, we decided to restock The Bar with Belarus's famous vodka. I chose a random selection from the vodka aisle (yes, a whole aisle) and left with 12 bottles of the stuff, having only parted with the equivalent of £20. We liked Belarus.

Outside of the capital, Belarus presented a different, more natural side, with quaint villages and miles of rolling greenery bordered by arrow-straight roads. The border crossing into Ukraine went without a mention of the shipment of smuggled vodka in The Bar and after avoiding the car insurance touts we drove out of the border complex and on to the slightly smoother roads. It is strange how crossing a line marked on a map almost always immediately changes the way mundane, everyday things look and this was no exception. The open fields were immediately replaced by diagonal rows of reddish pine trees, the low sunlight casting long shadows across the road.

Once again, it was dark by the time we made it to Kiev; so far we had driven after dark in every country that we had vowed not to. This didn't stop the Ukrainian police spotting us and instantly pulling us over, demanding our documents and asking us if we had any weapons in the car.

They were unrelenting in their interrogation and it looked like they were just about to find the stash of vodka when the officer who seemed to have a better grasp of English suddenly understood the purpose of our trip and explained it to the other. The mood changed immediately; packets of cigarettes were produced and offered around, and the officers even gave us a small wooden toy as a good luck charm, before releasing us with directions to the hostel around the corner.

The door was answered by a girl in her early 20s who eyed me suspiciously. When I asked her if she had space for three English guys she looked hesitant, no doubt her impression of us already informed by the many British stag parties that ravage the city.

'... and do you have anywhere we can park our car? We're, er, driving a black cab from London to Sydney,' I quickly added.

Her face lit up. 'What? Shut up! I have to see this car.' She pulled on her shoes and ushered me down the stairs.

As soon as she spied Hannah we knew we had a place to stay, and Hannah had gained another fan. Joanna absolutely loved the car and excitedly directed us to a parking space hidden away in some alley outside the hostel while quizzing us about the trip so far. Her cosy little hostel had the same atmosphere as a friend's house. We quickly settled in and got to know her and her guests, telling them about our big milestone: tomorrow would mark the end of our first month on the road and Paul's 24th birthday.

We tried to explain to Paul that it wasn't that we'd rather spend the day in a radioactive exclusion zone than with him on his birthday, but just that Leigh and I were desperate to go and visit Chernobyl and this might be our only chance. Paul couldn't really see the appeal of paying £70 to spend his birthday 'looking at ruined buildings and getting cancer'.

'We got you a birthday gift though,' we woke him to tell him just before we left at 7 a.m.

His sleepy face lit up briefly then immediately dropped as he saw the large shot of Belarusian vodka we presented him with and a cactus we had bought from a tiny *babushka* in a nearby underpass. He swore at us but took it in good spirits and we promised that we would take him out properly when we returned in the evening.

After handing over 1,000 Ukrainian grivnas to a dodgy looking fellow named Igor, we boarded the ancient minibus and made our way to the site of the world's worst nuclear disaster. In 1986 Reactor Four of the Chernobyl nuclear power plant exploded resulting in the eventual evacuation of the whole region, including the city of Pripyat and its 50,000 inhabitants. The resulting radioactive fallout spread throughout the entire continent of Europe, even contaminating sheep grazing far away in the Welsh highlands. Some areas in Chernobyl still show around 75 times the normal level of radiation today.

Thick grey cloud and heavy flakes of snow set the perfect atmospheric background as we drove into the deserted and decaying metropolis. The city centre housed an unused fairground, complete with a large fading Ferris wheel and mouldering bumper cars, that had been due to open the week after the accident. Now it lies rusting to dust after the inhabitants of the city were told they had two hours to pack their passports and a small bag, to evacuate for a few days. They were never allowed to return.

One of the most eerie areas of the town was the main school where children's drawings, a quarter of a century old, were still pinned to the wall next to crates of unused gasmasks and where posters still advertised the Soviet Union in all its glory. Everything was untouched since that fateful day; a sobering and eye-opening experience for both of us. Once we had been ushered back into the minibuses we sat in silence as they took us past the long-destroyed reactor itself, and mounds of dirt that buried entire villages. We wondered what Paul had been up to back in Kiev.

CHAPTER 13

NAKED COUNTRY!

Sometimes the miles just melted away and sometimes we had to drive every single one. The road to Poland was one of the latter long slogs and the police weren't as friendly as the ones in Kiev. Rather than giving us good-luck charms, these officers wanted hard cash, although it turned out to be surprisingly simple to barter them down; Paul got his 'fine' down to £6. I got away with giving them Paul's birthday cactus. Leigh was now the only one who hadn't been caught or fined.

After hopping through Austria our short time in Liechtenstein was characterised by a game invented by Hannah's newest passenger, Paul's friend Wikey. He had flown out to join us to celebrate his birthday on the road and his suggestion for the day's entertainment was to drive through an entire country naked. One of the benefits of having a country a hundred times smaller than Yorkshire was that this didn't actually involve all that much time being naked, so we agreed.

As we crossed the bridge that we thought signalled the border, the car, as one, yelled, 'Naked country!'

We pulled our clothes off and tootled along the lush green Alpine pastures, completely starkers.

A month living in the same vehicle had done strange things to us all.

'Wait a minute,' I ventured, looking outside, 'those are still Austrian signs, I don't think that was the right bridge.'

The others groaned and we pulled our clothes back on for all of 90 seconds, until we crossed the correct bridge and saw the Liechtenstein coat of arms halfway across and again chorused, 'Naked country!'

I've always had a fondness for Switzerland. Something about the perfectly ordered and almost unfeasibly clean place appeals to me. The beautiful, spotless Alpine villages almost look like some kind of film set. Unfortunately all this comes at the price of the country being horrendously expensive – even a simple meal at a cheap restaurant and a quick drink in a quiet bar easily smashed our £10 per day limit. It was interesting to spend some time with some of our friends from the other side: people who had graduated from university and gone straight into the corporate world, who thought nothing of buying a €50 round of drinks and then went home to their plush city-centre apartments.

There we were sharing a loaf of bread and a squeeze of bacon-in-a-tube on the bonnet of our car for lunch while these guys were living it up in posh cafes on the shore of Lake Geneva; we were sleeping on the floors of draughty farmhouses while they were lounging in king-sized beds in fully furnished bachelor pads. We admitted we had all had fleeting pangs of envy talking to these guys, but back on the road again it didn't take long for us to realise that we wouldn't swap places with them for the world. We were having the time of our lives.

Back in France, and the march ever southward had brought with it the kind of glorious weather you expect from the Riviera; a stark contrast to the biting cold of the frozen Paris suburbs we had experienced earlier in the year. We decided it was now warm enough to try out the pop-up tents we'd brought along as a money-saving measure, for wild camping in the warmer climates. We drove higher and higher up the sides of the valley in the foothills of the Alps and found a spot of grass marked as a 'Municipal camping ground'. As we were setting up camp, I saw Leigh tutting and shaking his head as he threw up his tent. The shop we had bought them from only had two green camouflage tents and one bright pink one left in stock, and Leigh had been cursing us for weeks that he ended up with the odd one out.

'If we ever get attacked in the night I guarantee I will be the first,' he always half-joked, 'they can see my girly pink tent from a mile away.'

In our haste to get on the road in the UK we managed to misplace a particular bag that contained half of our camping gear. This meant that although we each had a sleeping bag and a tent that was about it. An old roll of carpet we had found somewhere had been chopped up into makeshift sleeping mats and a pile of dirty laundry served as a pillow. Without proper gear, we shivered through the night, but we were rewarded the next morning with a stunning vista of the valley as the sun rose over the far mountains. Despite the low temperatures in the mountains our camping appetite was well and truly whetted.

It may have only been late March, but the sun was properly shining. Driving through the winding roads of the French Riviera from Nice to Monaco is one of the world's ultimate drives. It was perfect; the sun reflected off the gently rippling Mediterranean, which was only interrupted by the odd super yacht. I felt like I could have been Cary Grant. Except that instead of an Italian sports car, I was in a 20-year-old taxi, and instead of Grace Kelly – her headscarf flapping in the cooling breeze – I had Johno, scratching his balls in a pair of obscene cut-off Daisy Duke shorts.

Dropping into Monte Carlo, the home of the world's super-rich tax dodgers, we instantly found ourselves on the F1 track. We did a lap of some of the open F1 street-track – careering into the tunnel at a cool 30 mph to that epic Formula 1 sound, 'nneeeeeeeeaaaaaaaarrrrrrmmmph' (well at least that's the sound I was making to hide the gentle tractor-like hum of our diesel engine). I negotiated the dangerous chicane with ease and hurtled by the luxury yachts at 10 to 15 mph.

A scooter pulled up beside me and waved me to the side with a heavy arm with a large security badge on it. Expecting to be in trouble – which for us was beginning to feel normal – I pulled over to find that actually he was just a fan of the expedition who had been following us online and wanted to say hi.

We all had a go on the track and at making the obligatory sounds before heading up to the casino. The car parking was divided into an underground facility for mere mortals, and a show park for superstars and supercars out the front. The attendant took one look at our tatty old cab and waved us to the 'normal' zone, but we just smiled back, waved and drove past him into the exclusive zone, as brazen as day.

Hannah had been drawing attention ever since we had rolled off the ferry and into France. From the dollar signs rolling in the eyes of the Soviet cops to the wide grins and waves of what seemed like every motorist on the motorway in the Czech Republic, she was definitely causing a reaction. We parked up in front of a row of priceless metal and hopped out and started to take pictures. To our surprise, so did the rest of the tourists milling around – they were more interested in the sticker-covered, rusty black cab than the rare million-dollar machinery on display and, much to our glee, we were soon posing for a small group of German tourists. Even when the local police turned up to see what all the commotion was about they were soon happily chatting away to Leigh about how we had got here.

The reaction of the Italians was one of the best, and most stereotypical, so far. After leaving Monaco we were driving down the Italian motorway. As usual almost everyone was overtaking us when a throaty Ferrari ambled along next to us, inching past as the occupants enjoyed a slow cruise with the top down.

As we drew level, the passenger, a pretty, dark-eyed girl, caught a glance of our beaten-up London taxi with a roof rack full of junk and stared at us with an open-mouthed smile.

The driver, presumably her boyfriend, was still unaware, cool as could be, cruising down the road in his sports car. That was until he saw us, or more accurately saw the look his girlfriend was giving us. His mouth dropped open in disgust and somehow eyeballed all three of us at once as he made an unintentionally comical over-exaggerated display of putting his manly arm around the passenger before roaring off at 100 mph.

Staying true to our drunkenly planned task of driving to Australia via 'the longest route possible to rack up the fare' included driving across the top of Africa. Unfortunately, about a week after we left London a young student set himself on fire in Tunisia, successfully starting a revolution in the Arab world. Unbeknownst to him, he had also scuppered the plans of three lads in a black cab.

So, instead of taking a ferry from the southern tip of Italy and driving around North Africa and the Middle East to Turkey, we had come up with a new plan: the Balkans.

The first new country on our revised route was Slovenia, which was so miniscule that we managed to drive nearly all the way across it in two hours. Crossing the border into Croatia, we came across a cosy little hostel for the night.

We woke up the next day considerably more rested and relaxed than we had been for some time, at least until we looked out of the window. Hannah was parked right outside but even from our third-storey window it was obvious that something wasn't quite right. A large pool of some unidentified liquid had formed underneath her and when we got downstairs to investigate Leigh discovered that the ageing fuel tank had begun to split open along the seams, leaking diesel all over the road. This would either require a completely new tank – probably not that common in Croatia, we thought – or a very skilled welder to try to patch it back together. Fortunately our hotel owner knew the perfect guy, and within a few hours Leigh had explained all that Hannah needed and she was safely in the hands of a man who had just the right skills to make her as good as new.

With a forced exile from Hannah for a few days we decided to make the most of the free time with our latest Couchsurfing host, Igor, who showed us the city by day, and took us drinking by night.

We stayed with Igor for a couple more days until the car was repaired and we could hit the road again. Yet again, we struggled to find a decent camping spot for us all to lay our tents and ended up driving down an abandoned track into an incredibly eerie wood. Leigh outlined every scenario that happens to woodland campers in horror films, especially focusing on the popular modern trend for setting them in Eastern Europe. Driving past a particularly creepy abandoned hut was the last straw and, as the driver, I turned us around and drove out.

Not because I was scared though.

In the end we camped on a grass verge by an industrial estate – much safer.

CHAPTER 14

METAL MONDAY MORNING

We arrived in Split after a day of driving and exploring the stunning Plitvice Lakes. Driving for hour upon hour every day can, unsurprisingly, be quite dull, and the obvious way of keeping yourself sane while driving is to listen to music. Johno and I are both really into our music – Leigh, however, can count three Black Eyed Peas albums on his iPod and so it was agreed that his opinion was nullified. With opinions bouncing around the cab you would expect music choice to be a key point of contention, but fisticuffs were kept at bay by abiding to the simple taxi music rule – the driver is in full control.

However, by this point in the trip, we were all pretty bored of our choices and decided to jazz it up by having music-themed days. The Saturday drive from the verge of an industrial estate to Split in Croatia: Reggae Saturday. Consolidating all the reggae between us on to one playlist is easy – making it last for a day, however, isn't. Very soon ska was allowed in and by the end it was any punk band that had ever played a ska track. Needless to say, themed days took off and were going to stay.

We crossed into Bosnia and headed towards Sarajevo, following some directions to what had been described to us as the perfect camping spot. Soon we were crawling up a narrow track on a steep hillside far above the river below. Without saying a word we each took off our seatbelts and opened our windows, unspoken precautions in case Hannah slipped and tumbled into the rushing water below. The view of the impressive valley from the field made the sketchy drive worth it, although the high winds and chilly temperatures made for another fitful night's sleep.

After a brief stop in Sarajevo, although not long enough to do justice to the history-soaked city, we pressed on for the border with Montenegro.

Monday was Metal Monday, which meant all my old thrash metal albums got an airing, Leigh's Limp Bizkit came out and Johno introduced us to the rather unique Austrian Death Machine – a brutal heavy metal band that sing exclusively about Arnold Schwarzenegger films in a fake Austrian accent.

It was the perfect soundtrack for winding between the steep Montenegrin gorges, criss-crossed with Indiana Jones-esque rope bridges. The roads were tight, but well built – cut into the vertical cliff sides with sheer drops on one side protected by large concrete blocks.

Montenegro came and went, and we found ourselves at the top of a huge pass crossing into Kosovo. The Mediterranean spring behind us, it started to snow hard. The drive through Kosovo was grey and wet, and by the time we got to the border with Macedonia the rain was bucketing down.

Having been lucky enough to grow up in a time of open European borders and cheap air travel, we, along with most of our peers, hadn't really experienced the peculiarities that are land borders before departing on the trip. But over the past few months we had been thrown in at the deep end.

There was something horribly similar about all of the borders we had struggled through so far. All were bathed in harsh fluorescent strip-lights that never quite cut through the grey drizzle that always seemed to be falling. The barn-like structures, fences, concrete floors and constant throng of movement vaguely resembled some kind of human factory-farm and the constant bustle of human traffic belied any actual meaningful human contact. Although thousands of people pass through the barbed wire every day, none of them seemed to care about anything other than getting their own group over to the other side.

The officials seemed almost robot-like, dehumanised by the constant process of dealing with people as 'Approve' or 'Deny' stamps rather than as real people, and the Macedonians were no different. The border guards took one look at our Green Card insurance documents and refused to accept them on the basis that they weren't printed on green paper.

We eventually had to pay another £35 for Macedonian insurance. We passed through the border as evening fell.

After two and a half hours of driving through the darkness and rain – the occasional puddle splashing up through the gear stick hole and a continuous, tortuous drip over the driver's accelerator pedal foot – we exited Macedonia. Leigh poked his head out of his sleeping bag, having slept the entire way, as the border guard waved us through and into Greece.

Leigh was becoming more and more preoccupied by what was and wasn't allowed in Turkey. His main concern was whether we could take the pork we had stocked up on in Bosnia, but Johno and I could tell he was wracking his brain for any other items that may not go down well in a Muslim country.

'We don't have any booze do we?'

'Unfortunately not, plus it's not a dry country so we'll be fine.' I replied.

Back when we were in the Czech Republic, Leigh had been missing his girlfriend, Charlotte. So, as a good friend, I felt I needed to get him something to cheer him up. With few options in the first service station we stopped at, I selected the most depraved (and cheapest) hardcore Czech pornography mag, had it nicely gift-wrapped by the bemused woman at the till, and presented it to Leigh as a little cheer-you-up gift. It had since bounced around the back of the cab, spawning a new game; the game of hiding the porn mag wherever it was most likely that a person would discover it in an awkward situation (which was often the documents wallet that's brought out every time there's a police check or border).

'Oh God... did you guys throw away my... err, *the* Czech porn?'

'Yes, mate.' (We hadn't.)

'Are you sure?'

'Yup.'

'Good, because if we got caught with that, there would be all sorts of trouble.'

At that very moment, it was actually hidden in Leigh's hand luggage.

CHAPTER 15

THE GREEN CARD

Unfortunately the magazine stayed hidden across the border, but there was still the hope that Leigh's girlfriend would discover it when she came to visit us a few days later. The guards refused to accept our Green Card insurance documents and insisted that, even though it had 'Green Card' and 'Carte Verte' printed on the top, because it wasn't literally printed on green cardboard, it was unacceptable. A German couple in a camper van were having the same issue and despite the large man's angry, sweating protestations that, 'we already have zee GWEEEEN Card,' we were both forced to shell out handsomely for updated polices.

We made it to Istanbul in good time, but spent two hours trying to find the hostel we had booked into. We had arranged to meet up with an Irish couple we had met in a hostel back in Ukraine. They were brilliant photographers and cracking fun, but average at best at giving directions to hostels.

Eventually we found it and were let in by its owner – a Turkish Rastafarian, bottle of Jack Daniel's in hand, whose Thai Chang

Beer singlet hinted back to a better time. The building had been condemned and was set to be knocked down in the next couple of months, but that hadn't stopped the hostel being full and him double-booking us. Considering the effort it took to find the place, we weren't going anywhere else, so he offered us the kitchen floor and a piece of toast for breakfast for £1.50 a head, and we gladly accepted.

We spent the next day seeing the sights and lapping up their culture: the Blue Mosque, eating kebabs, smoking shisha, chatting with the wonderful Turks and wandering the Grand Bazaar, where we witnessed a fight break out that knocked over a charcoal kebab braiser and almost burned down the whole place.

The city break was not long enough, and before we knew it we had to go. It was approaching three months on the road and apart from four days in Rovaniemi and four in Croatia due to the fuel leak, we hadn't stopped anywhere for more than a couple of nights. We were exhausted. We had arranged a week off at a Turkish beach: a week off from driving, from moving, from camping and – most importantly – a week off from each other.

We had planned these breaks into the trip to allow ourselves to retain our sanity occasionally. Such a long time encased in a tin can in unbelievably close proximity inevitably creates tension, but nothing that a nice holiday within a holiday couldn't fix. To help us with our beach break, we had invited our girlfriends/girls-we-met-in-a-bar-in-Prague-who-we-somehow-persuaded-to-go-on-holiday-with-us along too. Their flights were due in a couple of days, and we had 500 miles to drive.

Driving in Istanbul was an experience, easing us into the erratic driving styles of the East. The sun was out and the windows were down as we weaved between the dense traffic to the large bridge that crosses the Bosphorus Strait. Passing over the small sailboats in the bay, we landed on the other side of the city and into the continent of Asia.

It was refreshing to once again be in a country larger than a few hundred miles across and the drive down the Mediterranean coast pleasantly surprised us all. The scenery of rolling green hills was perfectly offset by the agreeable warm temperature and nearly all the roads were either brand-new smooth blacktop or in the process of being upgraded. Every time we stopped for fuel – diesel for the car, and fizzy drinks and kebabs for the occupants – the pump-attendants, cashiers or waiters were effortlessly friendly and any language barriers just seemed to fizzle away. At one point we attracted the attention of a local scooter gang who, after saying hello and admiring the car, disappeared before returning with gifts of a single bottle of Efes beer, a packet of uncooked pasta and a loaf of bread.

Our week of freedom was absolute bliss. Instead of stuffy tents or cramped triple rooms we enjoyed four-star out-of-season-bargain luxury and did nothing more taxing than sitting around the pool or walking along the beach. Although we were all sad to see the girls go, by the time the week was over we were surprised to find that we were all itching to get back on the road again. We were still living our dream and we were raring to start the next section of the trip: the Middle Eastern leg.

Ever since we had changed the route to avoid Libya we had been constantly discussing the new path through the Middle East. The simplest route would be to drive across southern Turkey and into Iran, back on to the original line down to Pakistan. However, I was very keen to try to make it down to Jordan through Syria to see the famous rock-cut city at Petra. Leigh and Paul weren't so enthusiastic about crossing through shaky Syria due to the intermittent demonstrations that were breaking out in the major cities and our differences in opinion had been a constant source of simmering tension.

Although the mainstream media was reporting violent demonstrations and advising all foreign nationals to leave, there were still reports from independent travellers on Internet forums and from Couchsurfers saying that there was no problem, assuming you took sensible precautions like staying away from large gatherings within the cities. The discussion was still very much unresolved when we all reconvened and left Bodrum; Paul assumed I was being reckless with our plans, and I felt that Paul was being unduly influenced by his friends and family who had been reading the news reports. Leigh was sitting on the fence.

All we could agree on was to head over east in the general direction of Australia and try to make a decision in the near future based on better information.

CHAPTER 16

GALMAJUICE

A 20-year-old taxi that has been completely stripped and rebuilt with homemade modifications by amateur mechanics needs constant love and attention. On the road south we had noticed that the suspension, already famously uncomfortable, felt particularly weird. Upon closer investigation Leigh had discovered the problem. Although we had rebuilt the suspension with brand-new double-strength springs, these springs were still attached to the original early 1990s fittings and one of them had actually snapped its lower mounting, meaning that the slightest bump would start us pogoing around with a cringey 'pet-aaaang' sound.

We needed a very specific, very small and seemingly insignificant part. The closest we could find was back in England and would take days, and an extortionate courier fee, to arrive, so we chanced the drive over to the national park region of Cappadocia.

Cappadocia had been recommended to us by almost every person we'd met in Turkey and we could soon see why. The landscape was filled with amazing rock formations that formed phallic-looking 'fairy chimneys' and the area was peppered with underground cave cities. We found a cheap hotel, partially built into one of the termite-mound-like formations and caught up on the news. Our visa agent in Iran had emailed and told us that we'd have to wait another two weeks for our visas. Our spare part was due to arrive the following day so we were left with an unexpected chunk of time to fill.

Syria and Jordan had just closed their borders, removing one avenue of adventure, so we started to look further afield. We had met a Glaswegian Red Cross volunteer called Annaka who was living in Armenia and who had invited us to visit, but because of the various border politics we would have to enter Armenia through Georgia. All we knew about Georgia was that it was ex-Soviet and they had recently had a war with Russia. It didn't sound great, and none of us fancied braving Russian-style authorities again so we were pondering what to do out loud.

'Georgia?' chipped in an American girl who was frantically packing her bags in the dorm.

'Yeah, the country,' we explained, presumptuously expecting her to be talking about the American state.

'Oh, yeah… It's great.'

'Oh, you've been?' I asked, surprised.

'Yeah! I got there, and within two hours I was shitfaced drunk on homemade spirits, in a small village, shooting AK-47s!'

The room erupted into a whirlwind of packing – Georgia sounded like our kind of place.

We arrived in the country's capital, Tbilisi, a few days later, and went to meet our Couchsurfer host at his workplace. We made our way to his apartment, crisscrossing through the rush-hour traffic and between decaying facades of once glorious town houses. The city appeared to be in the midst of a momentous renovation project in the aftermath of the 2008 war, every building either falling apart or being rebuilt – yet nothing seemed quite finished yet.

It was impossible not to warm to George, and he immediately made us feel at home in his flat. He had an oversized mischievous grin permanently attached to his face, a face that seemed to be stolen from a much larger man. He appeared to have an aversion to wearing a top when inside his house, the tattoo of a cannabis leaf (which I assumed was the result of a rash decision in his youth) always on show just above his navel. His apartment fell into the pre-renovation category of Tbilisi buildings, on the third storey of an almost Dickensian block of flats that oozed as much soul as it did woodworm and rot. It had the air of a squat: it was clean, but the higgledy-piggledy furniture from various generations, lit by a dim bulb hanging from a chandelier mounting, gave the impression that at any time an aristocratic family may return from their summer retreat to reclaim it. Either that, or the whole place would be transferred and opened as a hipster bar in Shoreditch. The walls were covered with drunken marker-pen graffiti and framed paintings done by his friends; some were impressive works by talented artists, some destined to go no further than George's wall.

The *Lonely Planet* guide to Georgia basically says the most important thing to do there is experience the local hospitality, from which I inferred that they are a bit boring. However, it turned out to be code for 'get drunk with the locals', which is indeed the best thing to do in Georgia. We soon learned that '*galmajuice*' means both 'hello' and 'cheers', which perhaps says more about the Georgian culture than the attempts of any book.

George returned from work with a few litres of beer, a bottle of homemade wine and a water bottle full of unidentified spirit.

'Now, we get drunk.'

Some of his friends came round and we spent the evening enjoying Georgian 'hospitality'. It turns out the spirit, called *cha-cha* and derived from wine, ranges from 40 per cent up to 70 per cent ABV and is famous for turning people blind (but 'only temporarily' apparently). After one shot each, it was decided that now we were able to say we had enjoyed this Georgian speciality. One was enough.

By the end of the night, we retired to our respective sofas and George disappeared into his room with one of the girls from the party.

We spent the next day climbing a hill overlooking Tbilisi and discovered a half-built theme park at the top, with signs promising new rides coming in 2008 to provide 'new levels of excitement'. Using our basic knowledge of recent history, we calculated that this was just about the time the Russians invaded the country, understandably slowing general theme park construction.

We returned to find George in his room with a girl – a different one from the night before – so, taking the unspoken hint that we should make ourselves scarce (it was a small apartment), we headed out for dinner. I felt a tad rough and the last thing I wanted to do was go out drinking, and the lads agreed, so we were going to grab a bite to eat, let George do his thing, then retire for an early Thursday night.

This was our plan of action until I found myself in a shipping container in the car park of George's place, holding something that looked suspiciously like a ram's horn filled with liquid. We never made it to get food.

The next morning another Couchsurfer who happened to be a local TV presenter wanted to interview us on his show. We had found it quite funny that the first guy who offered to host us in Georgia was named George but it was just getting kind of strange when we found out that the presenter was also a George. Were all Georgian men called George? Was that the reason for the country's name?

After the filming, Georgian George the Second invited us along to a local wine festival. We had been repeatedly told that the Georgians invented wine and that Georgian wine was the best in the world. The festival was set in a tranquil wooded park overlooking the city and essentially consisted of many small tents set up in the forest clearings, each hosting an independent vineyard that wanted to prove they had the best wine by giving away as much as possible. We arrived fairly late so stocks were running low, but we discovered that it was impossible to have an empty glass for any significant period of time in Georgia, and soon we were sharing bottles with groups of families who were singing traditional chants and forcing yet more barbecued food down us.

I'm not sure what the conclusions on the primacy of Georgian wine were but we definitely did our fair share of field research.

Georgia is like no place I, or my liver, have experienced before. One of the guys from the shipping-container party had told us that the reason they drink from a horn is because you can't put it down until it's empty. This, along with their '*galmajuice*' greeting, seemed to summarise Georgians perfectly. Four days in Georgia is enough to drive someone to move to a dry country for the next two months just to recover.

Which, incidentally, was exactly what we did.

CHAPTER 17

STEPANTSKY-WHATEVER

With a bit of time to kill while we waited for our Iranian visas, we decided to visit Yerevan, the capital of Armenia, where we would meet Annaka. Ever since coming up with idea for the trip we had wanted to get a charity involved and to use the publicity from the record attempt to try to raise money and awareness for a good cause. The British Red Cross presented itself as an obvious choice; we had seen the enormous amount of valuable work that it carried out both in the UK and throughout the rest of the world. From our point of view, the Red Cross could also provide a lot of international support and expertise, and advise us on some of the more adventurous areas of the route.

After setting a fundraising target of £20,000, based on the mileage we thought we would be covering at that time, we became more heavily involved with the Red Cross, which culminated in a trip to their London headquarters for a planning session with their security consultant. Along with a book with the worrying title *How to Stay Alive*, she gave us some helpful advice on parts of the route we should avoid.

'Hmmm, Pakistan,' she had said, looking at our detailed route printout, 'you should be alright as long as you avoid the Baluchistan region. You're not going to Baluchistan are you?'

We shuffled uncomfortably. 'Erm, yeah, we kind of have to cross through that area, it's the only open border.'

She let out a loud exhale and looked at us over her glasses. 'OK, I'll get you some more copies of that book.'

The journey of around 200 miles between the neighbouring capitals was a slow one, particularly after we asked some Georgian farmers for directions to Armenia not far from the border and then blindly followed their advice.

Four bumpy hours later we reached the tiny border post, announced by a hand-painted sign at the end of a heavily potholed single-track road. We thought back to those bloody farmers, who gave us the wrong directions, and pictured them sitting down laughing at the gullible Westerners in the silly car (probably while sharing some cha-cha).

The day only got worse as we found that to temporarily import the car would cost us over £65 in fees; a steep price for less than a week in the country, especially on our shoestring budget. We thoroughly considered turning around and returning to Tbilisi but we couldn't stomach the thought of returning along that terrible farmers' track; plus we had arranged the date to meet Annaka, and we also had a passenger in tow – a German hitchhiker named Felix who was thumbing a lift from Georgia to Yerevan.

After some negotiation we knocked down the price slightly and eventually gave in, paid the fees and tried to make it to the city sometime before midnight. Unfortunately the Armenian roads were the worst we had yet encountered. Wherever small potholes had occurred, a giant chunk of the road had been dug out, ready to be refilled with fresh Tarmac, but the vast majority were unfilled. To make the day a little worse still, at some point during a driver changeover, I lost my iPod and headphones. Somewhere in northern Armenia a shepherd is probably sitting, watching his flocks by night, listening to Avril Lavigne.

When we arrived at Lilly and Annaka's lovely flat, we spent a couple of days catching up on the mountain of paperwork that comes with driving a car around the world; filling in more Pakistani visa applications; calculating visa requirements for plan Bs; filling in form after form and sending photographs of the vehicle from every angle to enter China; and watching two seasons of *Battlestar Galactica* (well, in Leigh's case).

Leigh and I were never granted Pakistan visas. Johno, being a filthy Yorkshireman, lived in a different consulate constituency to us where they are more willing to issue visas, but only just, so even after numerous visits to the embassy before we left, and then even more by a team of exceptionally patient friends of ours back home with our second passports, we were still visaless. The real problem we had lay in the fact that the car was registered in my name, so I had to be with it at all borders, and Guinness stated that two people must be in the car at all times for the world record. This meant that Leigh and I couldn't simply fly over Pakistan and meet Johno and Hannah in India. This left us with three options:

1. Persevere to get the visas and drive through Pakistan as one big happy family (complicated by Pakistan being a bit of a warzone, a kidnap hotspot and the scene of the killing of Osama Bin Laden a few weeks earlier).
2. Drive north out of Iran into the 'Stans' and enter China from there (missing India, Nepal and Tibet).
3. Pop the cab on a ship, parting with £2,000 we didn't have, and ship it to India.

We were in limbo – the whole expedition was hanging in the balance.

I was keen to go through the 'Stans' – it wasn't the most fun route but it meant the expedition was more likely to succeed and reach Sydney. Leigh and Johno were adamant about going through India and the Himalayas – more risky, but also more interesting.

So we waited on a final Pakistan visa attempt, and worried.

A few days after we arrived in Yerevan, we were told that the Iranian visas were ready for collection, two weeks earlier than promised.

We duly set off back towards Turkey, heading north into Georgia before hitting the turning for the Georgian Military Highway.

Supposedly one of the most impressive roads you could drive, it cuts deep into the Caucasus mountains and is closed for half the year due to snow.

The road climbed around switchbacks and past ancient monasteries. We stopped to explore an abandoned castle and even found an old ski resort close to the top of the pass, but the road kept on going. It had turned into an unpaved track that spent half its time beneath concrete avalanche tunnels, not large enough for trucks, but just big enough for a taxi. Deeply rutted, this inside road was occasionally lit by a shard of light where the concrete cocoon had split. We emerged at the end to find a queue of trucks waiting for the road up around the tunnels to be cleared of snow and rockfall from the winter. They had been there for days or longer and the road looked far from being clear, so their wait would continue.

Looking at the satnav we decided to make instead for the only name nearby, presumably a town nestled on the other side of the pass called Stepantsminda. We descended from the high mountains to a flat, grassy plain, walled on either side by high cliffs and hills, passing a small town. It was getting dark and, although now paved, the road made its way into a tight ravine, clinging precariously to the side of a cliff. We arrived at another queue of lorries where a raging torrent of a river looped around the road.

From out of nowhere, a chap in black robes and an unusual hat appeared and started to speak to us in broken, but proficient English. We explained why there was a London black cab parked in the middle of the Georgian wilds, enquired as to what the checkpoint ahead was for and asked him how much further. He told us he was a monk, that the checkpoint was in fact Chechnya and that Stepantsky-whatever was ten miles behind us.

Over the next few days we slogged back through Turkey driving solidly for two days on smooth highways, climbing ever higher into rolling mountain valleys that seemed to be populated only by herds of cows and sheep. The signs pointed to new unusual names that were beyond our lazy pronunciation skills; Erzurum quickly became, 'Er-zoo-thingy', far-off Doğubayazıt, on the border with Iran, became, 'Doggy-biscuit', and Noyemberyan became classic nineties power ballad, 'November Rain'. Eventually we started to see occasional signs for 'Irak'.

'Um, what's that ticking sound?' Paul suddenly said, quickly killing the conversation about the current state of Iraq.

'What ticking sound?'

'That ticking sound. The engine feels weird... oh shit!'

One look at the engine temperature said it all. The needle was beyond the red indictor, indicating clearly, 'You're screwed.'

Our feet had just about defrosted from the previous chilly evening's camping by the time we struck the small rolling hills. Having spent the night shivering with cold, the engine overheating was not at the forefront of Paul's mind.

Up came the bonnet and steam hissed everywhere – the classic breakdown.

The radiator had blown.

After some bodge repairs, we limped onwards, passing countless checkpoints and vast fortified barracks manned by teenage conscripts cutting their military teeth against the Kurdish rebels. They seemed undertrained, uninspired and very bored, and we had our first experience of feeling vulnerable in checkpoint queues.

We spent the night at a border town called Cizre, apparently built at the foot of the mountain where Noah's Ark came to rest. Although we stayed in a very shoddy resthouse, it turned out that three single rooms were about the same price as a shared room, meaning, tents forgotten, we each spent a blissful night alone for the first time since we left the girls in Bodrum.

CHAPTER 18

- - - - - - - - -

TURN RIGHT TO CERTAIN DEATH

The road was smooth, virtually empty and hot.

Johnny Cash sang out from the iPod and as the taxi drove towards the Iraqi border, it felt like the air got hotter with every mile and the land became more spartan and desert-like.

Eventually we saw the border in the distance. Like all crossings, it was marked out by queues of lorries looking to trade their wares across the country line. Capitalism in its purest form, there was everything from ice cream to motor oil, ketchup to cheap Chinese-made bathroom fittings – all evidence that people's desires for plastic toothbrush-holders-cum-mirrors often seem to supersede their interests in current affairs or the war that was raging in the southern part of the country.

Mr Cash was musing over the hot beverage and smoking choices of wealthy rail passengers as we passed through the Turkish side of the border, pausing to arrange vehicle paperwork with the typically Turkish border guard in his booth. He went through the taxi's various documents with a practised eye and I gazed at his cigarette as it slowly burnt down to the MARLBORO letters by the base, causing the scorched paint where he placed it on the windowsill to bubble and steam slightly. Leaving the cigarette burning, the border guard left his booth and headed towards the car, his ample midriff spilling out of his knock-off 'Tid Baker, London' T-shirt. Expecting a full car search, I watched his grave face suddenly break into a huge, sporadically toothed grin, and he asked me to take his picture with the car.

'What model? Mercedes?'

'No, LTI, it's a London taxi.'

'Ahh yes, Mercedes...'

'Um...'

'How old? Fifty years?'

'Twenty.'

'Oh, it looks older,' he said, looking mildly disappointed, and as he waved us through, it dawned on me that Leigh, Johno and I would have been barely out of nappies by the time Hannah rolled off the production line.

The area of northern Iraq is part of Kurdistan, populated by the Kurds who were continuously oppressed by Saddam Hussein until a no-fly zone was established there in the 1990s. Since the fall of Saddam, Iraqi Kurdistan has become a semi-autonomous region of Iraq and the Kurds are free for the first time in decades. It's now considerably safer for travel than the rest of the country, and is one of the very few places where George Bush Senior and Junior are both hailed as heroes.

On entering the customs office of Iraq, we were welcomed immediately by Kurdish hospitality. A cup of sweet tea was thrust into my hands and I was sat down on a comfortable leather sofa in a fresh, air-conditioned room. A man with a Wolverhampton accent introduced himself; he lived in Britain but had come to Kurdistan for his mother's funeral the following day. I made the right sounds, as one does in these situations, but I was cut short by his immediate invitation to come to his for lunch and to stay in his family home. This would have been a kind offer at any time, but being on the eve of his mum's funeral made it especially generous. It seems that nothing can suppress the famous Kurdish hospitality. I had to decline – joining a family of mourners had the potential for a few awkward moments – and besides, we had to get to the capital.

The next stage was to import the car into Iraq, a process that involved eight different windows, with eight different officials, armed with eight different red pens, date stamps and carbon paper – now a far more daunting sight than any soldier clutching a Kalashnikov.

But, Kurdish hospitality was again to prevail. Within seconds a short man with beady eyes and a calculating face had grabbed my arm and marched me to a window, announcing in perfect English that I would not be able to cope without his help. He whisked me through the procedure at each window and told me that if we had any problems at all, day or night, to call him. As he noted down a couple of numbers for me, he mentioned that his cousin also happened to run the Iraq–Iran border post. Checking the numbers thrice and waving him goodbye, I decided that he was a very useful person to know when moving forward into a country still ravaged by war. I also couldn't help but think how I had never seen a British businessman stopping in Heathrow to ensure a Kurdish family didn't have any problems with immigration.

Throughout the region shopkeepers often refused to allow us to pay for goods and people constantly offered us food and drink. One of the best Kurdish sayings we heard was 'A Kurd's stomach is never full'.

We headed down towards the regional capital – written as Erbil, Arbil, Urbil, Hawler, Hawla, or their equivalent Arabic, depending on which road sign you looked at – where we planned to spend a few days looking around and repairing the patched-up radiator.

We had been told that there was a certain turn-off on the highway with poor signposting where the secondary road split off towards the relatively safe Erbil while the main road continued on towards the extremely dangerous city of Mosul, the location of regular suicide bombings and extreme violence. With the help of the satnav and a quick look at Google Maps, it looked like it would be clear where we should and shouldn't drive. Unfortunately, Leigh looked up from his book at exactly the wrong moment, just as we passed a sign pointing the way to Mosul.

'Johno, stop, we can't go to Mosul, remember.'

'We're not, the road splits in a few miles and goes right to Mosul, left to Erbil.'

'Stop now! We can't go to Mosul!'

'Dude, I've been following the satnav the whole way, we're not going to end up in Mosul...' I promised, but his insistence overruled my internal GPS and we stopped to check with a passing truck driver.

'Erbil?' I ventured, pointing alternately in each direction.

He looked blank.

'Arbil?' asked Paul.

Nothing.

'Irbil?' tried Leigh.

'Ah! Orbil!' he erupted. 'Yes, yes, Orbil.' He gestured along the way we had been going.

'No Mosul?' we asked.

'Orbil,' he motioned forward and left; 'Mosul,' he gestured forward and right. 'You, no Mosul,' he said deadly seriously, pointing at us then drawing his finger over his throat.

When we came to the fabled junction we looked to the right and in the distance saw the largest military checkpoint yet. I doubted they'd let us pass even if we wanted to, but it was a stark reminder of the unrest that is still rife in the country and we were glad to be turning left down the road to Erbil.

Erbil's landmark is a citadel that sits on a hill in the centre of the capital and is considered the longest continuously inhabited urban dwelling on earth. Until fairly recently a large number of poor families lived in the citadel – almost as historical squatters – but the government decided that they were damaging the ancient buildings. They forcibly relocated all but one family, so they could keep the continual-habitation record going. The city sprawls in orderly ring roads out from the centre; the oldest in the middle and the new dwellings hugging the outskirts.

We were to collect our Iranian visas from their consulate in the city, our invitations having supposedly been sent there from Iran. So, duly, on the day after we arrived, we traipsed on foot for an hour in the midday heat trying to find the embassy, eventually discovering it down a neat residential street, only to be told they had no record of our invitation. Phone calls were made and we were told to return the next day. This happened for four days straight, which meant we spent what we had left of each day either sleeping off the midday heat or exploring the endless bazaar in the town.

Iraq is known as the cradle of civilisation, which makes watching the world go by an enthralling pastime. I would saunter through the tight, twisting streets, stopping to sit with the local old folk and sip from small glasses of black tea, served with a dessertspoonful of sugar.

The bazaar was hectic; the initial impression was one of utter chaos. However, order begins to become apparent as you spend more time there. Each area sells roughly the same thing. Babies' cribs are piled high for three storefronts, blending easily into the copper-piping stalls, which merge smoothly with bedding shops, before sacks of fragrant spices identify the spicemonger. Kebabs, fruit, honey, cheese, fake iPods and lingerie. If you know what you're looking for, then there will be a cluster of shops selling it. You just need to know where they are and that's no easy task in the alleys around Erbil bazaar.

Suddenly a sweat-drenched Leigh burst through the door into our blissfully cool hotel room.

'Did you not hear me outside?!' he panted, 'I thought I was being kidnapped!'

Leigh had been slaving away trying to fix Hannah's various ailments in the midday heat when a white van screeched to a halt alongside the taxi and three men grabbed him and started to bundle him into the back. Leigh fought back and started to shout, but was soon stopped as all three men burst into laughter and the owner of our hotel hopped out of the driving seat with a mischievous grin on his face in what was probably the most ill-themed practical joke this side of Baghdad.

Our new joker-friends gave us directions to the Auto Bazaar – a collection of mud buildings where any and every type of auto activity was being carried out. The place was a sprawl of garages with wrecked cars on top of each and oil-covered mechanics hammering, welding and fixing things.

A mechanical clatter and the smell of exhaust fumes permeated everything and the young boys rushed around ferrying cups of tea half-full with sugar to fortify the men hard at work.

As with the general bazaar, there were clusters of specialists for all types of parts, ranging from fan belts to exhausts and eventually we found the radiator section.

Leigh quickly negotiated a price and our piping-hot leaky radiator was immediately unscrewed and pulled out by the asbestos hands of a hardened mechanic. He held up the ailing radiator in one hand as the last of the dirty cooling water drained out and squinted at it, before grabbing another from a large pile and expertly braising on all the correct fittings by eye.

Half an hour later Hannah had a freshly working radiator, and the next day we were eventually granted our Iranian visas. It was time to move on.

CHAPTER 19

GUERRILLA CAMPING

After being granted our visas we had spent an entire day in the British Embassy, which was based in one of the only sparkling, glass five-star hotels that occasionally popped up out of the sand on the outskirts of Erbil. We had thoroughly made the most of the buffet, Wi-Fi and bathrooms. Unfortunately only embassy staff were allowed to stay overnight so we set off into the dusk to find a place to stay. Before long yet another car problem left us limping along in dire need of a proper mechanic. We decided that all we could do was find somewhere to camp in the Iraqi countryside and fix it the next day.

It was nearly 1 a.m. when we found somewhere that would have to do – a large stretch of wasteland, away from the main road and covered in spiky thorn bushes.

We pulled the tents down from the roof, found some bush-free patches and were about to settle down when an old man on an underpowered motorbike rode up out of the dark.

After a short conversation he got on his phone, started saying something about, 'Inglisey' and then motioned for us to follow him.

The day had already brought us the news that we might need extra permits as well as our Iranian visas to get across the border.

'You really think three young British men in a London black cab will be able enter Iran from Iraq without special permission?' the embassy official had asked us, with a condescending look that implied we had said we were going to do a naked-unicycle marathon through North Korea.

So after leaving the embassy earlier in the day, unsure whether we'd be able to leave the country the next day, we weren't in the most buoyant of moods. Then when Hannah broke down and a random man on a motorbike told us to follow him into the dark we all thought, 'Why not, how can our day get much worse?'

The motorcyclist led us out of the wasteland and up a dirt track into the lights of a village. As we approached a slight hill he raced off around the corner and when we caught up we saw that he had met up with another guy.

As we edged closer we realised he had an AK-47.

He motioned for one of us to get out.

'Shotgun not me!' Leigh and I both shouted. Perhaps a poor choice of words, but Paul cursed himself for losing and opened his door. He walked down the track with our potential captors, constantly looking over his shoulder at Leigh and I trundling along a safe distance behind.

And by safe I mean completely unsafe and well within the range of an AK.

We followed them into a courtyard where a humongous man who looked suspiciously like Jeremy Clarkson, but with a shock of white hair, was flanked by another rifle-wielding stranger. After a short conversation the three men beckoned for us to follow them down another dusty trail and Paul set off, as Leigh and I nervously made jokes about him being the sacrificial team member from the dubious safety of Hannah.

They took us to what appeared to be a deserted community centre and ushered us inside. We held our breaths as they showed us around, not sure whether to expect a torture room or prison cell, and eventually we were shown into one room full of beds. They quickly said their goodbyes and then we were left alone, seemingly having been given a free place to stay.

'I don't care if they do kidnap us,' shouted Leigh, 'this room has air-conditioning!'

We passed through the Iraqi border exit procedures with no problem; they had even given us tea to sip as they stamped our passports. That side of the border was never going to be the problem though; getting into Iran was and now we were approaching the Iranian border guards with nervous apprehension.

As Paul and I slowly exited the car on arrival, they fixed us with a solemn glare. Then Leigh shouldered open the stiff passenger door with all his might and in the process smacked the corner right into my head.

'OOOWW! WHAT ARE YOU DOING!' I shouted with anger as I jumped back clutching my scalp.

The guards looked at us then at each other before bursting out laughing. Our slapstick routine might have just saved the day.

Thankfully, the Iranian guards were very friendly and efficient, even giving us helpful advice on nice places to visit in the country. And then, just like that, everything was done and we were driving down the mountain road towards the city of Piranshahr, and our 30th country.

CHAPTER 20

SPECIAL BREW IN A DRY STATE

'I dunno mate, they all just look like squiggles to me.'

We were well and truly stumped. The Iranian border town was completely nondescript except for one aspect: neon. There were neon signs everywhere.

Growing up in the UK we had all come to subconsciously associate neon Arabic or Persian lettering with fast-food joints, but here it seemed that just about every establishment used neon signage, from shoe shops to lawyers to hairdressers. Everywhere apart from hotels.

We were trying to figure out how on earth we were going to find somewhere to stay when none of us had any clue what the Persian for 'hotel' was, when a friendly young man with impeccable English approached us and immediately invited us over to his place and then out to dinner. It dawned on us that we were still technically among the good ol' Kurds.

Over dinner in the city's finest fish restaurant we learnt that Ali and his friends were some kind of commodity traders, flitting between Iran and Dubai. They offered to let us stay at their offices for a few days, but more to our surprise, one of them returned from an errand sporting a plastic carrier bag stuffed full of cans of high-strength Special Brew lager: totally unexpected in what was supposedly a dry country. Each sip made us feel even guiltier as they explained that the cans were hiked through the landmine-ridden mountains from Iraq by poor smugglers looking to make a quick buck and so the alcohol-to-weight ratio was crucial to making it worth their while, especially as those who were caught were shot.

Iran regularly features in the Western media, but rarely in a good way. When you say you're going to Iran, most people's reaction is comparable to telling them you're going on a sailing excursion along the Somalian coast. However, although the government and its foreign policy supposedly presents one of the largest threats to 'Western' security, the country we saw was safe, pleasant and rammed full of some of the best sightseeing we had been lucky enough to experience.

The regime, however, is never far away. A few weeks before we arrived, the president, Ahmadinejad, announced that the rains had not arrived in Iran because the British had stolen them, and that is the reason why it always rains in England and not Iran. He also gave a speech to announce the celebration that Iran is completely free of homosexuals.

Iranian people, however, could not be more different from the image of the country portrayed in the media. Fiercely proud to be Persian (and not Arab; if you fail to make this distinction you will be met with some very stern looks indeed), they are articulate, intelligent and, from our experience, all appear to despise the government. Men dress in a Western manner with an open silk-shirted Persian twist; the women wear skinny jeans, inches of make-up and finely coiffed hairstyles. All this effort is covered by the mandatory hijab-veil and a shirt-cum-dress that does a very effective job of hiding their figures in accordance with the strict laws governing women's dress. But as soon as you enter a liberal Iranian home, the veil and dress-shirt are removed and their TVs display illegal satellite programmes from abroad that show you the real Persia, if its people were free to do what they wanted.

Variety shows in Persian, filmed in London, allow people a sort of escape from the constant repetition of the ruling ayatollahs' speeches and propaganda that infest the terrestrial airwaves. BBC Persia provides them with news from a different viewpoint, film channels from the Emirates beam Hollywood's banned finest into their front rooms, while soap operas from South America, Australia and the US provide housewives with badly dubbed distraction.

Although the roads up to the capital, Tehran, were smooth ribbons of new Tarmac, the driving was the craziest yet, especially in the cities and towns. Vehicles assaulted us from every direction and constant attention was required to keep track of the bikes, cars and trucks, which were all vying for space. Speed limit signs appeared to dictate the minimum speed at which to overtake an unusual foreign car before cutting it up and squeezing through an impossibly narrow gap in front of it. Everyone seemed to drive at breakneck speed lest they arrive at their destinations ten seconds late.

Upon the advice of a friend who had visited Iran a few years before, we decided to escape the never-ending traffic of Tehran and head up north to the Caspian Sea for a few days.

During the early route planning we had been surprised to discover that it's possible to ski in Iran. They have a proper resort with lifts and the works. This is because the hills north of Tehran are high enough that they are blanketed with snow for much of the winter.

However, in the middle of summer, it is very hot.

And those hills are still very high.

And slap bang between Tehran and the Caspian Sea.

And when your radiator is a reduced sized unit built in a yard in Iraq and you've been driving uphill for half an hour, your engine will overheat.

So we pulled into one of the many restaurants on the side of the road.

The restaurant we chose to eat at was colourful, with plastic tables and chairs overlooking the beautiful valley we had just climbed up. We settled down into a pile of cushions and asked the prices of the shish kebabs pictured in the menu.

'Two hundred thousand rials,' said the waiter.

We had been in Iran for over a week and eaten in myriad places, from seriously grotty roadside joints to some very fine establishments in Tehran, and had a pretty good grasp of the cost of living. The price of these kebabs was reasonable – not dirt cheap, but not expensive – so we ordered.

Our plates of charcoal-cooked spiced minced lamb arrived on a piece of flatbread as big as the table, with yoghurt and salad. Ripping off the bread and sharing the food is customary so we dug in and filled our boots as Hannah's overheated engine cooled in the shade of some trees.

The bill arrived; the meal came to 400,000 rials, about £2.50. This was extremely reasonable and it seemed like the waiter's meat prices must have been arbitrary as we handed over the cash.

'No, no, no, no,' he said, 'four hundred thousand toman.'

The value of one rial is less than 0.0001 penny, so, to make people's lives easier, Persians lop one of the zeros off and call it toman. However, there seems to be no logic or consistency with this practice, and in a country under strict trade sanctions you sometimes find the most bizarre things cost a fortune (eggs) and some cost next to nothing (fuel). As a rule of thumb you should always ask whether the price is in toman or rials, even if it does make you look a bit stupid.

We were also still getting our heads around the completely alien Eastern-Arabic numeral system, so we had always taken extra care to confirm prices before we actually bought things. After a few minutes of finger-counting and working out with a paper and pen, it became clear that this man was trying to con us. He tried to charge £25 for what we knew should have cost no more than a tenner. Johno and I left to start the car as the waiter carried on shouting at Leigh, getting redder and redder by the second. Eventually Leigh dumped £20 down and jumped in the car.

Now the waiter started to really lose it, following Leigh to the car and reaching halfway through my open window to punch me as we drove off, his legs flailing out of the side of the cab. He carried on trying to throw punches halfway up the mountainside, and when he eventually gave up we all breathed a sigh of relief.

It was 30 minutes later, the incident almost forgotten, when an old blue saloon slowly started to pull up close behind us, honking its horn and veering towards us.

It was the waiter.

And he had brought a gang.

We were now in a comically slow car chase in two overheating cars, over kebabs. I didn't want to stop for these crooks, but when we saw a set of flashing lights behind us we pulled over. Within seconds we were surrounded by an angry mob, with the waiter at the head of the gang spurring them on. Where so many people had appeared from was anybody's guess, but they all seemed hell-bent on attacking the three lads in the funny car. The police forced their way through the crowd to our windows but they barely spoke any English, so we couldn't explain that it was us who had been conned. It seemed the only way to break up the riot and save Hannah from the beating she was getting would be the old favourite – handing over a wad of cash to an undeserving party. The police tried to shoo away the crowd as we paid the waiter, but it didn't stop them kicking poor old Hannah one last time as we pulled away.

The whole time this was happening, a guy was having a long chat with Johno through the back window – apparently oblivious to the riot that was kicking off – asking him where he was from and whether he liked Iran.

CHAPTER 21

GLOBAL POSITIONING MELTDOWN

Despite a few more third-party attempts by helpful friends, Leigh and Paul had still not been able to secure their Pakistan visas. To the immense relief of their worried mums and girlfriends, it would mean they would have to skip this leg of the trip. Our most likely looking option was now to ship Hannah from Iran directly to India; a cripplingly expensive process that would probably have us picking fruit in Australia for years to pay off the cost.

With all this in mind I had been thinking about travelling through Pakistan on my own using trains and buses and meeting the guys in India – after all it seemed a shame to waste the visa it had been such a hassle for me to obtain.

Leigh didn't seem particularly bothered by my suggestion and although Paul tried to act unperturbed I could tell he was less than happy at the thought of missing out on such a gnarly section of the trip.

I was trying to explain my choice and we were talking through options when a familiar accent interrupted us. 'Alright lads, where you from?'

Mohammad was in his early 20s and had lived near London until he was 15, before moving back to his family's home country to study in Tehran. Like many of the Iranians we met – especially the more Westernised ones – he candidly told us his opinions on the failings of his government and explained that his overly vocal criticism of them had landed him in trouble with the religious police in the strict capital. This had led to him moving, or being moved, to study in the smaller coastal town where he would cause fewer metaphorical waves, although his beachfront house meant many more of the literal kind.

He invited us into the typically messy student digs that he shared with three friends and a ceiling fan that was on the verge of shaking itself to an early grave. While we waited for a takeaway meal they told us that their landlady was a crazy old woman addicted to opium who had died during a recent religious festival. Ever since then, no one had been around to collect the rent, which suited them just fine.

The next morning, Leigh was carrying out his usual tinkering with the car. Whenever we stopped for any length of time he loved to fiddle with anything mechanical or electrical, sometimes carrying out essential maintenance that Paul and I didn't have the skill or motivation to do ourselves (fixing our ever-breaking electrics, repairing the alarm, changing the oil), but often just meddling where no meddling was required (gluing coins to the roll cage, making new switches for the dashboard, recarpeting the footwells).

As part of the record attempt, Guinness needed many different types of evidence to prove that we were really driving where we said we were. This ranged from a witness book, signed by policemen and other officials (including Santa Claus), to news articles charting our progress. However, the most essential part of the evidence was the track provided by a second GPS unit that showed exactly where we had driven since leaving London. So far it read slightly over 14,000 miles. The only problem was that the GPS ran on batteries and we were constantly forgetting to recharge them and having to scrounge from cameras and torches mid-drive whenever we saw the dreaded 'battery low' message.

Consequently, Leigh had decided to attempt to wire the GPS into the car's electrical system. When I looked over and saw him with live wires in one hand and the open GPS in the other I automatically asked, 'Have you backed it up?'

'Yeah, yeah, of course,' he replied, reassuring me that the vital track was saved to his computer's hard disk.

So, when a few minutes later I saw his face drop and watched him frantically trot in and out of Mohammad's house with the GPS and various screwdrivers in hand, a feeling of terror hit me.

'Leigh, what's wrong?'

No answer.

'Leigh, is the GPS OK?'

'No, it just won't turn on,' he said, rapidly leafing through the instruction manual.

'But you backed it up.'

He didn't answer and carried on ripping through the pages.

'Leigh, you backed it up, right?'

We had lost thousands of miles of recorded route from the world record and now had no GPS unit to proceed with. Understandably, Johno flipped out.

Leigh managed to locate the only shop in Tehran that repaired and sold GPS units, but he told us we had to be there by the next morning or it would be shut for the weekend. After what turned out to be an all too brief 24-hour stop by the coast we headed back across the mountain pass to the capital.

As I manoeuvred my way through the lighter-than-usual traffic, we entered a large roundabout, ironically named Freedom Square, to find ourselves face-to-face with a battalion of riot police. A young man on a scooter sped past us and yelled through the open window, 'Bad timing, friends!'

It appeared we had inadvertently stumbled across a pro-democracy protest.

In Iran.

In the depths of the Arab Spring.

The GPS shop was now only ten minutes away and our eyes were anxiously darting around for signs of trouble at every junction we neared – crowds were milling around and the occasional gang of riot police stared out from their visored helmets. As we approached the final large intersection I was somewhat preoccupied and missed the signals of one of the many uniformed traffic police that were placed around the city. They were all dressed in a smart white uniform with a red cap, wore mirrored aviator sunglasses and sported designer stubble. They took the place of traffic lights at most junctions, and after a while they tended to just blend in.

A police officer stood bold as day, aviator glasses glinting in the sun, as he held his hand up in a stop signal. He couldn't have stuck out against his drab surroundings any more.

Johno ignored him.

By the time I had seen the particular officer, who had motioned for our lanes of traffic to halt so he could start moving the six lanes of buses, cars and bikes running perpendicular to us, I was already committed to crossing the junction and tried my best to weave through the impossible gauntlet of tonnes of metal approaching from each side.

Have you ever had one of those moments when you're certain you're going to die? I hadn't until Johno drove me through Tehran. The traffic came at us from all sides, just as Leigh started shouting, 'Shiiit!', I ducked my head down, closed my eyes and waited for the inevitable impact, metal on metal, metal on bone and flesh, that bright light in front of my eyes... are we covered by travel insurance in Iran?

Maybe.

Maybe it would help pay for the repatriation of what was left of our mangled bodies back to England.

I slammed the brakes on and waited for the seemingly unavoidable crunch, but it never came. Somehow, as if in a scene from an action film, I had managed to dodge everyone else (everyone else managed to dodge the idiot in the London taxi, more like).

Paul, who had appeared to be resting in the passenger seat, was jolted upright by a sudden increase in volume of car horns, the abrupt stop and the sickening sixth-sense feeling you probably get when a ten-tonne bus screeches to a halt inches from your face. In the back Leigh was clinging on to the old passenger handles so hard that I was surprised they were still attached.

For a second there was relative calm as the stunned drivers stared at the black cab wedged amongst them, then the horns blared with a vengeance and a mob of police ran over shouting and gesturing angrily.

Worst of all was the reaction of my terrified teammates.

'What the ruddy flipping hell did you do that for! He was telling you to stop you silly ninny!' I shouted (or possibly something a bit stronger).

Unused adrenaline was pumping through me with nowhere to go and the bus's radiator was inches from my face.

'I didn't see him.'

'He had to jump out of the way of the ruddy-flipping car, how could you NOT flipping see him?'

The police were shouting in Persian, my mouth was still wide open with the shock, but Johno just gave his best English, 'Terribly sorry', blatantly ignored their obvious commands to stop and drove out of the jumble of vehicles. Within a few seconds there were six lanes of moving traffic between us and them and they couldn't catch us anyway.

Soon, I pulled up outside the shop and sat shaking as Paul and Leigh went to find out the fate of our GPS. I took in exactly how close our near-miss had been while the local people gawked in amazement at the car.

The repairman told us he could recover most of the data, but that the GPS unit itself was truly fried, so all we could do was spend some of our dwindling supply of money. Obviously we were on a tight budget throughout the trip, but in Iran we couldn't withdraw any cash due to the strict UN sanctions and currency restrictions. That left us with the limited supply we had brought into the country in the cab's secret compartments. After replacing the GPS, which cost the equivalent of £150, we were left with a budget that fell below £6 a day each.

Another issue was that the new GPS had no maps installed. With no idea of where we were, we followed the compass south so we could get out of Tehran before we were killed by the protesters, the hordes of riot police or (most likely) Johno's driving. This technique eventually worked and we escaped Tehran after a few hours without engaging with any actual protests, and decided to put a bit of space between ourselves and the city.

We were soon in the desert, with nothing for miles except rocks and sand. After a good 50 miles, taking a turn-off and driving along an empty road for less than a mile, we pulled over into the desert and pitched our tents in the darkness, with only the lights from the motorway in view on the horizon and the gentle din of its users lulling us to sleep.

CHAPTER 22

- - - - - - - -

OUR FRIENDS, THE SECRET POLICE

As I stepped out of my tent into the sun-bathed sand of the Iranian desert, I stretched the last vestiges of sleep away and surveyed our surroundings. All around us was barren featureless wasteland, broken up by the occasional scraggly bush.

Then I saw it, about 300 m away.

'Is that...' I asked no one in particular, 'artillery?'

Leigh poked his head out and confirmed that we had indeed managed to choose a camping spot on a range of anti-aircraft installations and also pointed out the half-built oil pipeline a little further away. He nonchalantly went on explain that we were about 30 miles north of the holy city of Qom, infamous for being home to Iran's nuclear facilities. It would have been hard to find a more sensitive area if we had tried.

Leigh, always the last to be ready, was stuffing his tent on to the roof rack when our attention was drawn to one of the ubiquitous white Chinese pickup trucks that had just pulled off the main road and was now very deliberately approaching us.

This was not looking good. We were three British kids, driving a British car fitted out with cameras and GPS trackers and surrounded by some of the most sensitive kinds of installations to the Iranian government, in the middle of nowhere.

And to make it worse, the first thing Johno and I had done was to take pictures of the guns. Why would anybody photograph military installations erected to protect Iran's nuclear reactor from an Israeli airstrike? Well, firstly, we thought it was pretty funny before the secret police had turned up, and secondly and most importantly: we are bloody idiots.

Out of the pickup hopped two men; one of them was big, fat and sporting a pair of cube-shaped school-style shoes of the variety that your mum would dress you in on your first day back at school, and which your mates would then relentlessly mock you for. The other was short, thin, bookish and looked more like an accountant than a police officer. He would habitually remove his glasses and clean them when he spoke, revealing that his eyes actually pointed in separate directions, leaving you with the awkward worry of which eye to talk to. They each wore poorly made uniforms with hand-sewn police badges. Knowing that it's possible to buy these uniforms in the market and that fake police are a well-known scam in Iran, I didn't trust them.

'Passports,' they demanded.

'Who are you?' demanded Paul in return. 'Your uniform doesn't look real, I'm not letting you take my passport!'

I groaned, 'Paul, don't be difficult, they're obviously the real deal.'

They examined the passports carefully and relayed the details to an unknown accomplice on the other end of the phone then sat back to wait.

'Is there a problem?' we asked innocently.

'Wait, wait,' came the reply.

After half an hour fidgeting in the sun we found out what we were waiting for as another white SUV pulled up and two more men emerged. One was smartly dressed in black trousers and a pristine white shirt; the other sported a large beard and was wearing traditional Islamic dress. They conferred with the local police and examined our passports for a short while before approaching us.

The fat man with bad shoes had been quizzing me for what seemed like hours when he had a flash of inspiration. 'You… are Muslim?'

I mumbled a no.

'Are you a Christian?'

Now, this is where one should nod one's head vigorously, saying yes in as many languages as one knows and dropping to one's knees and reciting passages from the Bible. This is because, to Muslims, Christians are men 'of the book' and are generally respected.

I considered diving into an in-depth rhetoric about my Catholic upbringing, its lapsed status (once a Catholic, always a Catholic?) and what this means in the theological landscape of modern Britain. However, this just ended up congealing into a simple, 'No'.

At exactly the same time the skinny guy started to get in his pickup with our passports. He needed to photocopy them back at the base but I was not allowed there for security reasons. A Benny-Hill-like farce then unfolded as he tried to leave, and I refused to let him go.

He would get in the pickup, so would I.

He would step out, so would I.

He would get back in, closely followed by me playing dumb.

He would try to tell me, again and again, that I couldn't come. Each time I would hedge my bets by addressing a different eye, telling him in no uncertain terms that I was not leaving our passports. Eventually, after much deliberation, it was established that they could photocopy the passports at a service station and that I could come too.

I climbed into the blissfully air-conditioned pickup with him and the two of us made off across the desert, leaving the lads to sweat in the now fully risen sun with the remaining secret police.

This left Leigh and me with a confused pair of secret policemen and a whole new raft of questions. If Paul was not Christian then surely he must be Jewish, they reasoned. And if he was Jewish then surely he must be Israeli. And if he was Israeli then surely he must be a spy.

For the next 15 minutes we tried to explain that Paul was not Jewish or Israeli or a spy. In the end the subject was changed by the discovery of our Carnet de Passage document, which had the words 'Ex: Israel – Kenya – Iraq – Lebanon' in large letters on the back, to show the four countries our car passport excluded. The secret policeman's English was a little weak, but even to a good English speaker, the subtle 'Ex:' on the top of the Carnet could have been easily missed.

'Ah-hah, so you have been to Israel, yes?'

Cue an hour of arguments under the beating sun assuring the police that no, Paul was still not Jewish, and no, we had not been to Israel, and, most importantly, no, we were most definitely not Israeli spies.

While this was going on, I sat in a service station drying off in air-conditioning, drinking an apple-flavoured non-alcoholic German beer and eating dates with a pretty Iranian girl. My would-be-accountant guardian proved that there is a desk job somewhere in Tehran that is wasted on someone else, as he diligently photocopied every single page of all of our passports.

By the time we returned, the secret policemen had given up interrogating the boys and were now thoroughly searching the car.

I hoped they didn't notice my obvious nerves as I tried to imagine the consequences of being caught with an SLR camera with photographs of Iranian military installations on it. Only a few days before, Leigh had been talking about a British tourist who had been arrested and jailed for months for taking pictures of a landscape with pylons in the background. At the time I had questioned how anyone could be so stupid, but now the situation I was facing was even worse.

A god (Muslim, Jewish, Catholic or whatever) must have been smiling on us that day, and they somehow managed to miss

Johno's huge camera with the incriminating pictures and the GPS equipment we had picked up the day before. Well, maybe the search just wasn't that thorough, but to their credit the taxi was a characteristic shit-tip.

Fortunately the only camera they did find was Leigh's, with his almost-dead batteries. The screen flickered on for just long enough for them to see that the last picture taken was of a Turkish bazaar in Istanbul over a month before, and not at all incriminating.

The head officer turned his attention back to me. 'What electrical items do you have with you?'

I emptied my pockets. 'Just an iPod and phone.'

'Nothing else?'

'Nothing else,' I lied, praying to my non-existent god he wouldn't search the bag in the car by his side.

He studied my face for a moment.

'OK, you are free to leave.'

We had managed to get away with it, but we were clearly marked as suspicious. I wouldn't be surprised one bit if some poor junior intelligence officer had to trail us for the next two weeks writing detailed descriptions of how many cups of tea we drank as we wandered around ancient mosques, toured car bazaars buying spare parts and relaxed in the country's many leafy parks.

While we waited for the results of our thirteenth and final attempt at getting Pakistan visas, we had some time to kill in Iran. Luckily, Esfahan is scattered with various palaces, bazaars, antique bridges and mirror-filled mosques; you can wander and wander and always find something interesting and new. I met a couple of nutty Dutch fellas who had cycled from Istanbul, and after hanging out for a while, we decided to spend the evening sampling Iran's favourite pastime – picnicking.

In a country where you can't drink, watch movies, dance, talk to girls, talk freely, wear necklaces, sport a mullet (true story), swim in the same area of sea as the opposite sex, wear shorts, eat pork, get tattoos, own a pet, wear a tie, watch news, or (worst of all) use Facebook, you have to find other ways of filling your time. It appears the only option left is to sit, eat and chat, and when you don't want to do this at home, you picnic. The Iranians are master picnickers. They can and do picnic anywhere.

One of the favoured locations, I noticed, was the central reservation of a motorway. It's easy enough to do: just park up halfway on the reservation, half blocking the fast lane, whip out a Persian rug, snacks and shisha, turn up the car radio to deafening levels, and eat and talk (as long as it's not about politics, of course).

Meanwhile I was also wandering the tree-lined streets thinking about what it would be like to live in a state where extra-marital sex, even having a girlfriend apparently, is illegal. How did teenage bundles of hormones manage to live their lives within the confines of such strict rules? Surely you can't legislate against biology?

As I was musing this all over I saw one particularly pretty girl. Actually, I think I stared at her with my mouth agape because next thing I knew she smiled and said, 'Hello,' in a sweet singsong accent.

I was taken aback and managed only a grin and a 'Hi' as I carried on walking down the street.

But the encounter must have left me receptive to strangers because when a shortish guy walked up to the side of me and introduced himself I smiled and shook his hand, telling him my name was Johnathan and that I came from England.

So far the Iranians had been the friendliest and most outgoing people we had met. It wasn't uncommon for us to be approached every time we went out in public by local people inviting us for a coffee or asking what we thought of their country, so I didn't think too much of it as we walked along together.

'Can I... your friend?' he asked haltingly. I looked blank so he repeated, 'Can I, your friend?'

'Yeah, why not?' I said, assuming he was asking if we could be friends.

'Are you from Esfa—?' I started, but he cut me off.

'You are beautiful Yonatan!' he blurted out.

'Oh, er... thank you.'

'Can we,' he ventured, 'sex?'

'No,' I spluttered out in surprise. 'I, er... have, um... I'm married!' I said, grasping for the first polite excuse I could think of.

'But we can go get a taxi, come to room, we sex?' he protested.

'No, no... NO!' I told him, attempting to be firm. 'Goodbye.'

And with that I strode off with a spring in my step, feeling strangely flattered but confused.

After all, Ahmadinejad had assured us there were no gay men in Iran.

Our next destination was Persepolis, home to one of the greatest collections of ancient ruins in the world.

The day was spent wandering around the impressive ruins, which are amazingly well preserved and well worth the 18 pence entrance cost. The entrance gates are scarred with 200-year-old graffiti from British officers passing by, and rumour has it that the great explorer, Stanley, has even desecrated the monument (although I looked very hard and couldn't see his name carved with the others). The ruins are situated in the middle of the desert and present little or no cover from the 45°C sun. The Iranian heat is a dry heat that cracks your lips, evaporates sweat instantly and makes the car constantly run on the brink of overheating. The pedals and gearstick got too hot to touch, scalding air pumped in from holes in the bodywork and even with every window down, the desert wind provided little respite as we pulled over every hour to buy another two litres of cool water and the seventh bottle of Zamzam Cola that day.

The city of Shiraz (ironic, in a dry country) was our next stop, home to the best mosques in Iran and, apparently, a major crystal meth problem (it's cheaper than opium and when you don't have pubs...). We saw the sights and decided to sort out the car as it had started to really smell. The culprit was soon found: a rotisserie chicken had been festering in the desert heat for over a week and was well on its way to decomposition.

But the chicken was to be the least of our worries. We were headed to the mud city of Yazd where we would soon have to finally make a decision on the Pakistan problem.

CHAPTER 23

- - - - - - - - -

LEAVING A DYING MAN IN THE DESERT

'If we can get our visas, we're going across Pakistan, too — wanna come?'

'YEEEaah, if I tell me mates back home that I took a black cab across Pakistan, they'll flip.'

'OK. But you'll have to grow a bigger beard. We're trying to blend in with the locals you see, and the locals have big beards.'

Craig was a big Aussie, with a beer gut, half a beard, a seemingly mild temperament and a slightly gormless expression. Dressed in a sweat-stained T-shirt that looked like it had been hand-washed and bleach dried in the sun a thousand times, he was never found without his camera, and when he got excited, he started to resemble an oversized child on a sugar high after a birthday party in Maccy D's. He would fit in with us perfectly.

When you spend long months stuck in a small black cab with two other lads, the opportunity to have someone else along for the ride is great for maintaining team morale and sanity at healthy levels.

And besides, when we drove through Pakistan, we'd have someone to sacrifice to the Taliban besides Johno.

We met Craig in the Silk Road Hotel in Yazd – a breath of fresh air after weeks of camping in dusty deserts and staying on strangers' floors. The comfy dorm beds were located in a cool subterranean room, and the shaded courtyard was bustling with other backpackers and overlanders also keen for some conversation.

Three thousand years of desert living had left a unique mark on Yazd; the old city was a maze of mud-brick buildings topped with elaborate wind catchers or *bâdgirs* designed to funnel any slight breeze down into the semi-underground rooms to offset the sun's fierce heat. Far beneath the narrow streets, which were all-but deserted during the hottest hours of the day, water flowed in an ingenious system of underground canals called *qanats*.

A long-term guest of the hostel and de facto tour guide took us up to the roof of an unfinished mosque to watch the sunset. She was also originally from Australia but while travelling around Iran she met a local guy in Yazd whom she had fallen into a bit of a holiday romance with.

'So you don't actually live in the hostel?' we asked as we dug into her back story.

'No, my hubby works there but I live at his place,' she chirped.

'Your hubby?' asked Leigh, 'Do you have to call him that to avoid offending the religious police?'

'No,' she answered nonchalantly, 'we went to the Imam and he married us over breakfast, it means we don't get any problems down here.'

She explained that Yazd had a reputation as a deeply conservative town and relations between a local man and a Western woman would draw too much attention if things weren't official.

'When I want to leave,' she continued, as if it was a gym membership, 'we just go back to the Imam and he dissolves the marriage.'

She told us about a nearby Zoroastrian fire temple named Chak Chak, where an eternal flame burns. Legend has it that during the seventh-century Arab invasion of Persia, a Sasanian princess named Nikbanou was desperately fleeing from the advancing army and the gruesome fate that her capture would entail. As she moved further into the parched desert and her pursuers gained ground things looked hopeless, until suddenly the mountainside opened up and sheltered her in a tiny grotto complete with its own spring to sate her thirst.

Nowadays the cave is home to one of the most important Zoroastrian temples in the world and a centre for regular pilgrimages. The diminutive spring is little more than a trickle (Chak Chak literally means 'drip drip') but this tiny amount of moisture in an otherwise completely arid area has allowed a huge tree to flourish far up the mountainside.

We were given vague directions to the area and for a while we followed the road signs by figuring that two identical Persian letters next to each other must mean Chak Chak. However, soon these signs dried up, like the precious water in the hot sand.

As we drove along we scanned for someone, anyone, to ask for directions. Then we saw him. An old man standing next to a battered car that once might have been called white on the side of the road. When we pulled up beside him he appeared to not be the least bit surprised to see an old London taxi full of bedraggled foreigners.

'*Salam*,' started Paul, who was behind the wheel. 'Er... Chak Chak?'

The man beamed and vigorously nodded, 'Chak Chak!'

Paul glanced back around at us for guidance but meeting a sea of shrugs turned back to the old man.

'Chak Chak?' he repeated, this time pointing backwards and forwards along the road with an enquiring look.

'Chak Chak!' said the man.

Paul looked confused. 'Um, I don't think he knows the way guys.' He turned back to the man. 'Er, thanks... *shukran*... *merci*...'

He was just about to pull away when the man played his trump card: 'Chak Chak!' he said forcefully, this time holding his finger up in a 'wait here' motion.

He wandered around to the other side of his car, prised open the rear door and lifted something shiny out. He brought it back around to our open window and passed it to a very puzzled Paul who passed it to me.

I looked at the thing for a moment. 'I think it's an urn of tea?' I announced with uncertainty.

As I looked up, Paul passed me something else: a carrier bag of sugar and a collection of small glass cups.

'Guys... what's going on?' asked Leigh as the man locked his car, tugged our door open and planted himself firmly on the back seat next to Craig.

'Chak Chak!' the man cried triumphantly and pointed directly down the road ahead.

'Do you want us to...' Paul started ask.

'Chak Chak!'

'OK, so I'll just go...'

'Chak Chak!'

So we looked at each and started driving.

'Chak Chak!'

As the miles passed our new passenger made himself comfortable, singing Persian songs and chain-smoking next to Leigh. Any slight hesitation from Paul was quickly rebuked with the man's two-word catchphrase and a swift clip on the back of the head.

He was about 65 and barely pushing five foot tall. He had stickers all over his chest where an ECG had been attached, a hospital wristband on his arm and his left sleeve had a large blood stain on it, as though he had wrenched out a drip. He started to speak rapid-fire Persian, pointed to his chest and then made a cut-throat motion.

It appeared as though we had inadvertently picked up a dying man who had escaped from a hospital and were driving him into the middle of the desert to pray one more time before he died.

Out came a packet of cigarettes and the old man sparked up, right in front of the no-smoking sticker in the back of the cab.

Realising his rudeness, he offered them around (there were no takers), spilt ash in Leigh's ear and then berated me for driving too slowly. Trying to tell him that we were going up a hill in a massively overheating taxi with five people in it was beyond our two-word vocabulary and he continued to hit me and shout at me for my tardiness, occasionally sporadically breaking into song between drags because our sound system wasn't working.

We arrived at Chak Chak three cigarettes later and parked up. The temple is at the top of a hill and we started to make our way up. Our geriatric escapee, however, had other plans. First he insisted we share his tea – obediently we drank the obscenely sweet concoction – before setting off for the hill. The old man immediately started to lag behind, and looking back I could see him bent double, heaving, possibly just minutes away from death. I went back down to join him. He pointed at his heart, then coughed and spluttered and started to make his way up, only after insisting I take a photo of his bare-chested ECG patches.

The temple's caretaker was sat beneath a sign that informed women not to enter during menstruation and he greeted us warmly as we approached the gaudy bronze doors.

'Eternal flame?'

We nodded.

'Yes, yes, this way.' He hesitated, made a fist and flicked his thumb at us in the way that someone asks for a lighter. 'You have fire?'

We had been trying to explain to the dying man that we were planning to camp in the desert that night, and we thought he had said that it was OK as he was also going to stay at Chak Chak, but as the evening wore on it became clear he wanted to go back to his car. A little charade developed where we would all wave him goodbye and start towards our car with him waving us off cheerfully, but as soon as we started the engine he would hastily gather up his tea and sugar and come running to the back seat.

We tried in vain to figure out what to do.

'It's a two-hour round trip back to his car...'

'... but we can't just leave a dying man in the desert...'

'... nobody's leaving a dying man in the desert!'

'But we don't have enough fuel for a return trip!'

'Oh...'

'Well, we could, maybe...'

'Dude, we are not leaving him here!'

'Well who's taking him back then?'

As we debated the moral repercussions of leaving a dying man alone in the middle of the desert, I realised that our merry band of travellers would soon be breaking up. Leigh had received an email to say that our Pakistani visa attempt had failed once more. Luckily a friend of ours Leigh had contacted at the last minute, who had some contacts at the Pakistani Embassy in Dubai, had said he was able to pull some strings to ensure we could enter Pakistan, and so Leigh and Paul would be catching a coach back to Shiraz to get a flight to Dubai the next morning.

While we were arguing away about our unexpected passenger, the old man flagged down the solitary passing car, jumped in and drove off. Well at least one of our problems had been solved.

CHAPTER 24

- - - - - - - -

DEPORTED FROM IRAN

Raul was waiting for us in arrivals; cool as can be, in a smart, stylish skinny jeans and black waistcoat combo. Leigh and I, who 20 hours previously had been in what felt like one of the remotest spots on earth, were wearing very tatty jeans, ripped T-shirts, Iraqi Arab scarves and Talib-eards that would make any Pakistani militant proud.

Dubai is a big, brash, money-obsessed show town, filled with big brash, money-obsessed people, driving big, brash expensive cars to big, brash shopping malls, cinemas and American fast-food chains. It could not have been any further from the places we had been in the past three months and we were both suffering from the culture shock as Ferraris and Lamborghinis sped past us.

We stayed with our friend Jane, a war correspondent and probably the toughest girl either of us have ever met, on the 14th floor of a luxury tower block, where we made the most of the luxuries available. A courier from the embassy arrived, collected our passports and disappeared, leaving us with an unexpected free day. I would be heading back to Iran as soon as possible so I wanted to ensure I had lots to tell Johno as he was currently stuck in the desert with the Aussie. I bought cookies, Cadbury chocolate, crisps, coffee, cheese, English magazines and (most importantly) cereal and cold milk – the greatest Western invention not yet to have noticeably travelled east.

After a hearty breakfast and a dip in the pool, the passports were returned by the courier, who told us we had no fee to pay. After six months of angst, failed embassy trips and plan Bs, our visas to Pakistan were finally in our hands and we hadn't even had to pay for them.

Hannah had been having intermittent problems with her cooling system ever since we first experienced the rising temperatures of southern Turkey and northern Iraq six weeks earlier – a car designed for the soggy backstreets of London just couldn't quite cope with the deserts and mountains of the Middle East, especially at her ripe old age.

Now as we drove further south the problems returned and each slight incline saw the engine 'TEMP' needle slowly creeping towards the red danger band. The temperature sensor on Craig's watch showed 60°C and the gearstick and pedals became too hot to touch with bare skin.

Unfortunately, car whizz kid Leigh was now sunning himself next to a private pool 500 miles away, but before he left he had warned me not to let the needle hit the red under any circumstances.

During one of the frequent cooling stops, Craig and I were peering under the hood of the car and pretending we knew what we were doing when I suddenly noticed that the large cooling fan on the front of the engine had somehow wedged itself against the back of the radiator, leaving a scary-looking gouge in the delicate cooling fins. We would need a quick fix to get us over the hills that rose up on the path before us.

The only option I could see, short of taking everything to pieces by the side of the road, was to cut the fan down so it was clear of the radiator and try to reattach it to a shaft somehow. Thirty minutes later my soft middle-class hands were blistered from hacking at the tough plastic with the sweat-drenched wire cutters, but the fan was clear of the radiator and wedged back in place, and Hannah drove smoothly once more. Apparently I didn't need Leigh after all.

As holder of dual nationality, I was eligible to get a new visa-on-arrival for Iran using my Irish passport, but as a Brit, Leigh would have to meet the rest of us further down the route in Pakistan. So the next morning I enjoyed a delightful flight to Tehran, perched between Granma Omani and her family on their holidays, none of whom wanted to switch with me to be closer to their loved ones because it would mean forfeiting their window seat. This meant that they settled for shouting over me in rapid, spittle-infused Persian for the whole three hours.

Upon landing I went to the window marked 'Visas' and waited. A young, smiling Iranian prodded a form over to me, which I dutifully completed and returned to him, along with my passport, which he took away into the back office. I waited and waited, until I saw my young friend appear, trailed closely by a man in a neat suit and overly shiny shoes, who was clearly his boss. They pointed at me, looked at me sternly and then returned to their office, deep in serious conversation. Half an hour later the boss emerged and asked me the usual visa questions about why I was visiting Iran. I answered, and boss man disappeared for what seemed like an age.

Half an hour later I saw a petite and very attractive girl in a hijab wander past, clutching my passport and clearly looking for someone.

'Hi, can I have my passport back please?' I asked smilingly.

'Oh... are you Paul?'

I nodded.

'Ahh, I thought you were Iranian, sorry.' She looked at me askance. 'I was looking for an... um, Irish man.'

It appears I didn't fit her image of small ginger men in green, sat on pots of gold with shamrocks in their hats.

'I need two hundred euros,' she said matter-of-factly.

'I thought it was fifty euros?'

'Fifty? Most of them are costing four hundred, I've called in a load of favours from friends in booking to get you two hundred.'

I was confused. 'But everywhere I've read says it's a fifty euro fixed-price visa?'

'Huh? This is for your flight,' she said. Now it seemed she was the one confused.

'What flight?!'

'Home.'

'Home, what, where?' I stuttered, getting more and more frantic. This wasn't going well at all.

'I'm coming to Iran, not leaving it,' I explained.

She looked at me pityingly. 'Yes, you are.'

'No, I'm not, I'd think I'd know…'

'Yes you are, you're being deported.'

'DEPORTED?'

I've never quite understood those moments in films, when somebody gets some bad news and the whole world starts to spin, until then. This was it, the expedition was over, finished, kaput, and I was desperately trying to focus on the pretty girl with my passport.

'Is it because I'm Irish?'

'No, of course not, we always give visas to Irishmen.'

'But whyyy?' The 'why' came out as more of a suppressed primal yelp than a word.

'Something on our computers said no, your passport has been flagged and we can't let you in, I'm very sorry. If it was up to me…'

She trailed off as vivid images surfaced in my head of the policeman with squiffy eyes photocopying every single page of my passport asking why it was we found ourselves camping by all that firepower.

Every single page.

Eventually it sunk in, but still dazed I handed over the cash and was escorted to a cell with my own personal guard.

I had about £1 worth of credit, so I called Leigh. He didn't pick up.

CHAPTER 25

ARMED ESCORTS

After a long search through the abandoned streets of Bam, Craig and I eventually tracked down an Internet cafe, and after a quiet word with the owner fired up the illegal proxy software that would allow us to bypass the nationwide ban on our email and Facebook accounts and check for any news from Paul and Leigh.

The good news was they had finally managed to secure the visas that had eluded them for so long. The bad news was that Paul was being deported.

The only plan we could come up with was to meet in the Pakistani town of Multan, over a thousand miles away. I sat there as it sunk in that I would be doing such a huge and important chunk of the journey without the friends I had shared the past five months of trials and tribulations with.

But with our rendezvous set far in the distance, Craig and I traipsed back to the hotel, loaded up Hannah and headed towards Baluchistan.

Baluchistan is the name given to the large expanse of barren desert that straddles the Pakistan–Iran border. The desolate area was used by Pakistan for testing nuclear weapons less than 15 years ago. Over the past five years, Baluch separatists and bandits have carried out a spate of kidnappings of Western tourists. It is so notorious for drug-smuggling, banditry and kidnappings that all foreigners must be accompanied by compulsory armed escorts.

We had heard various unsavoury stories about the escorts so we were pleasantly surprised that the first group, a ragtag group of bearded Lawrence of Arabia lookalikes, seemed well organised and friendly. Still, it was unsettling to be ordered to hand over our passports and then watch them speed ahead to the next checkpoint in their souped-up four-wheel drive, while we gunned Hannah as much as we dared to try to keep up.

As Bam receded in the mirror and the signs for the city of Zahedan began to count down, each new escort seemed to pack more firepower. First AK-47s, then Russian PK machine guns and eventually truck-mounted 50-cals with about half a dozen soldiers.

It was when we got to the city that our problems began. Instead of nipping around the bypass and quickly covering the final 50 or so miles to the border, the escort directed us to drive into the choking traffic of the city centre and dropped us off at a police station. The next six hours were a nightmare of rising tempers as each new police checkpoint tried to organise the next escort to take us a mere few miles to the next one where the whole process would start again. What's more, the Rambo-eqsue escorts had now transformed into nervous-looking unarmed teenage police recruits sitting on the back seat.

As we crawled through the gridlock, we watched the clock tick towards the time the border would close for the evening and eyed the fuel needle edging towards empty with increasing frustration.

As we had got further south diesel had become harder to come by, and we'd heard that across the border in Pakistan the situation was even worse. As we edged into the last quarter of our modest fuel tank I was increasingly frantically looking around for the next gas station. So when one came into view I pointed and told our skinny police escort that I needed to stop and get diesel, or *gazole* in Persian.

'No *gazole*!' he said flatly, motioning ahead. 'Straight, straight.'

I assumed he must know a better fuel station around the corner, so I reluctantly continued forwards. When he directed us to pull up outside the next police station, jumped out of the car and walked off to the station, we were less than happy.

'Hey! What about the *gazole*?' I shouted.

'Yes, yes, after lunch,' he called back, disappearing inside with our passports.

'Wait, wha...' I trailed off as the door slammed.

We waited around for hours, growing ever more frustrated. Craig in particular was taking things badly – every time he spoke to the young recruits manning the front gate, he was told, 'Yes, yes, five minutes.'

I could see his internal temperature rising.

There's something in the psyche of the British public that loves a story about plucky explorers risking their lives for a distant dream. As kids of the 1980s and 1990s, we missed out on the heroics – and grisly ends – of Scott of the Antarctic and Captain Cook, but there still seemed to be something in our blood that attracted us to these dangerous, and (in our case especially!) ultimately pointless, journeys.

While it was undoubtedly reckless and a bit selfish to worry the folks at home just for the sake of our own kicks, the route and risks involved were very carefully thought out. What was perhaps less thought out was the fact that we were now putting the local escorts and police in extra danger for what was essentially our holiday. At the time we found it really hard to appreciate that they were actually there to help and look after us and we didn't show the patience or gratitude we perhaps should have done.

In reality, the conscripts were probably just bored, angry young men, co-opted into a job they didn't want or enjoy, and just as fed up and out of the loop as us. This translated into them subtly winding us up and I could see that if I didn't do something soon then the previously calm Craig would blow his top.

'Stay here and watch the passports,' I told Craig in a low voice, 'I'm going to get some fuel.'

Before the recruits could stop me I jumped in the car and set off for the fuel station we had just passed.

I was almost immediately flanked by a policeman on a motorbike, angrily signalling me to pull over. Against my better judgement I kept my eyes locked on the road for what seemed like an eternity, until we reached the gas station.

Of course they had no *gazole*.

Things were looking extremely bleak and I doubted we'd make it more than 30 miles with what was left in the tank, so I was reduced to pleading with the policeman on the forecourt to let me go to another station we had passed on the approach to his patch. I assured him it wasn't more than a mile and a half away and he finally relented.

Four miles later, after two and a half miles of more angry pull-over signalling, we finally made it to a station that did have *gazole*, as evidenced by the huge queue of trucks that we pushed to the front of. Here we hit the next issue: we hadn't ever been issued a special fuel card that was needed for diesel and so we had been reduced to sweet-talking truckers into selling us 30 or 40 litres from the hundreds their semis were swallowing. So now here I was trying to negotiate the illegal use of a diesel fuel card in front of the local police chief. The truckers were, unsurprisingly, not feeling particularly helpful this time. Thankfully the policeman jumped in and ordered a driver to give me fuel, although I was charged the outrageous price of 25p per litre.

When we were reunited with an immensely relieved Craig, I assumed that my newfound rapport with the police chief would mean he would quickly send us on our way but instead my insolence was rewarded with another hour sitting twiddling our thumbs. This was too much for Craig who finally boiled over and unleashed a tirade of choice four-letter words on the impassive young policemen.

Eventually the new escort arrived and we raced towards the border, trying desperately to make it before it closed for the evening. Unfortunately, all of the excitement was too much for Hannah and the 'TEMP' needle leapt up once again, warning us that the cooling fan had failed. We limped up to the final checkpoint to change escorts one last time. As our guard trotted inside to record our details, we noticed the police compound was full of dirt-covered men kneeling in a line with their hands on their heads. A young uniformed man standing on the steps of the building was searching the ground for pebbles to half-heartedly lob at them and an armed guard stood lazily watching what we assumed to be captured smugglers.

Thirteen long hours after we had started our day, we finally reached the Iran–Pakistan border. It was locked up and long deserted for the evening. The poor teenage escort – who had only been with us for the past five minutes of the journey – took the brunt of Craig's outburst and when the tirade was over he innocently informed us we would have to spend the night in the nearby border town of Mirjaveh, described by the British Foreign Office as 'particularly insecure'. This wasn't exactly shaping up to be the best day of our trip so far.

CHAPTER 26

POLICE CHASES IN THE WILD, WILD EAST

I waited alone in my holding cell for five hours for my deportation flight, finally arriving into Dubai's 'Terrorist' Terminal Two – so known because it's the jumping-off point for places such as Kabul and Mogadishu. My phone had barely any credit and if Johno couldn't take Hannah through the border then the whole expedition was in jeopardy. I started doing the maths of us driving back to London from Iran. Would it be enough mileage to break the world record? Possibly. But how could I look anyone in the eye afterwards? Things looked bleak.

In fact, things were bleak.

I sent a message to Leigh asking if he could pick me up.

> Sorry mate, we're in the cinema watching Transformers 3 on the other side of the city, meet us here at the Emirates Mall, it won't finish for another two hours

It wasn't Leigh's fault; he thought I was arriving the following day but I was furious, hopping mad.

It had been one of the worst days of my life. A day that had started with the promise of an end to the six-month long Pakistan-visa struggles and ended up with me being deported from a rogue state as a suspected Israeli spy, and to make it worse, I had little money left, after being made to pay for my own deportation, and Leigh couldn't pick me up because he was watching bloody *Transformers*.

Eventually I met up with Leigh and we went to our temporary home. An old friend of my mum's, a geologist working out in Dubai and an all-round hero, had invited us to stay in his huge apartment on the 43rd floor of the Radisson Hotel, overlooking Dubai in all its gaudy finest. It had a pool on the roof, a gym and even a sauna (a pointless extravagance in the Dubai summer, but that didn't stop me from using it). An expert and passionate chef, Chris housed, fed and watered us in a manner that one could easily become accustomed to, especially after suffering camel stew in the desert and my terrible camp cooking.

Hannah's health was dwindling, so while we were stuck at the border for the night I decided to try to find a mechanic to patch up the cooling fan. After driving to the town centre I popped open the bonnet and was almost immediately surrounded by curious white-robed men staring at Hannah's battered guts. The boldest one quickly grasped the problem so I nervously followed his pickup through smaller and smaller alleys and soon found myself sat outside a small garage with parts of the cooling system spread out on the dirt.

As the sky reddened a drink was pressed into my hand and conversation flowed freely as I thought to myself, *So, this is the place I need an armed escort?*

A young lad translated for me, 'No fix Mirjaveh, you go Zahedan for fix.'

It seemed Hannah couldn't be repaired here but that we would have to travel 50 miles back to the city where we had spent most of the day frustrated and stuck.

The only hotel in town was out of our budget, so we pitched our tents in their car park and after a fitful night's sleep we started the long journey back. It was an exact rerun of the previous day's bureaucratic bullshit, with all the same guard checkpoints putting us through all the same misery. By the time we reached the dreaded checkpoint, where we'd been held up for six hours the previous day, it was already mid-morning.

We tried patiently to explain that we needed to find a mechanic and get back to the border as soon as possible but it was clear that we would have to be more assertive. As soon as the guards went on their first break I grabbed Hannah's knackered fan and jogged off down the street to look for someone who might know how to fix a London taxi in the middle of the desert.

Miraculously, the first guy I came across recognised the broken parts immediately, and had just written down the address of a place that would be able to help us, when the fuming guards caught up with me. As I was frogmarched back to the checkpoint, I wasn't sure whether to laugh or cry – this whole situation was like something out of a pantomime.

While Craig was having a not-so-calm debate with our escorts, the younger recruits seemed to be taking increasing issue with me.

'Koola! Koola!' they kept saying, gesturing at a metal helmet, each time with more venom and less patience. It quickly became apparent that they thought we had stolen a helmet from them the previous day.

I shrugged my shoulders at them to show that I didn't know what they were talking about, but the more I played dumb the angrier they got. For some reason they seemed convinced that we were the culprits. One of the guards even grabbed a random passer-by from the street and put handcuffs on him, shouting some more about the 'Koola!' – no doubt trying to tell us that if we didn't give the helmet back then we would be arrested.

Their cursory search of the cab didn't uncover the elusive helmet, which deflated their theatrical display somewhat. With some angry gesticulating of my own I eventually convinced them that I didn't know where the bloody thing was, and after half an hour of harassment they finally left us alone.

By early afternoon we had found the mechanic's place, handed over the princely sum of £20 from our emergency stash for the repairs and were all set to make a break for the border again. Now all that we needed to do was to top up the *gazole* we had used going to the border and back.

We knew the fuel station we had used yesterday was close by, but the escorts wouldn't let us take another detour. This left us with two options: leave the already impatient cops and go to get fuel or follow them and sit around for hours more, probably missing out on the border crossing that day, and risk being stranded in the desert with no diesel. We blithely ignored their blatant directions and drove off. A few minutes later the police car screeched up by the side of us with sirens blaring. The driver looked like he was about to explode and his facial expression alone scared me into following them back towards the checkpoint.

There was, however, another turning which would also take us back to the petrol station. If I drove a little faster this time, I reckoned I could reach the station before they could catch up a second time. I turned off and floored the cab, heading for the fuel. We were almost there when their car raced up to us, but the livid gesturing of the two officers tightened my stomach and brought me out in an immediate sweat. These guys were seriously angry. We were definitely in for it. We pulled over a tantalising mere few metres away from the diesel pump.

It seemed that luck was on our side, because as soon as the guards stepped out of their car, they saw someone they knew and their faces broke into happy smiles as they walked over, embraced and started chatting. By the time they remembered why they were there, their anger had dissipated, and they waited while we filled up. It seemed that how to get your way with armed guards in Iran was to play chicken with them until they got distracted and gave up.

By 4.45 p.m. we had reached the final checkpoint just a few minutes from the fabled border we had been trying to cross for two days. It soon became clear they weren't going to let us cross this evening, and poor Craig's temper snapped, like a broken shoelace. He lunged towards the terrified escort, unleashing a uniquely Australian barrage of swearwords and demanded that we be let out of this 'fackin' shithole, you fackin' little caaant!'

Though Craig is a big and somewhat intimidating guy, I would have thought that having an AK-47 and a gaggle of other armed guards just behind him would have meant a rifle butt to the face of the yelling Aussie, at the very least. For a moment I was scared for my life, imagining our bodies disappearing under a huddle of hand-me-down boots, khaki shirts and badly fitting berets. But somehow the torrent of abuse that poured out of Craig's mouth made the soldiers cower in pure terror, although not quite enough to get them to let us through that night.

After another night in our car-park campground the next set of escorts suddenly became wonderfully helpful. We whizzed through with barely any trouble, even when the border guard realised that the taxi was registered in Paul's name and that my passport said Johnathan – in an area where smuggling is rife this was an understandable sticking point. Luckily we had thought this through, and the guard accepted Paul's letter giving me written permission to take his car through the border.

The official peered at the letter, tracing over the strange squiggles of the Roman alphabet with a filthy fingertip and mumbling syllables slowly. When he got to Paul's name he carefully crosschecked it twice with the car document and seemed satisfied; he had ticked all of his required boxes and dutifully stamped and signed the documents before beckoning forward the next weary traveller.

With a final, 'Yala!' the escort pointed us through the barbed-wire-topped gates and we were free. We had finally escaped from Iran.

The moment we pulled up next to the first Pakistani checkpoint, Craig popped the roof box open and pointed to the far corner with a mischievous smile.

'What the hell is that?' I asked, shocked at what lay before my eyes.

Partly hidden behind the piles of bags and spares was the policeman's metal helmet that had caused so much angst at the Zahedan checkpoint the previous day. It was a terrible thing, it had almost cost us the border but I couldn't help but let out a little chuckle.

Craig smiled for the first time all week. 'That, mate, is karma.'

CHAPTER 27

- - - - - - - - -

KIDNAP!

'Hello, how are you? I am fine thank you for asking!'

The Pakistani border officials spoke a charmingly quaint version of English and immediately seemed warmer and more helpful than their neighbouring counterparts. There were bristling moustaches and wide smiles everywhere, and insistences that we took their seats as they helped us fill in the importation documentation under a battered old parasol that stood over a small plastic garden table, which constituted the Taftan border office.

Despite being told that fuel was like gold dust on this side of the border, we soon came across a whole load of 55-gallon drums crowded by the side of the road and guarded by a grime-covered kid equipped with a hand-pump. A short exchange later we had all of our jerry cans and Hannah's main tank topped to the brim with diesel, as we set off parallel to the Afghanistan border, driving up towards the city infamous as the Taliban capital: Quetta.

By the evening we had swapped escorts many more times, each time at one of the tiny *levies* posts (old British army buildings from the previous century that still even sported the old regimental crests). The logbooks in which we recorded our details showed us starkly just how few Westerners ever travelled through this area. We had driven along the swathe of nothingness that was cut by a new ribbon of smooth Tarmac. When we reached the halfway point of the town of Dalbandin we were almost starting to wonder what all the fuss was about.

All this time, Leigh and I had been stuck in our luxury 43rd-storey flat, ignoring all the amenities, sitting at the computer, refreshing the browser and waiting for some scrap of news, unable to tear our eyes away in case something vital happened. We had been unsuccessfully surfing Google, news sites and blogs for any new info about Pakistan, as well as checking constantly for texts or emails.

Then Leigh suddenly called me over to the laptop and showed me the Pakistani news website:

*Breaking news: Two Western tourists
kidnapped from their car in Baluchistan*

No more details were known but there was probably no more than a small handful of tourists in that part of the world at once – it's not exactly one of the regular routes served by Thomson. It had to be them. This was it. The trip was finished: no expedition, no world record. I'd have to start writing a eulogy for Johno:

*Johno Ellison. An all-round good bloke. A traveller, a writer,
the master of fancy dress with an unhealthy love for Bonnie
Tyler and wearing Daisy Duke girls' denim shorts...*

All we knew about Craig was that he came from a made-up-sounding place in Australia called Wagga Wagga.

We kept pressing refresh for an hour and then a new story came up:

Two Swiss tourists kidnapped in Baluchistan

Johno and Craig aren't Swiss. There was hope!

It was hard to be too overjoyed when we thought of the misfortunes of the Swiss couple, but we breathed a sigh of relief that our friends were safe. We later found out that the couple were held captive for eight months before eventually being freed.

I was reading the latest in a series of increasingly desperate messages that were waiting for me when I finally got online at an Internet cafe in Quetta:

....

To: 'Johno Ellison'
Subject: !!!!!

If you've been kidnapped the world record is fucked!

....

I penned my suitably caustic reply, thanking them for their concern.

We had finally arrived in the city earlier that afternoon, driving through the black smoke of the makeshift brickworks that lined the roads. We had swapped our one-man escort for a ten-tonne truck loaded with soldiers in front of us and a pickup crowded with police behind us. After following them through the growing conurbation, and past a sprawling Tent City and a faded and chipped Pepsi mural daubed on a crumbling wall, we arrived at the Hotel Bloom Star. The desk clerk had smiled serenely at my attempts to haggle on price but knew he had us over a barrel – where else were we really going to go?

'Of course, do not worry, you will be quite safe here in Quetta,' he told us as he led us through the gardens – a pleasant oasis amongst the dust and heat. 'But make sure you do not leave the hotel after dark.'

That left us very little time to look around, so after finding a cafe for dinner, we ignored the stares of passers-by and had a look around the city, before checking in with Paul and Leigh online.

The tiny Internet cafe was packed with teenage boys somehow looking at the sort of material that teenage boys worldwide like to look at, and that was definitely censored under Pakistan's strict filtering system.

'Ah, Facebook!' they murmured as we got our communications lifeline up on screen. I looked squarely at my new buddies but they simply stared right back.

'Add me as friend?' asked one, leaning forward.

'Look, I'm terribly sorry, I really do need to check these messages, they're very important, do you think you would mind giving me a little privacy for a moment?' I asked him, never feeling more English in my life.

He looked mortified and barked something to the others in Pashto. His cohort moved back all of an inch then returned to their gazes. The leader smiled at me triumphantly.

The good news was that Leigh and Paul had suggested meeting us the very next evening in the town of Sukhor, a mere 250 miles south. We quickly agreed on a hotel to meet at and I logged off to hurry back to the Bloom Star before the sun went down.

The following morning, Leigh and I found ourselves on an Emirates flight from Dubai to Karachi, flirting with the Glaswegian stewardesses to get free beer (which turned out to be futile – all flights in and out of Pakistan are dry). Eighty people were killed in riots and violence the day we arrived in Karachi. We didn't fancy hanging around as there was a definite tension in the air, so we headed straight to the bus station. It was a million miles away from the subtle civility of Iran or the brash cleanliness of Dubai, with mountains of rubbish piling up against every flat surface.

Driving along the main highway out of the city, a man was squatting in the central reservation taking care of his business in full view of everyone. 'Welcome to Pakistan', we quipped.

I woke with a spring in my step. Today would be the day that I'd hopefully reunite with my buddies. The reassurance that comes from a group of trusted friends (especially when one of them is your mechanic) couldn't be overstated.

Craig and I negotiated our way out of the city along the road that hugged the winding path of the spectacular railway line south. Every bridge bore a nineteenth-century date and names like 'Mary Jane' and 'Windy Corner' hinted at the story of their construction under the British 200 years earlier.

When we reached the hotel we had agreed to meet at, we found that the owners had capitalised on their Westerner-friendly reputation by jacking up their prices. We had seen plenty of other hotels just around the corner so we went to find one more suited to our pockets.

Every place we entered seemed empty, but all presented us with the same stony response: 'No vacancies.' After five almost identical responses we were starting to get exasperated.

'Is it because we're white?' we finally asked, feeling a little like Ali G.

'Well, er, yes!' came the surprising reply.

After begging an owner and promising we would be discreet and leave first thing the following day, one hotel finally relented and allowed us stay. We popped back to the first hotel to leave a message for Paul and Leigh, telling them the address of our new hotel.

Half an hour later we were sitting on the beds in the tiny room, wondering if the note had worked, when the door crashed open and two familiar figures burst in, huge grins on their faces.

'Alright, wankers!'

CHAPTER 28

NO TENSION

I woke up wet, lying on a thin, bare mattress that was also soaked through. The windowless room I lay in was arid and airless, and the fan was silent. Another power-cut, I guessed, as I struggled to un-stick my back from the sodden mattress. It was early. We had agreed to meet the chief of police at nine – he insisted on giving us another slow and pointless escort out of the city, which would only manage to make us a larger target – so we decided we would be long gone by the time he called at our hotel.

After following the advice of the Red Cross's *How to Stay Alive* book and checking underneath the car for bombs, we set off, heading north towards the border crossing with India. I was feeling good to be back behind the wheel again, but the novelty soon wore off as the sun began to reach its full height. Soon wet through again, my black T-shirt became stiff with the amount of salt that had been deposited on it, leaving crystalline circles for all to see. The car was struggling in the heat, too, but not as much as Johno, whose sweat poured down his beard and dripped down his front, giving him the air of a dog drooling for his dinner.

We had all grown substantial beards by this point, in an attempt to blend in. As it turned out, the itchy, monstrous merkins on our faces were pointless because it appeared that generally Pakistani men only had moustaches. Who were we kidding though, we looked like lumberjacks on a day out. Beard or no beard, we were driving around in a London black cab, which was covered in stickers of Western companies. Hardly the subtlest vehicle to drive through Pakistan a month after Osama Bin Laden had been killed.

Every mile closer to the Indian border was a mile safer and according to the Red Cross the threat level for our next destination, Multan, was merely *Very high*, rather than the *Severe* rating given to Quetta.

What we had discovered so far echoed the experience of overlanders and travellers the world over: things usually aren't as bad as people with no direct experience make out. It can be easy for keyboard warriors in wooden-panelled government offices to release cautious travel advisories, but the only way one can really learn the true nature of an area is by visiting it themselves. Although the area undoubtedly had extreme dangers, it was one of the most unforgettable experiences any of us had ever had.

With Paul and Leigh in the taxi again it became clear just how much I had missed them over the past few days. Problems shared between us were now problems halved; difficulties finding places to stay, car problems and navigation worries weren't so bad with two others to help solve them.

The streets were packed full of people, animals and produce, and as we crawled along at walking pace it seemed the entire population of the city got a good look at us.

Eventually we found where the hotels were, but inexplicably every place that I tried told us they had no vacancies, despite all looking deserted. Puzzled, I headed back to the car and found quite a crowd, the lads looking stressed and Craig on the verge of getting shouty. Again.

'There is too much attention here, you are in danger – people will come for you,' a respectable-looking man told us, before adding, 'You should leave.'

We started to feel the mood around us change and wholeheartedly agreed. But leave to where?

Our saviour appeared in the form of an excitable young man who promised that he knew of the home of a local Englishman who would be sure to accommodate us. After quickly weighing up the scant options, and the risks, we decided to trust him.

We pulled up to the home of a lovely Pakistani girl who spoke perfect English. She informed us that none of the hotels would let us stay because we were targets for the local Taliban. If we got kidnapped (or worse) the hotel owners would lose their licence. There was a heavily armoured Holiday Inn for Westerners in the next town, but it was almost dusk and we would never make it (let alone be able to afford it). She began to curtly interrogate our new friend and after lending him her telephone he started to shout into the mouthpiece in rapid-fire Peshwar, before hanging up and announcing he knew a hotel that would take us. We double-checked that the owner understood our situation and upon receiving a confirmation we accepted our new friend's proposal to take us there in exchange for a few rupees.

'Go straight!' he shouted directly behind my head. I set off down the road and just as we reached a turn off, he yelled, 'Go right! Go right!'

Instinctively I slammed on the brakes to make the turn and he jolted forwards, bashing his head on the roll-bar.

'Oww,' he groaned, 'go slow on the corners.'

We twisted though the side streets as he constantly screamed last-minute directions that grated more and more with each passing minute.

'Do you want to meet my friends?'

'No. We are very, very tired. We want to go to hotel now, please.'

'OK, OK, go straight!'

'Hey, look at me, I'm in the crazy Westerners' car, look at me, look at me!'

It felt like we had been going around in circles. Checking the satnav, we had. He was making sure none of his friends missed this big event. He had already taken us on a 30-minute detour to show us his gym (called, believe it or not 'The Muslim Jim') and everyone in the car was beginning to get very tired of his games, as well as feeling more and more nervous as we drove around the city at night. Our increasingly irate protestations were simply met with, 'OK, no tension! No tension!'

Tension was building.

'Go straight… LEFT TURN, LEFT TURN, LEFT TURN!' he screamed into Johno's ear at the last minute.

'I don't think we'll fit down there, we're very high. Are you sure?'

'No tension, it not problem for height,' he replied.

Driving down a lane barely wide enough for the cab, we found that it was actually a very big problem for height as we came to a low bar we couldn't fit under. Traffic quickly backed up blocking our exit and although we got out to try to direct our escape, No Tension rapidly intervened and told the other drivers to ignore us and pull into the wall. With little more than half-a-metre of clearance on each side, there was no chance our 2 m-wide car could squeeze past a pickup truck, no matter how loudly No Tension was shouting at the driver.

Eventually we managed to get everyone to ignore him and reverse far enough for us to pass. We backed up and let the assembled queue past, and each of the drivers shouted what I can only assume were polite welcomes to their country, accompanied with some welcoming hand gestures I didn't understand.

Yet again we were drawing even more attention to ourselves. Obviously we were grateful for the local assistance but we were growing increasingly nervous about the situation: all it took was one guy to get on the phone to his local Taliban mate telling them that he had spotted a slow-moving British cash-cow doing circuits of the city (and local gyms).

We started going again but took a speed bump a little too fast, causing No Tension's head to crack against the roll bar.

'Owwww, go slowly, go slowly on bump.'

We went over another one and the same thing happened.

I could have sworn Johno had sped up.

The road turned into a heavily rutted sand track and we finally pulled up to a home-stay hotel with big gates and a perfectly Hannah-sized garage. It was just what we needed and No Tension beamed as he introduced us to the owner. Malik was tall and spoke excellent English, which he used, excellently, to tell us that there was no way we could stay.

It appeared that Malik, understandably, wasn't willing to take the risk for foreign guests and Craig, Leigh and I had reached breaking point. We were all very tired and scared, although nobody had mentioned it at the time, and possibly in the most danger we ever had been on the trip.

'I'm gonna fackin' kill you...' started Craig to No Tension, just as Paul casually sauntered over and closed the window, cutting him off.

Paul was our master negotiator whenever we sparred with hard-nosed border officials or tight-fisted hoteliers. So far today he had kept a calm exterior, but now it seemed that the friendly but firm owner would be the ultimate test of his negotiating skills.

We were desperate and I tried every single kind of persuasion tactic I knew. Eventually he broke and hurried to hide our car away in his garage in case anyone saw it. It was a genuine act of compassion, a huge risk for him and he didn't even charge us extra.

In the room Malik told us we were to lock ourselves in and not come out for anything; a motorbike bomb had gone off just over the road only the week before so everyone was especially jumpy. He told us outright that we shouldn't trust our new buddy; this was almost immediately proven when No Tension accidentally-on-purpose pocketed my phone after we paid him – biting our tongues at demands for extra money for the trip to the gym and other detours – and said what we thought were our final goodbyes.

'I come tomorrow. At seven, yes?'

'No thank you, we'll be fine.'

'OK, I come at seven.'

'No we don't need you, and we're not getting up until nine.'

'OK, seven.'

Ever the diplomat, Craig chipped in: 'If you come 'ere at seven, I'll fackin' rip your head off.'

'OK OK, no tension, nine, OK.'

At dead-on seven the next day there was a rap on the door and Craig had to be physically restrained from carrying out his threat. It didn't help when he discovered that a broken air conditioner had leaked all over his bags during the night, ruining the assortment of pristine banknotes that he had collected from every country that he had travelled through. Fortunately his anger was mainly directed at No Tension who, being brighter than we gave him credit for, had taken this moment to make himself scarce.

We navigated out of Multan and to the final stop before the Indian border: Lahore. It was the night of a huge religious festival; everywhere was a whirling tumult of sights and sounds, with men and women, and men dressed as women, spinning around to live music and dancing under showers of banknotes, thrown over them for luck. Hardly being inconspicuous, we were spotted by the organisers of the Sufi celebration and ushered up to take pride of place on the large stage erected in the town centre. The Foreign Office advice for Pakistan – 'Avoid large gatherings, avoid religious celebrations and do not draw attention to yourself' – flashed through my head as we nervously sat down, in direct view of the thousands of attendees, but it was soon pushed to the back of my mind as we were immersed in the celebrations. It seemed a world away from the pious Islamic rules of Iran.

Across the border and safely into India we said our goodbyes to Craig and headed towards Manali, a high hill station where the British Raj used to retire in the depths of summer to cool down. Hot, tired and relieved that we had finally conquered the hardest part of the expedition, we rewarded ourselves with a few days' respite from the incessant heat by driving into the low Himalayas.

But we weren't the only ones who had had this thought. Hordes of hippies with flowing robes and questionable haircuts had also made their way to Manali, but for them it was all about the spirituality of the Vashisht temple and spiritual healing of the hot baths; nothing to do with the pleasant temperatures. And it certainly had nothing to do with the fact that the best hashish in the world grows naturally and abundantly in Manali...

The hippies banged tambourines late into the night, improvising songs about fairies and their fellow travellers. Bangles and body hair replaced personal hygiene (ironic for a place famous for its hot baths) as they passed around chillums, and one adventurous soul broke out the sitar he had just bought but had yet to learn.

Leigh had been struck down by a nasty stomach bug, which unfortunately meant his sojourn consisted of trips back and forth to the toilet, where he was terrorised by the spider that lived there.

By a stroke of luck, one of my very good friends was also in Manali. Ellie was a trainee medic, who had somehow blagged the position of expedition doctor for a number of sixth-form trips that were exploring the area. It was nice to catch up with an old friend and even nicer to not have to go through the basics of getting to know someone in order to have a conversation. Meeting new people was my favourite part of travelling, however, after six months, it was nice to just talk rubbish to someone I knew so well who wasn't Johno or Leigh. But soon our time in the hills was up and we had to get going. As I gave Ellie a hug, it never occurred to me that within the week she might be responsible for saving my life (or at least saving me from a horrible stint in hospital).

The Taj Mahal, one of the most famous landmarks in the world, left us feeling a little underwhelmed. After the beauty of Iranian architecture, it just didn't seem quite as epic as we had expected. That we were all so jaded by such a technically amazing sight showed us how tiring driving through India had been already. We had only just had a break from constant driving up in Manali and now we almost immediately felt like we needed another one. Such was the stress generated by driving on the terrible roads of such a vast country in an old cab that now broke down multiple times a day. As we fought back to the car through the hordes of hawkers one at least brought a smile to my face: 'Sir! You buy fridge magnet? Twenty rupees!'

'I don't have a fridge,' I replied.

'It's OK, my dear, you can buy fridge here, too!'

India is a country of great contrast and limitless fascination. Its virtues could fill pages. However, so too could the subject most often spoken about during any conversation with anybody who has visited the country. That subject is poo.

CHAPTER 29

UNAVOIDABLE FACTS ABOUT LIFE IN INDIA

We spent the morning in Jaipur, where we heard the news that Amy Winehouse had died, joining the '27 Club'. This piece of information is of very little use to you, but having exhausted most topics of conversation after hundreds of hours on the road, trying to remember who else was in 'the club' (Kurt Cobain, Jimi Hendrix, Janis Joplin, Jim Morrison…), without the use of Google, was one of those amazing new conversations which could rejuvenate us and take up much of the day.

And it did.

The weather was wholly British as we drove out – overcast and muggy – except that in India your brow would rapidly bead with sweat as soon as the car stopped. We headed due south on the road to Mumbai, bouncing on unpaved roads, dodging rickshaws, cows and atrocious drivers.

We made good time at one point, actually finding a road that resembled a motorway, which meant we could gain speed. Indians are tremendously quick to capitalise on any situation. When a Western farmer sees a motorway built through his land he sees the business equivalent of a hooded character approaching, clutching a scythe that's clearly not intended for the harvest. However, when an Indian farmer sees a motorway built, he uses the newly laid, lush green grass in the central reservation to graze his cows on, oblivious to the cars zipping by at 75 mph.

So, there we were, speeding along, when I felt a twinge in my stomach. It was a slight twinge, but it was the kind that makes one sit up and say, 'Uh-oh' aloud. My stomach was quite clearly telling me, 'Paul, prepare yourself, all is not well in the world of your insides.'

India's fledgling motorway system consists of approximately 550 miles of expressways spread thinly throughout a country 14 times bigger than the UK and we were lucky enough to have a found a rare 60-mile stretch. However, smooth as it was, and central-reservation-cows notwithstanding, it massively lacked service stations or slip roads of any kind. Unable to stop the car, I held on for a bit longer, clenching every muscle in my body. The lads offered to take over driving, but I knew if I did stop to swap, I would be giving my body that little bit of permission to ease up, which would have dire consequences for the scuffed leather of our Cortina seats. A slip road eventually appeared, but it wound around for an eternity before leading us to the middle of nowhere. Things were getting pretty close to the line (or the cloth) by the time I pulled over at a farmer's shop, moving towards him in a half-clenched, half-jogging shuffle, shouting for directions to the toilet he didn't have.

I have been fortunate enough to experience toilet facilities in countries all over the world, and from what I've seen, India has a rather lackadaisical approach to sanitation. Human beings are fantastic at developing a system for getting rid of bodily waste, no matter how poor they are. From long drops in Africa and the communal troughs we were yet to experience in China to the patented water closets that adorn bathrooms across the Western world, they all manage undesirable outputs very well. In India though – for all its beauty and spirit – it appears that only the very privileged have flush toilets. For everyone else there's the side of the busy main road and a little bucket of water – it's a part of everyday life.

I have no idea why people think a road was more suitable than, say, the privacy offered by a bush or the semi-sanitary option of a hole, but performing one's ablutions in public is perfectly normal – old or young, male or female. Doubling the road network as a toilet network means the waste flows away, mostly, as it is trodden around into mud, sprayed up on to cars and moved onwards (presumably into roadside food stalls, vegetables and into the water network).

Not being a fan of the verge loo, the cow shed behind the man's shop was the next best thing for me.

We soon found the only service station on the brand new stretch of road, and pulled in for fuel. I had used the facilities three more times when I started to worry that this wasn't just the normal case of the trots. I self-medicated with a bottle of Coke; banking on its time-tested bacteria-killing abilities to eradicate the nasties from my stomach. But soon, back on the road, my stomach started to feel as though somebody had tied it in a knot and was slowly wringing it out, pushing everything either up, or down. Nausea overcame me and I informed the lads that we needed to stop. I then informed them again with more urgency, a few choice words and a very loud, 'NOW!'

The side of the road where we pulled over this time was rather typical for India; years of rubbish piled up around small bushes and everything was covered in an oily slime that smelt of sewage.

A small shop was open; I asked them if they had a toilet. Or, more accurately, I jumped around from foot to foot – my face distorted with pain – gesticulating and occasionally shouting words that sounded similar to 'toilet', 'loo' and 'owwwwww!'.

They looked at me blankly and started to call for other people to come over and see what was going on. I'd been through this process numerous times – it's part of the fantastic Indian desire to be helpful, something that seems almost wonderfully innate to every citizen. Three or four family members, old and young, would try to communicate with me, coming to the eventual conclusion that none of them could speak my language, I couldn't speak theirs and they didn't understand what I wanted. Then would come apologetic smiles and often a generous offer of some sort of hospitality, and certainly some kind of tea. However, on this occasion I just did not have the time to play.

I ran around the corner to a bush and threw up.

Flat Coke and stomach acid burnt the inside of my nostrils as I dry-wretched the last of my 'time-tested cure'. Out of the corner of my eye I could see four rickshaw drivers, nonchalantly sitting on their machines, observing the scene. As soon as I had finished, the wringing sensation started pressing downward, so down too came my shorts.

My audience just sat and stared. I caught one of their eyes from my squatting position and received a masculine nod, the kind that a man might give to acknowledge another man's pain as he struggles with something in the DIY shop, or follows his wife around yet another clothes shop.

'I feel your pain,' the nod said. 'It's something we've all gone through.'

This was one of my all-time low points. But it got worse: I soon saw that what was being wrung out of me was not normal poo or even normal liquid poo for that matter (if there is such a thing). It was green slime, marbled with a considerable amount of blood.

We needed a hotel – or at least I did – and quickly. After we eventually found one, we discovered that they didn't accept foreigners. Exasperated, I used their facilities and we found another. The same thing happened again and we moved on.

There are hordes of tourists in India, but as it's such a vast place there are some areas with few attractions and fewer public transport links that can only be seen if you're driving your own vehicle, meaning they're not used to accommodating foreigners. This started to get irritating after I shuffled off to another hotel's toilet for the sixth time. It dawned on me that the toilet paper I had acquired from the first hotel had run out at what can only decently be described as 'the wrong moment'. I shouted for Johno and Leigh, but what came out sounded more like a pathetic squeak. Apparently this was all I could muster. I squeaked a few times, but soon gave up. I leant against the white tiles that surrounded the hole-in-the-floor toilet, and, slowly slipping to the floor and feeling very sorry for myself, I cried for the first time in many years.

I decided that it was categorically the lads' fault that I had no paper.

It was their fault I was ill.

It was their fault nobody would accept us.

It was even their fault I was in fucking India.

Eventually, I plucked myself out of self-pity, used some initiative and made my way back to the cab, minus a pair of Marks & Spencer boxers. It was dark by now and the smooth road had turned very Indian again, each pothole and bump became agony, and it appeared that I had developed a fever and was now shivering violently. We found one more hotel but it was 50 times more expensive than anywhere else. They agreed to accept us, but it was way out of our budget. We decided to move on, but only after I had taken a trip to the men's. I soon remembered the paper problem had yet to be resolved.

But I only remembered when it was too late. By this point I was not in a state to care any more.

Things were bad. I lay in the back of the cab, shivering, cramping and covered in my own shit, wishing I had a bed, my mum, a shower, toilet paper and a hug; I was willing to pay any amount of money to get out of this bloody car, so we headed back to the hotel.

Leaving the boys to crack open our emergency cash supply and sort out registering I had to run to the room. I had nothing left in me, so I had a shower and curled up in the foetal position on the bed, forgetting that normal people clothe themselves after a shower. I felt like with one more whimpering trip to the loo, I might be a goner. Leigh and Johno must have come in and covered me up at some point, and I recall snippets of their conversation as they discussed what to do as I lay there 'moaning like a little bitch'.

When I was a kid my parents never took us to the doctor unless something was seriously wrong, like the loss of a limb. Once I was sure I had broken my wrist after falling out of a tree and it took a whole day of crying and begging until they finally took me to hospital for an X-ray. Of course, I was fine; they were right and I was wrong and since then I had learned to grin and bear it through gritted teeth.

By contrast Leigh's mum is a nurse and his dad is a paramedic and as such he had brought along a whole separate bag jammed with various bandages, tablets and needles. At the slightest sign of anything wrong he would be cracking out the antibiotics and rehydration salts while I rolled my eyes and reached for another cup of tea.

So when Paul started to complain he was feeling ill I told him to clench up and drink more water, but by the time we got him to a hotel he wasn't looking too great. Still, I was sure he'd be just fine in the morning...

Luckily, Leigh thought I was going to die. Ever the cautious one, I was glad that he ignored Johno's verdict and tracked down my phone from my shorts pocket – although I can only imagine what condition they (and it!) were in.

He called Ellie up in Manali, to get her advice. She asked to speak to me, but when she was told that I wasn't talking she came to the immediate conclusion that I *must* be ill. She diagnosed it as a nasty case of dysentery and said I needed rehydrating quickly and to get to a hospital. But seeing as there were no hospitals around, she prescribed some specific antibiotics that Leigh searched high and low for, eventually tracking them down in a street pharmacy after an hour of looking, and said that if I didn't improve during the night, we should find a hospital urgently; if I did, then keep taking the pills and I'd be fine.

I've known Ellie for many years, but, I must admit, I've always found it a little terrifying that as a doctor she is in charge of people's health. That day I must have gone to the toilet over 25 times, but after taking the drugs she prescribed within a few hours my fever had gone down, I stopped going to the toilet so much and I was actually able to sleep. The antibiotics had worked and Ellie's telephone diagnosis was bang on the money. I think I probably perpetually owe her a drink or two.

I woke up the next morning, naked, wrapped in a towel.

Where I had been sleeping, a large green patch had soaked into the bed sheets and the stench was unbearable. I felt like utter crap, I was sweating, I hurt all over... and I had clearly shit the bed during the night. Admittedly, I've had better mornings.

But, it was worse for Leigh who was just waking up. He had lost the rock-paper-scissors game with Johno the night before and had been sharing the bed with me.

CHAPTER 30

MISSING PERSONS

My convalescence was short lived, for, as always with the expedition, we had to move on. With the only hotel that would accept us unlikely to let us stay again once they had seen the room, we mounted up. Relieved of driving duties, I curled up in a ball in the back of the cab underneath my *hajji* scarf-blanket, sipped some foul-tasting World Health Organization rehydration solution and slept the entire way to Mumbai.

The sprawling capital's quirks and irks, beauty and dirt are far more mind-boggling than I could ever describe. It's vast and filled to bursting with people (60 per cent of whom live in slums) and then filled some more. Our destination was the touristy Colaba District where we knew we could grab a cheap bed in what turned out to be a surprisingly expensive city. The plan was to do some interviews with the Indian media, get Hannah in a Bollywood film and sample all the delights the city had to offer.

We arrived in the huge, bustling city with a terrible atmosphere in the car. Driving in India had been extremely challenging and tiring for all of us, and that day Leigh, still not feeling great from his illness in Manali, had hit a particularly large pothole at high speed causing one of our headlights to ping out of its mountings and smash on the side of the road. My less-than-diplomatic request for him to be more vigilant had led to an intense shouting match that had culminated in Leigh refusing to drive any further and me taking over for the gridlocked streets of the inner city.

As soon as we found a cheap hotel we checked into separate rooms. I dumped my bags in my two-metre-square box, splattered with the crimson stains of dead mosquitoes, and headed out to try to catch some of the tourist sites and walk off my bad mood.

The place where we were staying really was horrendous. Stocking up on toilet roll (I had learned the hard way…) and sleeping pills, I settled down to a night of toing and froing between my cell-like room and the toilet we shared with 30 Nigerian labourers, two families and a crusty hippy.

The next day, I carried on with the previous night's monotonous toilet activities, utterly drained (pardon the pun) by this point; Johno had gone out to see the sights of the town while Leigh sat and watched action films on his laptop, still annoyed from the earlier argument.

Eventually Leigh rose from his ancient, stained mattress and poked his head round my door. 'I'm going to get some lunch,' he said in a defeated tone.

'Cool, do you need some cash?' Leigh's card had been blocked so Johno and I had been subbing him until he had access to more funds.

'Nope, I found a hundred rupees in my pocket, should be enough for a samosa.'

An hour passed. Then two, three, four…

Johno returned.

'Seen Leigh at all?' I asked.

'Nope.'

'He popped out for lunch five hours ago.'

'Bothered.'

'He only had a hundred rupees.'

'Sucks to be him.'

His laptop lay on the bed of his unlocked room, paused where he had left it halfway through an episode of *Battlestar Galactica*. I was slightly concerned for his wellbeing, but figured he was a big boy and would turn up soon enough. I watched *Apocalypse Now* (the extended director's cut) with the odd essential toilet break built in. This had become the standard entertainment for the trip for when we were too exhausted to leave our rooms and explore. It seems that films and TV series are traded between travellers' hard-drives in hostels everywhere, so you can spend fortunes travelling to the other side of the planet just to sit in a hostel common room watching different movies on a tiny screen. The film was excellent, however the bit when Martin Sheen emerges from the water covered in browny-green slime was a little bit close to home for me at the time.

Midnight came around and there was still no sign of Leigh. I was starting to get really concerned – it was unlike him to do this, there was a monsoon blowing outside and he only had enough money for a cup of tea (hardly enough to nurture ten hours' worth of exploration). I left our hovel and paddled my way through the flooded streets to the local police station to give them my number in case a skint Brummie turned up.

When morning came around and there still was no sign of him, even Johno started to be a little concerned. We had no idea where to look; where do you start to find a missing person in a city with a population the same as Holland? We usually carried our passports at all times, and a quick search of his stuff confirmed he had his, so if anything had happened the British consulate was likely to be contacted. I called them up and asked if they had heard anything. They hadn't, but said I should call the local hospitals instead and emailed me their details. It was about 10.30 a.m. by this point and he had been out for 19 hours.

I started calling around.

'Hello, do you speak English?'

'Yes, some...'

'Did you have a Western man admitted last night?'

'Yes, what name?'

'Leigh.'

'Lee?'

'Yes, Leigh.'

'OK, how is that spelt?'

'L-E-I-G-H.'

'Le-yggy?'

'No, Leigh.'

'Leggy?'

'No – Leigh.'

'Ahh let me check.'

Ten minutes of noise followed, but I could make out the occasional, *'Le-gigigy... Leeeee.'*

'No, we have no man called Leggy here.'

'Are you sure?'

'Oh yes, sir.'

'Completely sure?'

'Yes sir, very. This is the Mumbai Hospital for Women.'

It had now been almost 24 hours since we had seen him and my animosity was long forgotten. We reasoned that since he had hardly any money he couldn't have gone out partying and the more time that passed the more nervous we both got. My mind was racing through possibilities. Could he have had enough of it all and got a flight home? Could he have been in an accident? Worse yet could he have been robbed or attacked and left in a gutter somewhere? I tried to think logically about how we could track him down but my thoughts jumped through all sorts of scenarios – would we be able to or even want to continue the trip without him? What would I say at his funeral?

> *Leigh Purnell – self-taught mechanic and master*
> *of roadside repairs who travelled around the world*
> *eating nothing other than burgers and chips.*
> *A true friend who would even share his bed*
> *with a leaking dysentery patient.*

I took the phone and dialled the next hospital.

It was about two in the afternoon when Leigh strolled in along the veneered, peeling corridor with an inane grin and a nonchalant, 'Hullo,' our argument the previous morning seemingly forgotten.

Paul wasn't quite so relaxed.

'WHERE THE FUCK HAVE YOU FUCKING BEEN?'

'I went out drinking, chill.'

'DRINKING? DRINKING! WITH WHAT FUCKING MONEY?'

I – understandably, I think, after the 24 hours we'd had – was annoyed.

The relief that he wasn't lying dead in a drain and the anger that he had been so irresponsible – combined with the fact that I had spent the past three days relocating my insides to my outside – manifested themselves in lots of loud noises and swear words.

'I had the kitty card on me,' he explained sheepishly, as a sizable crowd of Nigerian labourers peered out of their door at us.

The kitty was our shared emergency expedition funds, for times of real need and certainly not to be used for a day-long bender. This was the last straw.

'KITTY MONEY!' Paul exploded with rage and leapt at Leigh, fists in the air, venting all the nervous fury he had built up over the past few sleepless nights. Leigh was totally unprepared for this physical onslaught and looked shell-shocked as Paul flailed his arms at him. I jumped between them and soon managed to separate them, and sent Paul to calm down in another room while I explained to Leigh how we had spent the previous 24 hours and he told me his side of events. After weeks of being ill, bad driving and our huge bust-up he'd had enough and gone for a walk around the city to clear his head and try to process everything that had gone wrong recently. Craving some company that wasn't me or Paul he'd met a group of backpackers and was having a couple of drinks when the monsoon hit, rendering the flooded streets nigh on impossible to traverse and cutting off power in the hotel bar they were trapped in until the day.

It was the biggest argument of the trip so far and the first time any of us had ever actually come to blows. India had really taken its toll on us.

CHAPTER 31

BOND, HINDI BOND

Luckily after so long on the road together we had developed a kind of sibling-like attitude to arguments, where all it takes is a quick apology and half an hour apart and the rift is forgotten. In Paul's case the argument had blown over in the time it took for another of his still-all-too-frequent toilet breaks.

The following day, we were driving to the airport to pick up my girlfriend Katie who was coming out to join us on holiday for a couple of weeks. It was great timing as I was just starting to feel mildly human again after my bout of dysentery. However, after driving for hours in the muggy downpour, we were lost again and had to stop for directions. In my experience, Indians are almost always incredibly friendly and desperate to help – even if they haven't a clue what you're asking them to help with or the answer to your question. Requests for directions are always met with a beaming smile and a head wobble.

The wobble is a very Indian thing and quite hard to describe. Sometimes it's a clear sideways tilting of the head on either side; sometimes it's an almost undetectable inclination. I'm not 100 per cent sure on its meaning, but by now I'd seen it being used to imply 'Yes', 'No', 'OK', 'Maybe', 'Fine' and, most common of all,

'I'm sorry, I genuinely have no idea what you just said to me, but I'll make it up to you by wobbling my head!'

After two months apart, I had been expecting a dramatic, romantic reunion with my girlfriend. She appeared out of the arrivals gate and I felt a rush of joy at seeing her familiar face for the first time in what felt like forever. I beamed as she walked up to us.

'You're so skinny…' she said, staring at me in horror, 'and you look *so ill!*

'I love you, too,' I mumbled.

The first thing we did with our new passenger was to sign on for a typical tourist trap – a 'become a Western extra in a Bollywood film' experience. We were to feature in a nightclub scene for the upcoming blockbuster *Agent Vinod* – less of a typical all-singing, all-dancing Bollywood love story and more of a 'Bond, Hindi Bond' angle.

The five of us were sent to wardrobe for our attire, emerging one by one to hysterical laughter. Leigh in Versace and a nob-end hat, Johno looking strangely smart and me in skinny jeans, a Samuel L. Jackson cap and the most god-awful fake Ed Hardy T-shirt with a diamanté tiger on it. We looked like a bad teenage dance troupe about to appear at the local village fete – featuring on the bill somewhere between the raffle and the 'Dog most like its owner' competition. Katie emerged in a delightfully short skirt. After filming the same scene where we bopped away in the background for the hundredth time, we finished up at 2 a.m., exhausted but 500 rupees each – about a fiver – richer.

It was the first honest day's work we'd done in six months.

Katie's luggage consisted almost exclusively of spare parts. It was our first delivery since Turkey and Hannah was in desperate need of a new cooling fan and a few other vital pieces needed for the hot drive across India and into the Himalayas.

The next section of driving was one of the hardest of the trip. We knew the 1,100-mile slog up towards Varanasi and the Nepalese border in five days was going to be tough, but none of us anticipated exactly how bad the road would be. I had studied a map on the wall of the hotel before we left and seen a large road, National Highway 7, labelled as 'North–South Corridor', which almost exactly connected us to where we needed to go. 'If this is a major connecting road that's marked thickly on the map,' I reasoned, 'then it must be in fairly good shape.'

I couldn't have been more wrong.

The builders couldn't have made a worse road if they tried: large stretches of potholes slowed our progress and the heavy bumps battered Hannah's already ailing chassis and bodywork. To make things worse, frequent tollbooths actually asked us to pay for using these abominations. For the most part the drive was a crawl of intense concentration through the myriad hazards in the pouring rain and steaming heat. But the breakfast, lunch and dinner stops at the tiny roadside cafes, lines of bubbling pots of curry stacked outside, allowed us to experience more of one of India's great offerings: the tasty, plentiful and cheap food.

We often drove for more than 12 hours a day, from dawn until dusk. Road signs were sporadic, as were roads. Occasionally ten miles or so of brand new, smooth road would appear, but as soon as there was the slightest incline, decline, requirement for bends, junction or jungle, the road would give up. All that remained where a road should have been were gaps between dense jungles that resembled the no-man's-land at the Somme, only not quite as smooth.

We had an average speed of 20 mph and those five days were some of the most uncomfortable of the entire trip. It wasn't too much of a burden for the lads and me, but Katie only had a few weeks off from her intensive final-year studies to become a doctor and this was supposed to be her holiday. We arrived at Varanasi at sundown, and collapsed in front of a steaming plate of butter chicken, happy to have got there and looking forward to a day off from driving.

Katie and I wandered the streets to discover the holiest of Hindu cities. Varanasi is a city on the holy Ganga (Ganges) River, and it's the place where the Hindu dead are burned, their ashes spread into the river. It is also the perfect microcosm of India's ability to warm your heart and turn your stomach at the same time. Nestled among smouldering funeral pyres with charred limbs protruding at grotesque angles, we watched an eldest son dress his father's body in bright, expensive cloth and carefully build a fire around him, liberally spreading it with spices and flowers in a sombre ceremonial manner. Amazing temples line the banks, their bright gold and orange contrasting with the dull brown of the river. As children ran, bathed and swam right next to the sewage outlet, the corpse of a sheep became caught on a boat's anchor a few metres away while a 'baba' holy man watched over in a meditative state from the bank.

We hopped on a boat at dawn and watched the sun rise over the city as throngs of devoted men, women and children came to bathe themselves in the holy waters.

But again we had to move; after all the delays, the Indian visas we had been granted back in the UK before the expedition started only had three days remaining on them and we had to make the 200 miles to Nepal before they expired. We drove all day along the same kinds of roads and got to within a few hours of the border, eventually holing up in a mosquito- and bed-bug-ridden 'hotel' when it got too dark to drive – India was the one place we stuck steadfastly to our no-night-driving rule. We all felt physically drained from our time in India, and after being overcharged one time too many for our meal in the hotel, we agreed we were thoroughly ready to leave. To be fair, we hadn't really seen India at its best, so we resolved to return one day to give it another chance.

We left as the sun rose. For once the temperature was pleasant and it had stopped raining. A cool, low mist snuck between bushy outcrops and rough pastures as their lumbering bovine residents began to move for the day. The dawn chorus of a hundred different kinds of birds singing as one provided nature's soundtrack to the sight of whole families – mothers hitching up their saris, old men crouching their knees to breaking point and kids, naked as the day they were born, doing their bit to ensure the side of the road was fertilised. We were being treated to a rare insight into the rural Indian morning routine as we counted 35 people squatting, each with a small pot of water, on the road within less than two miles.

Passing the border without too much trouble, the road suddenly changed: it became paved and started winding through the Himalayan foothills, where we encountered something we had not seen since Europe. As we came up behind a slow moving truck, he pulled over to the side to let us overtake. He didn't have a problem with his truck, he didn't need to stop, he was just letting us pass because he was a nice guy.

I thought, 'I'm going to like Nepal.'

But nothing confirmed this more than the sign we passed that confirmed the end of India and its running theme:

Welcome to Pokhara Region, Nepal.
An Open-Defecation-Free Zone since 1995

CHAPTER 32

LEIGH'S LISTS

We were all overjoyed to be in Nepal, where things appeared to be completely different from India: the roads were good, the people were tourist-friendly and seemed to take real pride in their surroundings, and best of all we could finally go for the steaks we had been salivating over since before we entered the largely beef-free state of India.

In tranquil Pokhara we had a final team meal and some beers for our last night together for a week or so, then we each took off in our separate directions for a much-needed break from each other. Leigh was planning to rent a motorbike for a few days, Paul and Katie were going to find a hotel with room service and I had decided to go hiking around the Annapurna region.

Towards the end of our minibreak, I had set off early to scale one of the mountains of the region. Woefully underprepared, however, I suffered the early signs of altitude sickness as I struggled my way up to the top of a mountain. Rushing back down again I caught a bus back into the city, which soon rounded a corner and swerved sharply to avoid a vehicle – a rather familiar taxi-shaped vehicle – haphazardly parked on the side of the road and missing a front wheel.

It took a very stressed-looking Leigh a second to register who I was as I jumped down off the coasting bus, but once he did the relief on his face was incredible. He had spent the past three days welding, cleaning and rewiring Hannah but now another of the troublesome ball joints had broken apart causing the entire front wheel assembly to come loose. In a way we were extremely lucky it had happened here in the city and not earlier, on the tight mountain roads flanked by sheer drops hundreds of metres deep.

With help from the assembled locals and some soldiers from a nearby army base, Leigh and I found a temporary fix for Hannah and took the short drive across the capital to meet up with Paul.

As Katie and I arrived in Kathmandu a week before the lads, it was my job to track down a suitable hotel. It had to be cheap and it had to have some sort of parking where we could – literally – rebuild Hannah, again. Katie and I had had a wonderful week of relaxing in chai houses, and it was strange to wave her off at the airport and meet back up with the lads. But after regaling each other with our stories of Johno's altitude sickness and Leigh's fallout with the Pokhara mafia over a flat tyre on his motorbike, everything quickly fell back into place.

By the time we got to Kathmandu, Hannah was in a terrible state. As well as the dodgy front wheel, which had literally fallen off, the black cab body had sheared away from the chassis, a suspension mount had snapped, we had an ant infestation, another ball joint was going and we had no headlights. Rust had crept into everything, causing many of the electrics to fail and our roof boxes – which were great at letting water in but less so at letting it leak out – were reservoir-esque.

The sound system, however, was still banging... until Leigh discovered the source of the ant invasion was a colony in our subwoofer. We tried all the dubstep we could get our hands on, but it appears that not only can ants survive underwater for two weeks (true story), but they are also impervious to Skrillex. We even tried Johno's disturbingly extensive collection of Bonnie

Tyler, but 1980s power ballads didn't have the same fumigation effect on ants as they do on a dance floor. The sub had to go.

To nobody's surprise, we couldn't find spare parts for a London black cab in Nepal... so we made our own with low-grade metal and welding torches. For headlights, Leigh found a pair of similarly shaped motorbike lights and mounted them in the gaping holes where the old ones once lived.

Johno's friend Matt flew in to join us for the next leg. He was an RAF fighter pilot who had been made redundant in the recent cuts and so flew straight out to meet us. We also had another useful pair of hands in Binay Lama: a friend of Katie's who was in the area and who was quite possibly the loveliest person in the entire world. He owned a tour company and used the profits to build schools and help the community back in his village in the remote mountains. We were also joined by another familiar face a day or two after Johno and Leigh arrived. There was a note on the door:

I'm in room 201
Love
Craig

Our favourite potty-mouthed Australian had made it to Nepal on his circuit of Central Asia. We were glad to note he had purchased a new T-shirt soon after he left us, but it didn't look like he had changed it since.

Meanwhile, Leigh had been preparing a list. Leigh's lists are a very serious thing. They contain everything that needs to be done to the car and even more that doesn't. Leigh is an incredibly talented mechanic and electrician, and pretty much the only member of the team who actually mattered. However, his prioritisation skills leave a lot to be desired. Johno and I – although very untalented mechanics – had become very talented at prioritising Leigh's lists. So when we'd find Leigh applying stickers to the roof rack when there was a host of essential complicated electronic work that only he was able to do, we'd gently encourage him to do those instead. This would then be followed by an argument where Leigh tried to persuade us that cutting out the outline of a sponsor sticker so that it looked prettier was more important than having headlights. Then Johno and I would pretend to take over the sticker-cutting (stopping as soon as Leigh looked away, of course), and Leigh would start working on the vital headlights and the list would gradually start to decrease.

Johno had told Matt about 'the lists', but he didn't believe us. That was until I saw him looking at the car with broken suspension, dodgy steering and no lights, but its entire contents strewn around midway through a spring clean, with a puzzled look on his face.

'There's so much to be done... why has Leigh asked me to scrunch up tin foil and clean the rust off the chrome of the side walls so they shine? We're about to drive over the bloody Himalayas!'

We were on the eve of the next leg of the trip – China, which was always a vastly expensive but necessary part of the trip. Myanmar was closed to vehicles, so we would be spending over £4,000 on visas, paperwork and guides to pass through the country. Not that we weren't looking forward to China, it was just that we were loath to have to use a guide for the first time on the trip. However, with no knowledge of the Chinese government system and even less Mandarin between us, it would be impossible to do it without help.

Because of this, none of us had researched China very much. In fact, in all honesty a part of us probably doubted we would ever get this far, so our research of anywhere on the trip past

Iran was imperfect. However, to get to China, first we had to pass through Tibet – and to get to Tibet we had to drive the Friendship Highway.

For me, the Friendship Highway that connects Kathmandu in Nepal to Lhasa, the capital of Tibet, was one of the sections of the trip I'd been looking forward to the most. It carves its way through the 23,000-foot peaks of the Himalayas before gliding across the expanses of the Tibetan Plateau, finally terminating in the relatively lush farmlands around the capital city of Lhasa. And now, against all the odds, we had actually managed to get Hannah this far.

We couldn't wait to start.

CHAPTER 33

CLIMBING EVEREST

We said our goodbyes to Craig again and followed the road out of Kathmandu, ascending through pleasant hills and small villages in stunning weather. Finally out of the sweltering heat of Iran, Pakistan and India, it was sunny but comfortable, reminiscent of the ideal British summer's day. We had received word that the mudslides were nearly cleared and there would be no rain for a few days. Conditions weren't perfect, but we decided to give it a go.

Busy buses and small cars occasionally passed us, but the surroundings were otherwise peaceful and the road was quiet. The soft hills gradually transitioned into high mountains partitioned by sheer valleys, the thin road precariously clutching to their sides. We had heard that landslides meant this road could be impassable for weeks, even months. Two-wheel drive vehicles were out of the question in the wet season and four-wheel drives unreliable at best. Calculating that Hannah would do just fine (basing this on nothing in the slightest, other than the fact we couldn't turn around now), we decided to push on, having no idea what lay ahead.

We passed a few flatbed trucks loaded with mud-splattered earthmovers, returning battered and bruised from the landslide-clearing front line. Reaching the first rockfall, it became clear how the road could be shut for weeks on end – half the mountain seemed to have crashed down, taking everything with it. This was obviously an old slide, as a new 'road' had been carved into the embankment. Deep grooves showed where bigger, more appropriate vehicles had negotiated the track. Gunning the engine to gain speed, I tried to balance on the ridges between the ruts as the rear wheels fishtailed to and fro on the slick surface and the lads shouted for, 'More beans!'

Splashing through a stream, the tyres gained purchase as the mud turned to gravel and we were soon back on the relative solidity of the potholed, concrete road.

This scene would repeat itself throughout the day, sometimes with added vehicles coming the other way and sometimes resulting in Hannah getting stuck in the mud, and everyone having to get out and push, losing multiple flip-flops along the way.

On top of a foundation of unstable, wet mud was not the most reassuring place to be.

As I slowed for a turn, a battered old coach appeared. It wasn't going to stop for us, instead subscribing to the time-tested technique of using the horn instead of the brakes. We couldn't back up, as it would mean sliding down the big hill, or worse.

We were stuck.

Everybody was shouting in different languages, trying to take control. Beyond the bus the road widened enough to pass, but he refused to back up. He edged forward and it became clear he was going to push past whether we moved or not. I reversed the cab a few feet, and then slammed the whole car forward, embedding the bumper into the muddy embankment on the non-chasm side of the road.

The coach managed to pass, its wheels churning through the mud just inches from the edge, before sliding dangerously out of control down the hill. Our tiny wheels, however, were well and truly stuck. Everyone got out to push, cursing the monsoon for its lack of sympathy.

We traversed muddy pass after muddy pass, landslide after landslide. It was getting dark and our makeshift motorbike headlights were doing a poor job of illumination. Just before pitch-blackness covered us, the track became a well-sealed road. Within a few minutes we could see the lights of the border town of Kodari. Triumphant, we soared towards it, jubilant at having managed the pass successfully – albeit with a few helpful pushes and a trail of flip-flops in our wake.

Finding a cheap hotel, the team celebrated with our final Indian curry dish and slept soundly with the gentle thunder of the Bhote Kosi River in the background – the official boundary to the most populous country in the world.

A large bridge marked the border with China, the previous two having been washed away in floods. Bored-looking guards on little red platforms stood to attention for the handful of people who passed. Squat Nepali women, swaddled in thick cloaks, trekked back and forth across the bridge, carrying burdens three times their size. Because no trucks are allowed through this border, porters carry all commerce between the countries. The contents of a Nepali truck would be unloaded into bags secured by a strap around the women's foreheads. The women would go through a scanner to confirm they weren't transporting nuclear weapons and then lug the cargo to a waiting truck on the other side. On the return journey, slyly tucked into their shawls, were bottles of cheap whisky to be sold on the black market in Nepal.

To drive a foreign vehicle in China, it is a legal requirement to have a guide with you at all times. The reason for this is slightly unclear, but China is not a place where you will find an abundance of reasonable answers. Our guide would meet us at the border with the paperwork, all organised by an agent. With no idea what to expect, we only knew his name was Fred and that we would be spending the next 25 days in very close proximity.

We were all quite nervous about meeting the compulsory guide who we had paid through the nose for and would be covering thousands of miles with. My biggest worry was that with us three strapping lads plus Matt already in the car we would now have to potentially squeeze a shuai jiao wrestler in there, too. I sincerely hoped he would be a little fella.

We stood around amongst the huge sacks of flour being ferried around and tried to spy our guide through the automatic gates and rows of guards.

After a while we saw a tiny Chinese woman with a backpack and folder waving frantically at us with a grin. She looked like a lot of fun and would definitely be able to fit in the space in the back seat; could it be that she was our guide, Fred?

No, no it couldn't.

After a quick chat we found that she was waiting for someone else, but she did agree to go back through the border and find our guy. Before long we had met Fred Jin – a middle-aged man wearing a fleece, walking boots and a floppy sunhat, clutching a wad of papers, who was at least six foot tall – and crossed the border into Tibet, or as he swiftly corrected us, the People's Republic of China.

There was only one road out and it disappeared in a cloudbank as it switchbacked up the side of a cliff. Shrouded in clouds, we quickly lost sight of the border as Hannah's tired diesel heart was urged further into the thinning air.

We were pleased to discover that China has lots of good quality Youth Hostel Association hostels spread throughout its four million square miles, and that one of them was located in the first town we came to.

I was less pleased to find out that the Chinese have a strange habit of making toilets with no doors. I discovered this when I knocked on Fred's room door and he yelled for me to come in then looked almost as surprised as I was when I marched in and came face to face with him, pants around ankles. I felt like knowing each other for five hours (or a lifetime for that matter) wasn't long enough to find ourselves in these circumstances.

The next morning, from our hotel at 5,500 feet we climbed up the seemingly never-ending mountain hairpins and on to the Tibetan plateau. The road was truly amazing; a magnificent feat of engineering far from the landslide-strewn track we had been told to expect. As we chugged higher and higher we appreciated the views, snatched through the gaps in the clouds, down into the lush valleys, but Hannah didn't feel the same way.

Passing 12,000 feet the car started to feel more sluggish than usual and began to belch out thick black smoke. The highest point on the Friendship Highway was about 16,000 feet and I was really starting to worry: if we were struggling now, with 4,000 feet of oxygen-starved air still to go, how would we ever make it over one of the highest roads in the world and into the rest of China?

Somehow Hannah crawled up the slopes and we crested the pass at around 16,800 feet, all five of us feeling a little weird from the altitude as we stepped out to breathe in the crisp mountain air amid the flapping prayer flags and yak bones.

Tibet is a very poor place, but the road we were driving on was brand new and smoother than anything we had experienced since we left Iran. Built as an example of Chinese superiority, it cuts through some incredibly inhospitable and remote areas, and bears a stark contrast to the rest of the country. Tibetan people live in traditional abodes built with rough stone and topped with red roofs. Each had a perimeter wall with ornately decorated ends, on which piles of yak dung – used as heating and cooking fuel – dried in the sun.

The people – their hardy, warm faces, wrinkled by years of driving winds, sun, and tough living – stared as we drove through. Their wise, laughing eyes were a world away from the Chinese – most of whom were pedantic officials and bored young conscripts in oversized uniforms, with their helmets resting low over their young, hairless faces.

The road wound with racetrack-perfect arcs between the small hills that rose from the plateau as hamlets appeared and disappeared. We reached the hotel Fred recommended at dusk – a launch pad for Everest Base Camp. Lined up outside were eight new Land Cruisers and entering the restaurant was like walking into a North Face convention: the room was crowded with middle-aged wealthy men whose beer guts strained at their gilets, as they discussed the extortionate amounts they had paid to fly in and be driven to the top of the world. The rooms were triple our usual budget, but as it was the only place for miles I negotiated cheaper accommodations in the workers' quarters – much to Fred's annoyance.

We chatted with a few beer guts about the next leg of our journey, driving Hannah to Base Camp. They all looked at us with concern, each one of them repeating that the 65-mile track is just not possible in a two-wheel-drive car. Young, foolish, reckless, and with little point of reference other than the knowledge that we had managed to get this far, we decided we'd give it a go anyway.

Long before sunrise we stripped the car of luggage, spares and camping gear, leaving the extra weight in the hotel yard, and set off. The sun crested the distant peaks, revealing a table-flat plateau. We were in a huge bowl, surrounded by the world's tallest mountains. The sun, low and yellow, streamed through, bouncing off lakes and silhouetting the small Tibetan bungalows.

The first 40 miles continued on the stunning Friendship Highway, and the sight of the low sun reflecting off the pools of standing water amidst the high meadows kept us wide awake.

At the turn off to Mt Qomolangma (Everest's Chinese name), Fred assured us it would take only two hours to get to Base Camp. The road turned to heavily rutted dirt as it wound up lazy hairpins on a meadowed hillside. We presumed Everest would be on the other side of the hill, but no. As the altimeter rose steadily, 14,000 feet turning to 16,000, Hannah's engine strained in the thin air. Johno revved her engine, pumping more and more fuel into her oxygen-starved cylinders, which was only to be pumped back out in thick clouds of smoke. Progress was slow.

After Fred's two, incredibly bumpy, promised hours we had only covered 12 miles, and were forced to reconsider our plans. We figured if this kept up it would take us all day just to get there, not to mention returning. Disheartened, we cursed every Land Cruiser that zoomed past us at twice our speed and with half our shakiness.

Our spirits were buoyed into continuing at the top of the first peak as we surveyed the epic mountain range spread out before us. With 50 miles to go we were certain Everest must be one of the big ones directly ahead of us.

'Is that it?' Matt asked.

'Erm... I'm not sure.'

'What does it look like?'

'Ummm, like a big triangle I guess...'

In a small village in the next valley I went in search of water. When the tap I scouted didn't work, an elderly lady (though she could have only been in her 40s, it was impossible to tell) offered help and invited me into her house. Inside, the main area had the feeling of a farm building; mud floor and ancient farm equipment piled against the walls. In the living room, every inch of wall was covered in decorative murals. Furniture, crafted from crudely cut wood, was made beautiful by intricate carvings. The woman didn't speak English, nor did I speak Tibetan, but the water bottles in my hands made it clear. She led me to a giant bowl covered in wood. Ladling fresh clear Himalayan water into the bottles, she gave a toothless, maternal smile.

As we arrived at the lower slopes of Everest, the four-wheel drives from the hotel were already on their way back. Tussock grass gave way to a scree valley with a few bitterly cold concrete and stone buildings. To reduce air pollution, we found that no vehicles were allowed to Base Camp apart from the pricey government tour buses. We pleaded with the official, 'just for a picture' and 'we've driven all the way from England for this', to no avail. We paid the overpriced fee, piled in, and sped off to do the last three miles on the bus in a thick cloud of fumes. At the top we found that the no-car rule was strictly enforced: unless, of course, you were affiliated with 'the ruling party', in which case your Land Cruiser apparently doesn't emit pollution and you can just drive yourself up.

We'd managed to drive Hannah, a wholly unsuitable London black cab, to one of the highest points in the world. And as much of a dump as Base Camp was (we dodged mini cyclones of used toilet paper and sanitary towels while taking our pictures), and even if the summit was completely obscured by cloud, we were jubilant.

CHAPTER 34

- - - - - - - -

THANK YOU, HELLO AND DIESEL

By the time we reached the bottom, the new headlights had almost fallen off, the fuel cap was missing, the reverse light was gone and we'd sheared our Nepali backyard welds on the body mounts. Fred huffed sulkily as another Land Cruiser steamed past in a cloud of dust, chastising us for refusing to hire a four-wheel drive. We limped back to the hotel 18 hours after leaving. We were exhausted.

The next morning, with a breakfast of dumplings and tea inside of him, Fred was in considerably better spirits as we drove to the next town.

Since Georgia, the three of us had had a long-running joke about finding a McDonald's, our sacred Internet connection spot. Now we decided to bring Fred and Matt in on the joke.

'Will there be a Maccy D's, Freddyboy?'

'A Mack Eeh Dez?'

'You know, McDonald's.'

'Oh yes, very big town. Definitely McDonald's.'

Instead we found a small completely McDonald's-free town, but the joke had been set.

Based on previous experiences in Russia, our car was quite a large target for police checks, and seeing as we had over 4,000 miles to cover in China and that none of us had a fond desire to complete a term of hard labour in Inner Mongolia, we decided that it would be best to at least attempt the official Chinese driving test and try to get the correct licences.

We had heard mixed things about the test, ranging from, 'Don't bother with it, just bribe your way out of any document checks,' to 'It's a two-hour written test with a hundred questions and a 90 per cent pass mark. And it's in Mandarin and you're not allowed a translator.'

We turned up at the police station in the late afternoon. Paul was quickly scooted off for an inspection of the car while Leigh and I nervously awaited the dreaded test.

With Fred accompanying us to the police station, we waited as he talked to the paper-shuffling, noodle-eating, tea-drinking officials. Periodically, an officer would make a grotesque honking sound, as though to simultaneously relocate their lungs and transfer their sinuses to their bowels. They would then get up, walk to a pile of empty noodle pots in a shallow cardboard box and spit their phlegm out. And that was just the women. We were just beginning to learn how Chinese culture was completely alien to anywhere we had experienced so far.

It was now time to do the test in the taxi. The lads stayed at the station and I went with a policewoman to get the car checked. I had been in the country for a few days and had picked up a few choice words; *nee-how* (hello), *she-shia* (thank you) and my proudest achievement, *chaaay-un* (diesel) – said with a focus on 'aaaaayyyy' and an abrupt 'un'. She could count to seven in English. Amazingly this limited shared vocabulary kept us going for 30 minutes.

I think she was trying to remember how to say eight so much that she missed my absent-minded driving on the wrong side of the road.

I was apprehensive about the vehicle-worthiness test. Our brakes were shot, we had a crack in the windscreen and our headlights, which had been reattached with duct tape and epoxy glue ten minutes before the test, pointed in different directions. I smiled and said my three words in various sequences to the test man. He looked at me, bored and confused at this Westerner grinning like an idiot and periodically shouting 'thank-you-diesel' and gave me a piece of paper.

Hannah and I had passed.

Apparently, there was no need to test Johno and Leigh's driving, so we returned for the theory test. These first two checks had been somewhat less than comprehensive, but the theory test was the bit we had been dreading.

The head policeman, portly and smiling, invited us to sit on a long sofa and began to fire Mandarin at us. We smiled while Fred listened and translated.

'In China, we drive on right.'

We nodded yes. The policeman glared at us. There was an awkward pause.

Fred intervened, 'That OK?'

We realised that was the first question and it required an answer. 'Um, yes,' we replied in unison.

He broke into a broad grin – we had clearly answered correctly. He carried on while Fred translated: 'The speed limit is one-hundred kilometres, but forty in resident areas... or by school.'

There was another awkward silence before we realised this was another test question.

We again replied, 'Yes,' nodding and looking serious.

'Tibet is very big place, you must use conscience and not break law because there not many police.'

I had mastered this by now, nodding furiously, turning down my lower lip and creasing my brows to show I had harnessed the gravitas of the situation. 'Yes.'

Johno and Leigh had also clearly mastered this skill.

The policeman smiled and started speaking in Chinese. 'It must be time for the written test,' Leigh guessed. The basic rules of the road had been outlined, now things were going to get hard. We shot each other nervous glances.

Fred translated, 'OK. You pass, collect licence from window in main room.'

That night in the hotel, thanks to the slightly lower altitude, I slept properly for the first time since reaching Tibet. I also discovered that it is normal behaviour for Chinese men in their mid-50s, to strip to their white Y-fronts and wander around hotel rooms getting in uncomfortably close proximity while bending down to take things from their suitcase.

Licences in our pockets and a laminated Chinese number plate on Hannah, we set off to Lhasa on one of the greatest days of driving I have ever experienced. The plateau transitioned into a large valley with snow-capped mountains rising to either side. The road wound around a large unnaturally blue lake, then climbed through the occasional 16,000-foot pass. Fish, hung on racks by locals, dried in the brisk wind.

Occasionally, we'd pass someone lying on the side of the road. Dressed in a thick leather apron, and with wooden paddles attached to their hands, they would occasionally kneel up, slide their pads forward, and then return to a fully prostrated position a few feet further along. Over a period of months, the devotees would make the long pilgrimage to Lhasa (which is literally translated as 'place of gods') in this form with the purpose of praying at the Jokhang Temple, the holiest site in Tibetan Buddhism, and heading to bow at the tombs of former Dalai Lamas.

I couldn't shake the impression that the approved-for-foreign-eyes Folk Heritage Museum, set in an old feudal manor, might be slightly different to the rest of Tibet. Everything was just slightly too well ordered and picturesque. When we reached the servants' old quarters there were signs everywhere proclaiming how much the lives of the peasants had improved since China 'liberated' Tibet in the 1950s:

Pintsochuochun used to receive only 16 kg grain a year.
Since she stood up for liberation her family now have
seven cows, one horse, one cart, one TV set and
one plough! She need not worry for eat, live and use!

Fred saw us studying the boards and mused, 'Ah, Chinese propaganda!'

I was surprised at his frankness, but it turns out that his translation of the word 'propaganda' just meant literally 'government-provided information'. In its traditional English usage he would have been correct.

The final pass yielded to a deep valley and the final descent to Lhasa. The oxygen-rich air provided a new lease of energy, not only for us, but for Hannah as well. After an hour of riding the brakes, they began to overheat and we worried they would eventually fail. Stopping to let them cool, we chattered energetically about what Lhasa would be like. Even Fred seemed happy, telling us about some of its history, explaining how it was the religious and political centre of old Tibet before the Chinese 'liberated' them.

Reaching the bottom of the valley, we were now in rich farmland. Sheaves of corn had been bunched for collection in the fields and orchards lined the side of the road. One could have mistaken it for somewhere in the Mediterranean.

Lhasa, a broad and sunny city with a heavy Chinese influence and designer shops on every corner, could not have been more different from the rest of the country. Finding a hostel, we parked and headed out for a beer or two.

At first, decked out in our cleanest clothes and ready to party, we were highly disappointed. Every bar we hit was overpriced and under-occupied and it looked like a quiet and short night lay ahead. So naturally we started asking the bar staff where was best to go and after a short while we found ourselves bundled into a taxi (a strange sensation given our mode of transport for the past few months), destination unknown.

Ten minutes later we pulled up at what was possibly the most exclusive club I have ever seen. The queue that snaked away from the door was populated by hip young things clad in expensive-looking designer clothes. High-end 4x4s and sports cars surrounded the building. Even the bouncers looked like fashionistas and the doorway into the club was made up of a row of green lasers.

I immediately felt out of place in my shorts, sandals and T-shirt.

Inside, banging house music mixed with clouds of smoke and flashing lights. Every table had stacks and stacks of unopened beer bottles on it and people in various stages of drunkenness waltzed around.

The only thing on my mind was money; this place was going to be cripplingly expensive. However, I had a plan.

I walked up to a table near the bar that was covered in full bottles of Budweiser and put on my best stupid-foreigner routine. 'Excuse me, do you know if we just, er, order beers from the bar, or is there a waiter?'

A guy at the table smiled and without a word opened a bottle and passed it to me.

'Thanks! Uh... my friends are also...'

He opened three more and passed them around.

Here we learnt that in Chinese culture, if you get bought a beer, you lose face. We also learnt we had no real affection for our faces and started losing them on a regular basis.

CHAPTER 35

RECORD-BREAKING HIGHS

When we first conceived the idea of the expedition, one of our mutual friends had drunkenly confided what he thought our reasons were for going on the trip.

'Leigh is all about the world record and the charity aspect, whereas you just want to tick as many countries off your list as possible,' he told me, 'and Paul, he just wants to be able to use the stories to chat up girls.'

In a way he was right; whereas Leigh saw the world record as by far and away the most important aspect of the trip, I saw the record as more of a means to an end, a way of helping to secure the corporate sponsorship that was bankrolling some of the journey. Our first passenger, Chops, had left us with the parting words, 'Even if it's not written in some book or verified by some organisation, you still know that you have the record in your hearts and you will still have had an absolutely amazing adventure along the way,' and this summed up exactly how I felt. However, when we woke up on the morning of the 194th day I couldn't deny that I was at least a little bit excited about what lay just around the corner.

Earlier that week we had crested a pass on the highest road of the trip, a staggering 17,162 feet, and we were talking about whether we would also qualify for the record for the highest ever journey by taxi when I realised we were approaching the previous record point. I had won a coin toss, officiated by Craig before we left him back in Nepal, which meant I was to be the one driving when the record was broken. I had been keeping an eagle-eye on the GPS.

After over half a year of driving along some of the world's most exciting and picturesque roads, we broke the record on an utterly dull, if beautiful and deserted, section of highway in an obscure province north of Tibet. As the meter ticked over to 21,691 miles, Paul, Leigh, Matt and I erupted into cheers and jubilant shouting, while Fred sat sandwiched in the back a little bemused; the concept of a world record was still not fully making sense in his head.

At an unremarkable milepost, 1,996 miles from Beijing, on the China National Highway 109, surrounded as far as the eye could see by rolling steppe and distant mountains, we jumped out to slap each other on the back and take a photo to commemorate the moment. Matt grabbed the camera out of my hand, and said 'You three get on top of the car, Fred and I will take some photos.'

We clambered on to the roof rack and Matt arranged Fred in place with the camera, whispered a few words to him, stepped behind the car for a moment and reached down.

'Congratulations!' he shouted, as he ran forwards spraying a bottle of champagne over us. He must have had it hidden in his luggage the entire time. Most of it covered the car, but at that altitude it was probably best that we didn't drink more than a mouthful anyway.

When we had calmed down I clambered off the roof and retrieved the camera from Fred, and eagerly looked at the photos. He had completely missed the shot.

Eventually we reached the edge of the huge elevated Himalayan plateau and descended for many thousands of feet down the edge of the immense mountain range. The towering peaks gave way to fields of rolling sand dunes as we approached the fringes of the Gobi Desert.

We were all staggered by the Chinese infrastructure; ever since we had left Lhasa we had been following the seemingly never-ending railroad and almost all of our time in China had been on smooth, wide and well-built roads. Often they were clearly just finished; some hadn't even had the road markings painted on yet and most were almost completely empty of traffic. It was impressive forward-planning on behalf of the Chinese government, meaning that the burgeoning middle classes of the next 20 years would have somewhere to spread out to.

Our impression of lots of countries tended to become coloured by service stations and truck stops, and in China this meant communal squat toilets, which left something to be desired, and small roadside shops that baffled us with their lack of any recognisable Western-style food.

When we arrived at Dunhuang, home to what we were told was 'the largest Buddha in the world... in China', we were pleasantly surprised to find an attractive little city with a bustling night market selling all different types of food and drink (but still no McDonald's). After checking into a virtually empty youth hostel, we left Fred recuperating on his own and went to explore the markets.

Even though we had some disagreements with Fred we couldn't deny that he had been excellent at ordering us brilliant local meals at bargain prices and we quickly found out that without him things wouldn't go so smoothly. After looking around the stalls and seeing what I thought was some kind of prawn or shrimp stir-fry with vegetables I asked the price and ordered a dish. When it arrived I got stuck in, trying to look like a natural with the chopsticks. I soon discovered my mistake.

'Erm, why have these prawns got claws?' I asked anyone who was listening.

Leigh peered at the dish and burst out laughing, his mirth spurred on by my earlier scorn for his safer order of something Western. 'You've ordered chicken feet!'

I looked closely at the prawns and saw he was right – each was a fleshy leg ending in three long talons. I was determined to follow Fred's example of not losing face and so forced as many down as I could, lying to a smug Leigh that they tasted just like chicken wings.

When the bill arrived my second slap in the face hit me: the price was not 15 yuan as I had confirmed four times but 50 yuan. This called for a beer.

That evening we had a Chinese lock-in; somehow we had acquired the keys to a bar and climbed on to a roof where we stared up at the clear desert sky and chatted about the crazy chain of events that had led us here.

Waking the next day and feeling somewhat precious, we pored over the route plan. We were about 60 miles from the Mongolian border and none of us had any idea why we were so far north. Letting someone else plan our China section of the trip without checking the route properly had been a bad idea, but we were now at the furthest point and would just have to carry on with it.

To meet our schedule, we would have to drive for six days a week, which meant that our main viewings of China were through a windscreen. In India we had encountered the most atrocious driving skills, but at least the quality of the roads meant that people couldn't drive at speeds of more than 20 mph. Here, on the road to Xi'an, the smooth new roads meant that expensive BMWs and Land Cruisers would hurtle along at 90 mph, side by side with the donkey carts and pedestrians who continued to use the highways. This didn't seem to be too much of a problem, though, until it rained.

A weather front caused by a typhoon in the South China Sea had moved in and, although the full force of it had exhausted itself by the time it reached us inland, the rain was incessant. It literally drove down non-stop for four days, flooding fields, roads and black cabs.

I had already been terrified that I would hit somebody as they wandered out into the road, or I would try to avoid a ditch without looking for fast-moving cars, but as soon as the rain started to fall an accident became almost inevitable. We saw six major accidents that day, including a brand new BMW that had rolled over and been crushed like a concertina. Every bit of it was smashed, yet luckily the passenger compartment was still secure and the driver and his family walked out with little more than a few bruises. It was a triumph of modern safety engineering – and also a sobering reminder that if we crashed, we would not be so lucky in our 20-year-old taxi. The over-laden roof rack, the homemade roll bar and excessive weight in a car without even an airbag would mean a completely different story if we so much as slid a little bit.

The rain didn't seem to dampen Leigh's determination to get to Xi'an, home of the famous Terracotta Army, as quickly as possible, and for the second time that day we asked him to reduce his speed a little. His nonchalant reply wasn't the most comforting: 'If we hit something today we're dead anyway, the speed doesn't matter.'

CHAPTER 36

THE ABDUCTION OF FRED JIN

Xi'an was the first proper city we had visited since Mumbai: it had Starbucks and KFC and, finally, a McDonald's! The running joke with Fred had been weeks in the pipeline, so regardless of whether any of us were fans of the golden arches, we felt obliged to get a Big Mac. But, as I finally dug into the familiar flavour of a lukewarm beef-flavoured patty with soggy fries and a watered-down Coke, it dawned on me that the roadside fare Fred had been ordering for us was some of the best food I'd ever had.

The next morning, when Johno, Leigh and Matt went in search of an Egg McMuffin, Fred and I dug into a piping hot batch of steamed pork dumplings with chilli and soy dipping sauce.

After we'd had our fill of the Terracotta Army's pottery soldiers, archers and horsemen, Fred, Leigh and I set out to find some flesh-and-blood mechanics. Despite the impressive infrastructure, the 2,500 miles we had covered in China over the previous fortnight had caused another of our long-suffering front-suspension spring brackets to snap off.

We parked outside the first in a line of garages and showed them the shattered plate and bent shock absorber. Fred spoke to the teenage mechanics at length, explaining our problem while occasionally referring back to the broken parts Leigh and I stood holding.

Fifteen minutes later Fred turned to us. 'They say it is not possible to fix this.'

We were pretty stunned. 'What do you mean? Of course it is, the shock absorber just needs hammering straight.'

'No, this is not possible,' Fred replied.

'Yes it is, we just need a big hammer,' we said, looking around until we saw one suitable, 'look can we use this? Do you have a vice?'

Fred spoke to them for another few minutes. 'No,' he said, 'there are no vices here. This whole street is tyre change only.'

'But... this is a mechanic's, there must be a vice!'

'No, they do not have such a thing.'

Leigh and I walked along to the next workshop and immediately saw a chunky vice. We asked the mechanics if we could use it briefly, and two minutes of hammering later we had straightened the unfixable shock absorber. After the friendliness of the Indian people we had met, and their eagerness to help, the defeatist attitude on display here was something of a surprise.

To be fair to Fred he was usually exceedingly patient with our unusual and sometimes demanding requests and, sure enough, three hours and much discussion later we also had a brand new bracket, hewn from a sheet of scrap metal, to hold the shock absorber in place.

Our next stop was Chengdu, in Sichuan province. Fred was very excited by this prospect as he told us it was home to the most attractive girls in China.

'They have big eyes, like whales, filled with water,' he said.

Some of the most impressive feats of engineering we saw on our journey were the huge elevated skyways that sliced through steep winding valleys across China, cutting our journey times dramatically. Unfortunately, in southern Yunan we had arrived six months too early, and so a whole day was spent crawling up and down mountainous B-roads while staring longingly at the unfinished six-lane monsters towering high above us.

Still, these slow routes allowed us more chances to meet local people, and we soon found the Chinese to be as welcoming as the Indians – if a little more pessimistic. We spent an enjoyable few hours being treated to lunch one day by a car full of young locals, who kept repeatedly calling Matt, 'Big Ham'.

'Do you think they're calling me Big Ham because I'm sat at the head of the table?' he asked.

'Dude,' Paul chuckled, 'they're calling you Beckham!'

He wasn't too impressed.

The final large city before leaving China was Kunming, home of a sprawling market that sold everything from live bugs, birds and animals to hand-made stone stamps. It even had an entire shop stocking surplus police gear including radios, weapons and fully kitted-out police scooters. We realised that we were now into our last few days in China and we had encountered surprisingly few problems on our extremely tight schedule of manic driving. However, we still had 48 hours left in the country before we could declare China trouble-free.

'Stop!' yelled Fred. 'You must take me to hospital now!'

It was lunchtime on our last day in China, and Fred had been pushed over the edge.

Maybe Fred was used to overland expeditions with rich, middle-aged Westerners in roomy air-conditioned 4x4s and luxury hotels, because it had only taken 23 days with us for him to reach the end of his tether. Though we had explained about the shoestring nature of our trip before he signed up to be our guide, it seemed to have gone in one ear and out the other. He seemed to think we were deliberately torturing him with our small food portions and irregular stops, not realising that we were all sharing the same frugal conditions. On this day we had decided to have a late lunch to coincide with a telephone interview we were doing about the trip, but Fred seemed to think that the sole reason for the late lunch was to deny him food for a few hours more than normal.

It was Leigh driving past a service station that provoked this outburst.

'You must take me to hospital now!' he demanded again.

'Hospital?' we asked, shocked. 'Why, what's wrong, are you OK?'

'No, I am malnourish!'

We spluttered in disbelief, 'Fred, we just told you we are stopping later because of the interview!'

'No,' he shouted, 'stop now!'

'I can't stop now,' blustered Leigh, 'we're on the motorway.'

'Stop or I will tell police you kidnap me!'

We were all relieved a few hours later when we reached the border, where we could say goodbye to our hysterical passenger and say hello once again to our freedom as Hannah crossed through the ostentatious display of wealth and power that was the Chinese border. A large shining arch with Chinese writing and the Chinese flag marked the spot where the road that represented communist superiority crossed into Laos... and turned into nothing more than a jungle track.

CHAPTER 37

VOLLEYBALL DIPLOMACY

The feeling woke me up.

It was the feeling of a million feather dusters tickling my entire body, coupled with the sensation that my skin had been flayed raw. A cursory glance in the mirror revealed that my entire chest was covered in a rash – a battalion of insects (or maybe one very hungry one) had feasted heartily on my skin all night long.

I ran to find a shower, but soon I remembered that I was in a jungle shack a long way from running water. All I could find was a bucket of stale water to soothe my itchy, burning skin.

I poured it on my head.

Out of water and utterly unsatisfied, I tried to find something – anything – in the car that would fix me. The lads woke to a series of bizarre squawks, the sound a horse with Tourette's might make if it accidentally sat on a traffic cone. My frustration that no amount of scratching would sate the itch was escaping in uncontrollable blasts:

'Eeerrrroooooo aaahhhhhhhnneeeeehoooo WHERE'S THE FUCKING ANTI-FUCKING-SHITTING-HISTAMINE!'

Bang.

I'd kicked the car, which was rather ineffective at stopping my chest from itching, but served as an excellent way to make my foot hurt.

'Nneoooood-assoooooo-fucking itchy.'

'In the med kit, mate.'

'WHERE'S THE FUCKING BLOODY MED KIT AAAAHHHHHNNNNGGGHHH.'

'Here...'

It was sat just in front of me.

I ripped it apart and rubbed an entire tube of cream all over my body and chomped down five times the daily dose of antihistamine pills, made a few more noises, decided now would probably be a suitable time to clothe my near naked self after my bucket shower and sat down.

Johno calmly looked over: 'Looks like you got some bites, mate.'

We had been in Laos for less than 24 hours.

Laos's official name is Laos PDR. Ostensibly that stands for People's Democratic Republic, but we had heard people say it should be Pretty Damn Relaxed. Needless to say we had been excited to experience a proper taste of the South East Asian vibe. Although we were well versed in border wild-goose chases, the sunny jungle backdrop made this one seem so much better than the drizzly murk of the Eastern Bloc.

We had paid for and collected our visas and everything seemed to be going swimmingly, until we went back to the immigration window and found the office empty and closed. We quickly spotted the immigration officer, along with the rest of the border staff, fooling around on a tired volleyball pitch that had been cleared from the jungle undergrowth.

'Time is now four o'clock: you pay overtime fee!' he informed us when we finally dragged him away from the game. He pointed to a hand-written notice hastily propped behind the window. When we refused to pay the fine, the officer brought down a barrier in front of Hannah and padlocked it so we couldn't get through. Though he was only asking for a few extra dollars, we weren't prepared to give in to this sort of low-level bribery.

Taking matters into his own hands, Paul challenged the staff to a game of volleyball. Paul has a fantastic ability to push things just slightly further than the average person would be comfortable with – cringeworthy to watch at times, but it wasn't half great for getting things done.

'Right!' he announced defiantly. 'Here's the deal: I'll play all of you together and if I win you'll release our car!'

The Laotians slowly gravitated to the other side of the tattered net while Paul held the ball at arm's length and sized up his serve. It was as the ball sailed straight into the net that I remembered that, like me, Paul has no sports skills whatsoever.

The Laotians won hands down, but Paul wasn't about to give up so easily. Insisting on a rematch, Paul flailed out at the first ball to come his way, sending it over their heads and deep into the vegetation. The guard's smile flickered into a grimace as he rooted around the bushes for the ball, and when he finally found it and restarted the game, the same thing happened. It was almost as if Paul was trying to hit it as far out as possible.

Eventually his strategy worked, and his skill, or lack thereof, broke the will of the guards who finally agreed to let us through in exchange for a quiet, bush-free life and a chance to enjoy a proper game.

It was virtually dark by the time we got to the first town. With torrential rainstorms forecast we didn't fancy camping, fearing our single-skin tents were not up to the task. This was less a town than a crossroads with a few houses, and the four of us ordered random food by pointing at a menu and secured some beds in a guesthouse of sorts. It was nice to be away from Fred; there was a feeling of freedom akin to being home alone as a kid, of being allowed to do whatever you want away from your parents. We were back on the road again, the three of us and Matt, getting into scrapes and trouble, and everything was better. That was until we had to order from a menu of unidentifiable food and we realised how valuable having a translator had been.

Still caked in anti-itch cream, I decided to drive for the morning to take my mind off the continual desire to roll across spiky gravel just to soothe my screaming bitten torso. The track into Laos from China gradually became what you could call a proper road, and was only built by the Chinese in exchange for Laotian timber. Although we no longer had to persevere with driving through mud, the latest problem was that the road wound through the mighty, mighty jungle.

The Asian monsoon moves gradually east from the Indian Ocean. It hit Mumbai two days before we set off across India, moving at approximately the speed of a black taxi across the country. We had finally left it behind as we rose up into the high Himalayas, but it had caught us up in China. Reaching Laos just before we arrived, it was still doing its best to deposit the majority of the Indian Ocean over the jungle that clutches inexplicably to the sides of the Laotian hills. Bushes and trees grow out of almost vertical hillsides and create a beautiful and impressive, if a little intimidating, landscape – until the monsoon arrives. Their untenable position then becomes highly precarious as the soil becomes loose and the whole hillside slides away – often on top of, or with the whole road. Large earthmovers had been battling valiantly to either flatten or move the landslides, but they still left massive piles of mud to negotiate. Everything that wasn't a four-wheel drive was getting stuck and, even with seven months' experience of negotiating terrible roads, we found we would slide around next to steep drops before eventually finding solid ground and plodding onwards to do the same at the next slide a mile down the road.

But we did finally get to use the winch. Its fitting caused untold headaches, weeks of delays and cost over £500 and God-knows-what in fuel due to the extra weight, but it was finally put to good use when we rescued a small truck from one of the larger landslides. It had slid out and found itself positioned perpendicular to the road in two feet of sticky mud, blocking all traffic. Leigh and I wedged the taxi into a giant lump of mud, built stones around it so it wouldn't move and then clipped the winch to the truck's rear axle. We pulled it back into the tracks and it eventually caught traction, and made it across.

Covered from head to toe with mud, and having lost our flip-flops yet again, we were triumphant with our good use of the winch. Johno, in his self-appointed position as photographer, clambered in almost spotless from a tiny dry patch of the road.

Just before we set off, I nipped into the bushes to have a wee. It felt a bit weird and when I looked down I discovered to my horror... It wasn't just my torso that the insect had feasted on.

Some idiot was bearing down on the cab in some sort of ancient car. Right in the middle of the road, he just drove at us, honking his horn. Slowing and pulling to the side to let the imbecile pass, it gradually dawned on us that this wasn't just some old car – this was a 1928 Graham-Paige.

We had bumped into Chitty-Chitty Bang-Bang in the middle of the Laotian jungle. To add to this, out hopped the von Trapp family, a perfect line of tallest to smallest. Our amazement about coming across a Depression-era roadster in the jungle was equalled by their bemusement at coming across a black cab. We exchanged stories and took photos.

They were an Argentinian family who had been driving that car for 12 years. Having driven across the entire Americas, they were making their way up from Australia. Their three children, born on the road, had never known a home. When the final child arrived, limited for space, they simply got a coachbuilder to extend the length of the car's cabin. We could have chatted all day long with these fascinating people, but they had to make the Chinese border to meet their guide and when we told them about the landslides they started to look concerned – compared to their wooden-wheeled car, our taxi looked like a positive off-road monster. The dad clutched us in a strong, sinewy handshake; his casual and relaxed manner and perma-smile gave the impression that this fellow was probably the happiest man in the world.

Either that or he had been driven truly mad by living in a car for 12 years.

We were just starting to settle into the day's driving when there was a sickening scraping noise and an obvious pull to the left. We coasted to a halt and set about our diagnosis. It was the brakes. Again.

Jungle roads tend to either be unbelievably crap or surprisingly excellent to drive on. Full of potholes or smooth as a Radio Norwich DJ and we discovered that in Laos the best ones tended to occur in the middle of nowhere, away from the daily wear and tear of people and their various loads. The road we were stranded on was smoother than an ice rink.

Two small parts had snapped in the front left brake and gone spinning off into the steaming undergrowth at some point in the morning. This meant that the brake pads had slowly wormed themselves out of position and were now wedged against the front brake disc. We took the wheel off and pondered the problem for a while before concluding that the only thing for it was to replace those lost parts. But where would we find two retaining pins and clips for a 1992 Fairway Driver in the middle of the Laotian jungle?

'See what you can do here, and we'll go and see what's around the corner,' I told Leigh and Matt, as Paul and I set off down the road.

After a mile or so we came to a village and at the far end, much to our relief, stood a grimy shack with an old car wreck next to it. It had to be the town mechanic. The mechanics looked surprised to see the two of us: a skinny white guy in denim cut-off shorts and bright blue plastic sandals, and a tall topless man covered in a rash and carrying a large chunk of rusty metal. I approached the older-looking of the two and set about trying to explain with hand signals and pantomime what we needed.

'No.'

'No? You mean, what? You don't have them? Damn. Well, can you make them?'

He shrugged, 'No.'

'Um, well... can I,' I looked around the cluttered workshop for inspiration, 'can I make them?'

He waved me off and turned away.

The floor was covered with metal off-cuts and ancient tools. We eventually found an old discarded coffee can that looked about the right thickness and cut the parts by hand as best as we could. By the time I was finished, the mechanics were actively helping us, suggesting tools and even bringing us some tea in chipped and stained cups.

When we trekked back out of the trees, Leigh was lying on his back under the car fiddling away. A small gang of kids sat on their haunches a safe distance away watching him silently.

The part worked exactly as we had hoped and soon we were back on the road, stopping only outside the mechanic's to wave a cheery thanks as they stood open-mouthed, cigarettes stuck to lips as a London cab passed them by and re-entered the jungle.

CHAPTER 38

- - - - - - - - -

IN THE TUBING

Of the 25 days in China, we – four sweaty lads and a flatulent Chinese guide – had driven for 23 of them, often from dawn until past dusk. Although not actually falling out, by this stage we were pretty bored of each other's company so Matt insisted that we check out 'tubing' at Vang Vieng.

'It's a tiny village with one street and a couple of guesthouses and restaurants – all of which play *Friends* on repeat on the TV. It's super chilled out; you can get a tuk tuk up the river, hire a tractor inner tube, and float down on its gentle stream, stopping at a few small bars on the side.'

This sounded like the perfect place to stop for a couple of days and regroup our thoughts. My two sisters were flying out to see us as well, so we agreed to meet at this small village.

As predicted, the road became atrocious the closer we got to the town. Large potholes, big enough to rip the undercarriage to pieces if hit with speed, covered our path. To make matters worse, the evening monsoon started and the road became like a stream. Muddy water filled all the holes, making them all look the same. You would expect a three-inch hole and find, with a horrifying crack, that you had just driven into one a foot deep.

All black cabs of the same era as ours have a peculiar quirk: there is a leak into the dashboard that drips water over all the electrics and then on to the driver's accelerator foot. This has two outcomes: firstly it creates a Chinese water torture effect on the driver and secondly it short-circuits the headlights. Fortunately, we had a couple of spotlights remaining, which was lucky, but their power was minimal – having the effect of driving by the light of a torch. The driving was made all the more challenging by the tiny ineffective windscreen wipers that failed miserably at holding back the monsoon. Twenty minutes turned into two hours of some of the worst driving of the trip as we broke the cardinal rule, yet again, of driving at night. We told ourselves that we would be fine because crashing into one of the two cars that passed per hour was unlikely to have much effect at the 2–3 mph we averaged. The far more likely possibility of driving off a cliff or into one of the raging torrents never to be seen again was never brought up. But being halfway between the last guesthouse and our destination, turning back was just as risky, so onwards Hannah rattled.

A large river appeared beside us, occasionally lit by the cab's spotlights as we wound around the bends, revealing a grossly flooded mass of muddy boils, bursting at its banks.

This had to be the Nam Song river, our tubing destination.

'We're going down *that river...*'

I've been kayaking for most of my life, a sport enjoyed with the utmost respect for water and for the safety precautions. When I kayak white-water, it's with helmets, life jackets, and a group of trusted and highly experienced friends, all of us armed with rescue ropes and trained in complex rescue techniques and first aid.

'... completely shitfaced...'

The spotlights lit up the water, I caught sight of a tree floating down, occasionally sucked down by the violent whirlpools and eddy lines.

'... on tractor tubes!?'

'Yup, it's great!' Matt reassured me. 'But... it wasn't this big when I last went.'

Things didn't improve as we continued south. By seven it was dark – really dark. The rain was coming down in huge waterfall sheets and it filled all the deep potholes, meaning our previous swerving techniques were useless and every 20 seconds we were all pitched up out of our seats. The feeble headlights did little to fend off the gloom as we forded broad swathes of road covered in rushing water.

'The potholes are getting really bad,' someone shouted over the dim of the downburst, 'we must be getting near the town!'

Sure enough, bright neon lights appeared from the blackness. We had made it to our destination. Relief to be almost off the road and out of the rain washed over us when suddenly a man appeared on the road ahead of us. The topless figure wandered over to the window and grinned. He was covered in fluorescent body paint and spoke with a shockingly familiar accent.

'Maaaaayyte, is this a Laandan cab?' He stared into the cab, identifiable as a Brit by his drunken demeanour as much as his cockney tones.

'Yup.'

'Amazin', 'owd you get it 'ere?'

'We drove it...' said Leigh, holding back the entire extent of the distance.

'Ahh, right, you buy it in Bangkok and drive it up?'

'No, we drove it the whole way.'

'Oh, wow, from Singapore? That's a long way.'

'No, from London... We drove it from London,' Leigh grinned.

The lad's jaw looked as though it would have hit the floor, if he wasn't so preoccupied with grinding it against his top teeth in an attempt to alleviate the pent up tension and energy caused by whatever he had been shoving up his nose that night. His eyes bulged, unblinkingly – his pupils occupying the majority of the socket.

'Naaaaaahhhhh, maaayyyyte. That is AWESOME!'

'Thank you.'

We were feeling rather proud. When we were in India we had met Europeans, but India felt like a place that you could drive to – it was on the hippy trail and someone always had a parent who had driven a VW camper there in the 1970s via Afghanistan in a haze of hash smoke. We were now in Laos, South East Asia. Half a world away.

As we bounced further into Vang Vieng, it became clear it wasn't a one-street town any more. Large bars blasted chart hits, filled with hundreds of half-naked Westerners, soaked and oblivious to the pouring rain. The bars all had remarkably similar menus, ranging from innocuous milkshakes and pizza to bags of opium and hash cakes for the more adventurous.

We had all expected Laos to be chilled out, but none of us had expected this.

After meeting up with Paul's sisters, the six of us found a chilled-out guesthouse, overseen by a surly Laotian grandmother, and crashed out.

The following morning we were making our way along the muddy river path and out of the trees on to the waterfront when a voice shouted a greeting, 'The taxi boys!' It was the guy from the previous night, who was a rep for one of the bars. He quickly introduced us to 'snake wine' – a local delicacy of rice wine infused with a whole dead snake – mixed with whisky, as we surveyed the scene. The fast-flowing river was lined with banging bars made from bamboo and palm leaves. Each had a thumping sound system and hordes of attractive young backpackers.

'So, you are the taxi guys?' shouted another rep, brandishing yet another bottle of spirits. 'Come here – you're legends!'

And so the day began.

Apart from a night in Nepal and a few awkward nights in China, we had not been out partying since Georgia, four months previously. Suddenly we were three red-blooded males thrust into the backpacker party scene. The 60 pence bottles of whisky, pounding chart tunes – unfamiliar to us at the time, but apparently six months old in the UK – and English speaking revellers were a culture shock… for about five minutes. We acclimatised very quickly. Especially when we found we were pseudo famous – word got round the small town about the guys who had driven there in a taxi, and one or two people had even read about us in the newspapers or heard the radio interview that caused Fred to cry 'kidnap'.

We decided to whole-heartedly embrace this bizarre hedonistic Wild West where gap-year kids swung from homemade rope swings and got hammered in swimwear, while modest locals looked on from their ramshackle huts on the bank. It was either that or sit in a cafe and watch *Friends* on repeat.

A rickety boat took us across the river to the first bar, where it seemed the biggest party was in full swing. Leigh somehow managed to acquire a full bottle of whisky from one of the backpacker employees: a girl covered in obscene slogans spray-painted on her body with car paint. Before things got too hectic and hazy, Matt and I decided to try out the tubes and jumped into the fast-flowing river.

I paddled with all my might and, just as I thought I was going to miss the bar and float off down past the town all the way to the sea, an unfeasibly muscular pre-pubescent local boy wolf-whistled and threw me a Coke bottle half-filled with water tied to the end of a rope. I scrabbled around to grab on to it and he hauled me in effortlessly.

We only made it down to the third bar before the party moved back into the town, and, still only the middle of the afternoon, the last thing I remember was Leigh, barely able to walk from his whisky adventure, staggering towards the main bar strip.

'Dude, you need to go to bed,' I slurred.

He tried to focus on me and composed his words with much effort. 'You,' he emphasised with a beaming grin, pointing at me and swaying around, 'need to go to bed!'

Though we had a lot of fun in Vang Vieng, it didn't surprise us to hear that a year after our visit the government had severely clamped down on the tubing enterprises after a surge in the number of deaths, as tourists tried to swim in the river when drunk. From the look of the brown, bubbling river, it seemed like a very logical decision.

It appears it is almost impossible to take your own vehicle into Vietnam. It was one of the countries Leigh had wanted to go to the most, and Johno and Matt were also keen to visit, so we agreed to travel our separate ways; the three of them through Vietnam while my sisters and I would drive Hannah through Thailand to keep the world record valid. We'd be reunited for the continuation of our trip in Cambodia.

After two days of partying, the lads were in a sorry state as they climbed on to the early morning bus with the other zombies – all still covered in florescent pink car paint, and worse – from the night before.

CHAPTER 39

LAOSY MEDICAL CARE

Early the next day, my sisters and I began the journey from Vang Vieng to the Laos capital, Vientiane. Although the capital is a relatively unremarkable place – a few pretty French colonial buildings house various different business fronts and restaurants – its laidback atmosphere was warm and inviting. Which is pretty amazing considering Laos is the most bombed country in the world; during the Vietnam war (a war in which they were not involved) more ordinance was dropped in Laos than on the whole of Germany and Japan during World War Two.

Driving was becoming a bit of a challenge for me. A small chip of what was presumably a Beerlao bottle, hidden in the muddy banks of the Nam Song, had managed to get lodged deep in the heel of my right foot, and it was really starting to hurt. I had to get it removed before the infection took hold, which could happen all too easily in such tropical climates. So, after attempting an operation in the hotel room with tweezers and a scalpel from the med kit, and discovering that it was in too deep, I limped to the city hospital.

The air was heavy with bleach and rows of beds lined each wall; some with curtains pulled around them, from behind which the sound of retching and the odd moan of pain and agony could be heard through the thin fabric barrier. Archaic equipment was strewn against the wall and blue paint flaked everywhere, showing the bare concrete or rusted metal beneath.

I was led to a bed – which was basically a sheet of green vinyl – and told to lie down. However, it was obviously designed for the average Laos patient's height and not my six-foot-four-inches frame. My feet stuck out over the edge, just far enough for an absent-minded nurse to walk into them, lending my own cry to the cacophony of moans that surrounded me. A doctor gave me a big grin – this was clearly hilarious to him – and nodded that he would be with me in a moment, before he turned to the patient beside me. Middle aged and overweight with a healthy moustache, the patient had a boil of some variety, blushing, bulbous and red, on his naked lower back, lying no more than a metre away from me. The doctor injected some sort of anaesthetic into the lump before taking his scalpel and delving deep into the boil. The anaesthetic clearly had little effect as the man groaned and the doctor cleared over a teacup-full of bloody pus from his back, before throwing it into the bin a few inches from where my head stuck out from the short bed.

I turned, stared up at the ceiling – desperately trying to hold down the vomit that was building pressure in my gullet – and started to assess my life decisions that had got me to this point. I came to the conclusion that I would never drink snake wine ever again.

The smell of the pus in the bin by my head, combined with the general shit state of the hospital, got too much for me and I tried to get up and leave – landing heavily on my bad foot and wedging the glass further in.

Oh yes, I thought, *that's* why I'm here.

This was the best hospital (or at least the only one I knew of) in the country. I reprimanded myself for being a pussy and settled back down. Once the doctor was finished, he washed up (thankfully), brought over a fresh tray, put on new gloves and went about anaesthetising and cutting open my foot with brand new needles and scalpels. (I carefully checked each one myself to ensure the packet was properly sealed, much to his bemusement.) Cutting down about 2 cm into my heel, he rooted around for about five minutes as I grasped the sides of the bed and gritted my teeth.

'Ahh-haaa,' he said triumphantly, standing up to show me what he had found. 'You want?'

'Want what?' All I could see was a bloody pair of tongs.

'Glass, see...' I could just make out the tiniest shard, 2 mm squared.

'No... errr... thank you,' I said. I wasn't really sure how I would store it for safekeeping, how I would tell the lads why I was carrying around a minuscule piece of glass, or why I would want to keep it in the first place.

'I think there is more. I'm pretty sure there's almost a beer bottle in there,' I told him. 'That bit seems too small to cause that much pain...'

He rooted around some more, while I grasped the side of the bed again. There was nothing left – it turns out I was just being a pussy after all.

I was given antibiotics, spare bandages and paracetamol and sent on my way after parting with a fiver for the lot. I felt bad for being so judgemental – those doctors were doing a fantastic job and each with a beaming smile on their face.

We were heading south, to where beautiful beaches and islands lay. Arrival at the Thai border coincided with the wearing out of the anaesthetic on my foot. I limped from window to window, getting paperwork stamped and paying standard border charges, my foot gradually becoming more and more useless. By this point I couldn't drive – resting my heel to use the accelerator was agony – so my sister had to take over.

I was happy.

The sun was shining, I had some peace and quiet from the lads, and I could spend some quality time with my sisters. I commented on how amazing the driving was, how smooth the road was and how civilised the drivers were, as I sat chilling, bandaged foot stuck out the passenger window, unaware that that's an incredibly offensive thing to do in Thailand. My sister, apparently, strongly disagreed – swearing and sweating – as big trucks undertook her in the slow lane. Coming straight from the UK, Thailand was hectic and the worst driving she had ever experienced. However, to Hannah and me, it was the most civilised road system we'd seen since Turkey. I told my sister this, with characteristic sibling understanding.

'Fuck off, Paul. I don't care. Your fucking brakes don't work.'

'Oh yeah, they don't really… you need to shift into a lower gear to slow down well in advance of any hazard… do you know that they're made out of old coffee cans put together in the jungle? Pretty cool, eh?'

'No, not cool. Terrifyi— STOP FUCKING UNDERTAKING ME IN THE SLOW LANE!'

I left her to it and went to sleep.

Even with smooth roads, things are never easy when you're driving Hannah. After two days of driving, there was a familiar 'clunk' and I had to repair another ball joint. Fortunately the girls had brought a load of spare bits and pieces for us, so while I was at it I also fitted a new steering arm and a brand new shock absorber, and replaced a suspension plate. The lights were still broken from Laos, but I had no knowledge at all regarding them – the intricate electrics system had been built when John Major was still in power and they had since been customised by Leigh's very own and unique DIY approach. This meant that even if I did know anything about car electronics (which I don't) I was still going to have to wait for Leigh's master skills to fix it in a week's time.

I would just have to avoid driving at night.

Over the past eight months we had become accustomed to eating from roadside food stalls, due to their convenience and ultra-low cost. But now I found that I actually preferred this way of eating, even if I'd had the choice between a small shack and a Michelin-starred restaurant. If it's good enough for the locals, then it was good enough for us. Travellers often avoid them for fear of getting food poisoning, but other than my case of dysentery and Leigh's food poisoning in Manali, we'd had no trouble whatsoever by following four basic rules:

1. Don't drink the tap water in any way. This one is obvious, but it also includes ice cubes and anything washed in the water.

2. Don't eat the salad. A cursory wander around a market will reveal piles of lettuce and vegetables on the ground, often accompanied by the odd goat relieving itself on it. And besides, it's often then washed in the dirty water anyway.

3. Make sure it's cooked. This rule negates the first two; if it's piping hot and cooked through, it's generally fine. Some people avoid meat in bad places, but if it's been cooked to death, it should mean death to all the nasties inside it.

4. None of these rules count when you're drunk.

We had been having a gastronomic adventure, tasting the freshest and most authentic food each country had to offer, usually ordering by pointing at random things with a big dumb smile on our faces. And in my opinion, for street food, Thailand is without parallel the best in the world. From barbecues to curries to the simple but always perfect noodle soup, three times a day you can eat good, healthy food that puts a huge smile on your face – even if it's often accompanied by a sheen of spice sweat on your brow – for next to nothing.

Although China had felt modern in its own very Chinese way, Thailand was modern in an American, 7-Eleven on every street selling hot dogs and iced coffees, Starbucks and MTV kind of way. We wanted to find an island, to get away from the hustle and bustle where we could chill for the last few days of the girls' holiday.

We eventually found ourselves on a southern island called Ko Chang, where a couple flagged us down. They were English and were fascinated to see such a familiar sight so far away from home. They told us they'd show us a good place to stay if we gave them a ride there in our cab. 'You'll have to let us buy you a beer when we get there,' they proclaimed.

They took us to a charming palm-fringed beach with an excellent restaurant and bar, and little wooden huts where you could stay for next to nothing. We were assured that the views were stunning as well, but all we could see was the monsoon bucketing down. Sheltering from the rain, one beer turned into three or four, as we sat at the bar with white sand beneath our feet. It turned out that Ian and Mish had led fascinating lives. Ian had been a session musician for some of my favourite bands, playing with The Prodigy, Massive Attack and the Smashing Pumpkins, before moving to Cambodia. They now volunteered for a local charity, working to stop the child sex trade, rescuing children and teenagers and providing them with an education.

Ian's job in particular shocked me. In his own words, he's a 'dodgy looking bloke', his greasy black hair falling down to his chin and with the red complexion and brown teeth of a forty-a-day man who drinks a vodka-orange for breakfast. Looking the part, his job was to act as a 'John' in sting operations to catch madams peddling underage sex. He would also go along with Cambodian police to arrest Western men in the act, and ensure they don't get the chance to bribe their way out; apparently a mere £1,300 is enough to ensure the police and the child's family get paid and heads look the other way. It was all quite shocking stuff.

Then he told me an interesting story from a time he visited Cambodia ten or 15 years earlier with another prominent musician. Cambodia was still recovering from the vicious Khmer Rouge regime and was relatively lawless at the time. Ian and his pal were invited to shoot AK-47s and roll grenades under cars in the jungle. Apparently this was something that tourists liked to do. So, for a few bucks they got to shoot 30-year-old Vietnam War-era ammunition at trees, while feeling very concerned about the condition of the weapons they were using. Once they had finished, their guide asked them, 'So... you want to shoot cow with rocket launcher?' He then winked in a very obvious and overt way. Ian declined.

'Are you sure?' he said, winking again. Again, Ian declined, but eventually the story came out about what the guy *really* meant.

Apparently, if you wanted, you could shoot a person – a real, live, breathing person – dead. There are a very small number of customers (interestingly, it was apparently an almost exclusively American clientele) who have the desire to pay to kill another person. Older Cambodian men would volunteer (although by 'old' he meant 'about 50 or so') and the money would be given to their family to ensure they could eat. Obviously shocked, Ian was curious how much this cost and asked the guide, to which he replied between £3,000 and £4,000. For £3,000, the victim stood stationary; for £4,000, he would run around for sport.

CHAPTER 40

- - - - - - - -

THERE *AND* BACK AGAIN?

A few days later I was on the road again with Ian and Mish. I had to meet the lads in Phnom Penh, but first I had agreed to give Ian and Mish a lift home to Cambodia.

The road clutched the coast, passing beautiful resorts and tiny villages. The closer we got to the border, the thicker the jungle got, but the close, humid temperature was blown away by the fresh sea breeze; perfect driving conditions.

On reaching the border, I began to have a minor panic that I had only known Ian and Mish for a couple of days and had no idea if anything they said was true. For all I knew, their luggage might be stashed full of drugs. But after some delays, where I ended up basically doing the border guard's job for him (months of border crossings had obviously taught me more about importing foreign cars than he had been trained for), we crossed into Cambodia.

It started to get dark when we were still 60 miles away from our destination – stuck in the middle of nowhere with no lights, no hotels and no mechanics. We *had* to keep going. Luckily, our trusty spotlights in the middle of the bumper were working, so I could just about see the road in front. The problem was that we looked like a motorbike to the trucks that were driving towards us. It was terrifying. I needed to find a way to let the trucks know that we were a 2 m-wide car and not a little bike that could pull into the side of the road. I searched the car for a solution. I found every torch and reflective item in the car and set about lashing them on to the front of Hannah. The cab looked very strange, but it just about worked.

Three nerve-wracking and painfully slow hours later, having succeeded in not hitting any wayward pedestrians, wild dogs or articulated lorries, we arrived, triumphantly, in the town and I was introduced to the folks who lived in Ian's hostel. The town had a Wild West atmosphere to it, where traveller hedonism met the numbing poverty and rampant corruption of Cambodia. Add to this a well-stocked pharmacy with no prescription laws and beer that cost 30 pence, it very quickly became apparent that Sihanoukville was a bit of a party town. I spent a few happy days there before realising I had to move on; it was time to be reunited with the lads.

Our long-term passenger Matt finally had to fly home so I met Johno and Leigh in Phnom Penh, the country's capital. Wanting to know a little more about the country's devastating history, and on the recommendation of numerous friends, we visited the S-21 Genocide Museum. Cambodia was ravaged by one of the most brutal regimes of the twentieth century from 1974 until 1979. Pol Pot and his Khmer Rouge cronies killed and starved to death nearly a quarter of the country's population, often for no apparent reason. They picked out anybody who posed a possible threat, famously killing everyone who wore glasses, for instance, which were seen as a sign of intelligence.

The museum was an old school that had been used to interrogate and detain 17,000 prisoners. There were only seven known survivors. Juxtaposed against the decadence that has become the South East Asia backpacking circuit, this was a grim and sobering experience for all of us. It was disturbing to think that this wasn't distant history – it had happened only a few years before we were born.

Our next destination was Angkor Wat, the eighth wonder of the world. However, we had no map of Cambodia – because, as previously mentioned, we're complete idiots – so it took much longer to get there than expected. On top of this it was still raining and it appeared as though the whole country was flooded – roads were becoming rivers, every field was underwater and torrents gushed off the roofs of every house.

Holed up to avoid the rain in a dirt-cheap hotel in fuck-knows-where, we were catching up online. Johno was, for once, the bearer of good news.

'Erm, lads… I think we have a solution to our problems.'

Our problems actually all boiled down to one single problem: money – or more accurately, the lack of it. What we had was rapidly running out. When we left England we had enough cash to pay for our visas, our fuel, our shipping, ourselves and maybe even for a few beers. We also had buffer money because we expected problems. The problem was, we were three months late. Delays, breakdowns and a hike in fuel prices left us running on fumes. Three extra months of personal living costs, multiplied by three, had eaten all the contingency money. Most of our arguments had been directly or indirectly related to money, and there was always a tacit worry simmering away that one of us was going to burn through his nest egg before the others and have to be bailed out somehow.

'What are you talking about?'

'Well, someone tried to add me as a friend on Facebook. He's called Nimrod, he's from Tel Aviv and dressed in a white suit like some mafia don… so obviously I thought it was spam and just ignored him. But he just sent me a message…'

We all crowded round to read the message on the screen:

....

To: 'Johno Ellison'

Dear Jhono, I would like to compliment you on your inspiring journey to break

> the GWR and I would like to use this
> opportunity to offer you and your team
> a sponsorship which will enable you
> to achieve your fundraising goals and
> more... Let me know if you find my offer
> interesting and relevant?

....

'Spam,' I replied.

'Does he just need our bank details to free up a small fortune left to him by a Nigerian prince?' Leigh said.

'That's what I thought, but I've spoken to him a bit more and they basically want to pay for us to drive Hannah back to London. I've done a bit of cyber-stalking and from what I can see his company is genuine,' grinned Johno. 'They're a taxi app startup company that has just raised millions of pounds in venture capital funding... I think this really is a real offer guys.'

The following conversation went something like this:

'Fuck.'

'Fuck.'

'You're kidding?'

'No!'

'Fuck.'

'Fuck.'

'I know!'

'Shit.'

'Fuck.'

'Well, do you want to drive back?'

The answer was unanimous.

'GOD NO!'

What happened next, strangely enough, considering that this was technically fantastic news, was a huge argument. Leigh and Johno had a major falling out. Although he never said it, I think Leigh was overly cautious and wanted to be extra careful with anyone hopping on the back of our recent world record triumph.

Johno was characteristically obtuse about the matter and with no real ties back home, wanted to continue putting off getting a real job for as long as possible.

Personally, I didn't want to drive back either – driving back through Asia was a trip we all feared neither the taxi or her team would survive – but this company clearly had money to spend and wanted in on our expedition. There was another option, it was expensive and difficult, but it would be a dream come true.

I ventured, 'Why don't we ask what this company thinks about driving across the USA and doing a full circumnavigation of the globe back to London...'

Negotiations began in full swing via email, staying up late into the night to allow for the Cambodian–Israeli time difference.

GetTaxi were a company that ran a taxi-ordering app for smartphones in London and Israel and they thought we seemed like the perfect fit for their huge marketing budget. At first they were hesitant about our American proposal, especially seeing as they weren't yet launched in the States, but they started to come around to the idea when we described the photo opportunities of the taxi – draped in GetTaxi livery – in front of the Hollywood sign, or the Golden Gate Bridge.

There was an issue, though; Nimrod had to have this all wrapped up by the end of the week because he was going on his honeymoon. We congratulated him and asked where he was going.

'Ko Pha Ngan, it's a Thai island.' The island is home to the infamous Full Moon Party, something that can't be missed when driving through Thailand.

'At the end of the week?'

'Yes, it's going to be amazing.'

'We'll be on Ko Pha Ngan, too... at the end of the week.'

This must have been fate. We arranged to meet up on the island and discuss things from there.

CHAPTER 41

HOW TO NAIL A BUSINESS DEAL

I stood in our hotel doorway, watching the monsoon rains that had relentlessly followed us ever since India, waiting for Leigh and Paul to check out. The entire drive from the capital up towards the ancient and impressive jungle ruins of Angkor Wat had been accompanied by pouring rain and it looked like most of the country was underwater.

'I was going to go to Siem Reap and Angkor Wat but I think I will not bother because of this rain,' said a voice beside me.

'Well, we're going soon and we have a car,' I told the tanned French guy, his mass of curly hair almost obscuring his face. 'If you want to come with us, you're more than welcome...'

'Hmmm,' he pondered, 'you are going right now?'

'In ten minutes, yeah.'

We watched the sheets of water pelting the street for a few more minutes then he spoke. 'Yes, I will check out of the hotel and I will join you.'

Kevin had an acoustic guitar and was even more chilled out than Anders the Swedish rockstar. He had worked for months in Australia and was making the most of the strong currency to travel around Asia and using his French charm to sleep with as many impressionable young backpackers as he could along the way. When I mentioned that we were aiming for Darwin in Australia he smiled to himself.

'Oh, I had a funny time in Darwin,' he started, wistfully looking into the middle distance.

'Oh, yeah? Go on...'

He obliged with a graphic and entirely unrepeatable story involving his 'relations' with a local lady, a shopping trolley and his tripping on acid. His colourful stories certainly cheered up a dismal day, and the stunning ruined temples of Angkor Wat, nestled in the jungle amongst obese trees, vines and creepers, left us all in awe.

As we were leaving the temples a boy of about seven ambushed me and set about trying to sell me some bracelets.

'You buy bracelet!'

'No thanks, I already have some.'

'You buy for your girlfriend!'

'I don't have a girlfriend...'

'You know why you not have girlfriend? Because you not buy her bracelet!'

Our next stop was Bangkok, the home of backpacker folklore. The very name conjured up visions of bustling, steamy backstreets where wizened old women sold fried insects on wooden skewers. In the smoky rooms above, people of questionable gender would be doing even more questionable things with ping-pong balls and hordes of short fat men would be betting wads of money on bare-knuckle boxers, fighting to the death.

The ride into the sprawling city dragged on and on. We had been given some sketchy directions to stay with a friend, most of which related to a motorway and a tall building, both of which Bangkok has many of. We had been squabbling over which tower block was which, and driving up and down the same stretch of freeway for nearly an hour.

Our plan was to head to Khaosan Road, the backpacker centre of South East Asia and meet up with some new friends we had met earlier in Asia. The packed, neon-soaked street seemed to suck in Western travellers from miles around and within a few hours we had bumped into three other groups we had met over the past two weeks.

On the journey down the coast to the Full Moon Party, we thought about our options and realised we had none. Throughout the trip money had been a major issue for all three of us. The fact that we had worked so hard to save all of our pennies meant that each one was precious; squeezing nine months of existence out of our six months of budgeting was no mean feat.

This was all before we had even considered how we were going to be able to pay to get both ourselves and Hannah back home from Australia. It was looking like we would all need a summer spent picking mangoes in Queensland in order to put away enough cash to fly cattle-class back to Blighty.

Even Hannah herself was causing problems. Besides the money we had spent on repairs and the costs of importing her to China, the fee for shipping her across the sea to Australia was growing with each passing week. We couldn't even leave her Down Under because we would be hit with crippling vehicle-import fines so we had to either somehow ship her back home across 11,000 miles of ocean or completely destroy her in the Outback, 'by mistake' of course. We were even half-genuinely considering getting hold of some Australian mining dynamite and blowing our baby sky-high so we could get around the import fees that we couldn't afford. With so many issues to contend with, we were more than happy to hear out Nimrod's sponsorship proposal, even if we were suspicious that it definitely sounded too good to be true.

'Leigh, you can't go like that, this is a business meeting,' lectured Paul, the business graduate, pointing to Leigh's freshly painted neon-pink and bright-green toenails.

'Tsk! Don't worry,' replied Leigh, the design graduate, and we rattled and creaked over the island's lush interior and through the swish hotel gates.

I immediately felt scruffy as Nimrod strolled up, flanked by his beautiful new wife in her designer bikini, and ushered us with smiles to an exquisitely laid table. The wine-and-dine experience was a little overwhelming, and we tried our best to remain serious as we told some of our calmer stories and listened to the proposal from GetTaxi.

Nimrod told us that he had independently come up with an idea to break the current world record, but when he had googled the idea he had been deflated to see we had already broken the old record back in Tibet in August. Then he thought: if you can't beat them, join them. The fact that we both happened to be heading to the same island in Thailand made it seem as if cosmic fate had drawn us together. Either that or a really slick scam was about to take place. But who were we to scam? Three unemployed British guys with barely the price of a bus fare between us, soon to be stranded in a sandy country thousands of miles from home and surrounded by the world's highest concentration of poisonous animals?

By the end of the meal we had come to some sort of initial agreement. GetTaxi would give us a crazy sum of money and in return we would travel around advertising their brand. This would enable us to continue avoiding growing up and carry on driving around the world, albeit now with slightly different stickers on the car and with no more money worries.

As we shook hands and walked back to the car we were all trembling. We were barely able to walk straight with the effort of keeping our exteriors vaguely professional; someone was going to pay us to go on a road trip around the world! It still sounded like some kind of dream. What's more, tonight was the

Full Moon Party, only the biggest party in all of South East Asia. All I wanted to do was get in the car, drive around the corner and scream at the top of my lungs.

'Just one more important point,' Nimrod called after us, suddenly serious.

Uh oh, I thought, here it comes: the deal-breaker. The part where we all have to sell our firstborns into taxi-dom and have GetTaxi tattooed on our foreheads.

'Leigh... my wife really likes your nail polish!'

Our pent-up excitement roared out in waves of laughter way out of all proportion to the joke and we made ourselves scarce before we messed up the greatest deal of our lives.

CHAPTER 42

- - - - - - - -

THE SWANSEA MASSIVE

The Full Moon Party. The 18–30 holiday for the noughties. Sun, sea, sand and Rihanna. Every single bar since Vang Vieng had played a loop of the top ten dance-pop tunes and Ko Pha Ngan was no different. As we were driving back from Nimrod's, an Englishman on a scooter pulled us over, told us he owned a club in town and that if we parked the cab in front of it we could drink for free all night. This day was getting better and better!

Later that evening, Leigh was so high on the local energy drinks and booze that he was raving in front of a speaker stack. Johno and I got to the solid task of getting shitfaced on free booze while sat on the taxi outside our new friend Woody's Club 9, absorbing praise like the couple of attention seekers that we are.

'Maaaaaate. I love your taxi.'

'Thank you.'

He was a Welshman of mammoth proportions – covered from head to toe in tattoos and a three-foot-wide pure Swansea steroid-enhanced mass. He glared into both of our eyes, slowly enunciating each word, dripping with venom and intimidation.

'No, I LOVE your taxi.'

'Errrrm… cheers?'

'I mean, like, I really LOVE it… can I fuck it?'

'Fuck it?'

'Yeah, fuck it... can I fuck your taxi?'

Unwilling to provoke this behemoth of terror from the Valleys (and equally as interested to see what it would do next), we said, 'Sure.'

A broad smile spread over his face and the atmosphere changed dramatically.

'Really? Awww, thanks boyos.'

With that, he knelt down by the exhaust and pulled down his swimming shorts and started to touch himself. A crowd was starting to form and Johno and I were laughing so hard we fell off the cab.

We had seen some weird things on our travels but this had to be one of the most bizarre. It seemed that he had imbibed a few too many buckets of Thai whisky and was struggling. After two more minutes of feverish agitation, and at risk of giving himself a friction burn, he pulled up his shorts and gave up.

'I'm sorry boys, I just can't do it, too much booze ya see... maybe next time, yeah?' He looked at us questioningly, genuinely checking whether he'd blown his one chance at having a London black cab in the exhaust on a Thai Island.

'Um, sure...'

'Thanks, boyos,' he said, and with that, he disappeared into the night.

Leigh and I had both managed to cut our legs on coral while swimming in Thailand. Coral wounds can instantly become infected and, combined with the unsanitary conditions of living in a London black cab and swimming in the vomit- and urine-filled waters around Ko Pha Ngan at the end of the Full Moon Party, meant we were both healing slowly even after Leigh had spent 24 hours sweating out a fever in the hostel in Kuala Lumpur. Our main weapon in cleaning out our pus-filled gashes was a bottle of deep-red iodine antiseptic from our first aid kit. As I sat on the porch one evening, redressing my leg, I reached over and grabbed the bottle of rich dark liquid.

'Is this the new iodine, Leigh?'

'No, that's soy sauce.'

'Haha, very funny,' I said as I poured it liberally into my cut. I looked up to see a table full of shocked faces at just about the time when my leg started to scream.

'Dude, I did tell you...'

With Thailand behind us and with potentially only three countries ahead of us, things now seemed to be moving way too fast. In theory it could all be over in a month. Now instead of running from corrupt police we were showing our car to hordes of schoolkids as we stayed with a friend of Paul's who was a teacher out in Malaysia.

Malaysia's perfect roads still had a few surprises in store for us as we suffered our first major blowout while powering along the motorway, but our spirits were raised when a couple stopped behind us as we tightened on the spare tyre and they invited us for lunch at the next service station.

Following the usual questions of where the idea came from and what our favourite country had been, things suddenly got a whole lot deeper than normal.

'So, how do you feel that you have spiritually fulfilled yourselves on this journey?'

I felt uneasy. Was this the prelude to us being 'saved' by some crazy cult leaders or were they ramping up for a rant on personal social responsibility? Thankfully it was neither; they were actually on their way to speak at a conference in Singapore and wanted to use our story as an example of people following their dreams. It felt great to have inspired some total strangers enough to want to share our story.

The car was due to be shipped from Singapore down to our long-awaited destination of Australia but due to the crippling expense of just about everything there, we decided to hole up in a Malaysian city called Johor Bahru, right on the southern tip of the Malay peninsula. The guesthouse was within metaphorical spitting distance of the Straits of Singapore and was looked after by a spirited couple who had been travelling for most of their lives.

Although he was in his late 60s, Tom still had the rugged looks of a film star and he was a master storyteller who regaled us with tales of being arrested in England in the 1960s for being over-generous with his employer's whisky. His current lover was a feisty Spanish woman named Emma and they had both left their previous spouses to travel the world together.

They became almost like surrogate parents to us during our stay, making sure Leigh's and Paul's Full Moon war wounds were tended to and helping our preparations for the upcoming shipping. However, when they thought they were out of earshot, while we were trying to sleep on the rock-hard concrete slabs covered in inch-thick mattresses that passed for our beds, we would often hear them arguing away like they had been married for decades. Apparently all was not quite as well as it seemed in paradise.

Hannah was soon stowed away in a shipping container and I was stuck in the middle of Singapore's giant port with a flight to catch to the island paradise of Bali. It had transpired that it was cheaper to fly to Darwin via Bali than direct, and with at least seven days of ocean transit, it would be rude not to check it out.

Leigh decided he'd also like to visit Bali, but we were quite looking forward to some time alone so I took my two-day head start and ventured off to Kuta Beach – the Indonesian equivalent of Magaluf. It was full of 'bogans' – a kind of Aussie chav, but one who is generally ripped and tanned and showing off their tattooed arms in baggy singlets. I didn't exactly fit in.

However, I got wind of a beautiful little island half a day's boat ride away that was largely bogan-free and didn't have any motorised transport on it. This sounded great, and would be the perfect place to get some peace and quiet.

Sunning myself and enjoying the view of perfect white, palm-edged beaches, and what seemed to be the entire female population of Sweden – tanned and in bikinis playing volleyball (seriously, this may be the greatest place on earth) – I was suddenly brought back down to earth when I heard dulcet Midland tones sneaking up behind me.

'Alright dick-cheese.'

Damn.

CHAPTER 43

QUARANTINE

To me Australia had always been a land of stereotypes and I had seen half of my list within 15 minutes of stepping off the plane. First and foremost was a leathery old man yelling, 'Criiiiikey!' quickly followed by a group of fully grown men wearing backwards baseball caps, and playing 1980s arcade machines in the arrival lounge.

Out in the unfeasibly clean parking lot, sun-bleached mulleted kids tore around and an Aborigine with a flowing white beard wandered past me in a daze. All I needed now was a guy in a hat with corks hanging off it, a boxing kangaroo and a lovable rogue to tell me, 'that's not a knife maate!'

While Leigh and Paul were relaxing with the Swedish volleyball team in the beach paradise of Bali, I had caught a later flight directly to Darwin. Our old gal was supposed to be waiting for us there, ready to hit the road, but unfortunately, despite the shipping company repeatedly increasing our quoted costs, the ship itself was running almost a week late. Paul and Leigh had extended their Swedalicous break while I tried to scope out the importation situation and have things ready to roll upon their arrival.

I wandered down to the shipping office at Darwin Port and was told, 'Yeah, no worries mate, the ship is due in on Wednesday, just pop down.'

That was coincidently the day the others arrived, so on Wednesday morning we strolled down, backpacks and all, to the dock, rather naively expecting to be on the road that afternoon. However, we were quickly coming to learn that what shipping agents told us and what actually happened were two very different things. The ship had already been delayed by a week and now we were told matter-of-factly that it still had to be unloaded and inspected and that the car would probably be available, 'sometime next week'.

This was a disaster. Darwin is a pleasant little city of 130,000 people and was definitely a nice relaxing and well-ordered place, especially after the manic streets of Asia. The problem came with being in a country where the minimum wage was about £12 an hour, meaning that everything is horrifically expensive. This was even more acute in the remote north and, although the hostel I had been staying in did have a hot tub, it also cost more for one night in a grotty dormitory bed than we were used to paying for a full week in a private room back in Asia.

We racked our brains for options and only one presented itself: on the flight over I had gotten talking to a local headteacher. After explaining our story she had invited us round for dinner. We figured that just maybe, we could be cheeky and ask her if we could camp in her garden for a few days.

We were halfway through the bus journey to her house when we suddenly realised that the tents were in the car, and the car was on the ship. We had been living out of hand luggage for approaching three weeks now.

Over an amazing meal we told Bernadette about the car situation and without hesitation she invited us to stay with her while we got ourselves sorted out; we hadn't even got to the bit where we asked to camp in her garden. It was just one more example of the sterling hospitality we had received throughout our trip – we had learnt that this kind of generosity and welcome was not restricted to just one country but seemed to be a worldwide phenomenon.

As Australia is essentially a huge island populated with a load of deadly and unique creatures, the Australians are understandably very serious about maintaining their uniquely isolated ecosystem, meaning that quarantine is a very big deal. We had all heard the horror stories about tourists being fined hundreds of dollars for accidently bringing a banana into the country, but our case was slightly different and we were rightly worried about Hannah's filthy innards when she was finally let off the ship that Friday afternoon.

Although she had been fumigated in the container and we had spent many hours in Malaysia cleaning Hannah, we realised it wasn't good enough less than a minute into the inspection. The officer headed straight for the back rims, felt around underneath and came up with his fingers covered in dirt from Asia, India, the Middle East, Russia, probably even London itself. Now the car would have to be cleaned 'professionally' at the cost of £50 per hour. Worst of all, it wouldn't be re-inspected until at least Tuesday, so we returned to Bern's with the bad news that she'd have to put up with us a little longer.

After giving some talks to her schoolkids, cooking her a few meals and generally trying not to be a total hassle for Bern, our D-Day rolled around again and we traipsed back to the port, awaiting the verdict of the quarantine officer.

Mercifully he passed us this time, but there were two rather irritating factors that came from the procedure. Firstly, rather than power-washing Hannah in an enclosed space, as you would expect, they blasted off all the dirt, seeds and other 'sensitive ecological' crud that had accumulated over 30-odd-thousand miles straight into the sea, where bits of it floated back into the port anyway. Secondly, when we mentioned we needed to change our oil to the Holy Environmental Protector of Australia™, he just suggested that we drive into the Outback and drain the old oil straight out into the dirt.

Luckily we had some good luck in store.

'I've been waiting for you guys.'

This didn't sound good. We had no idea who the chap in the Import Office was, but when a legal officer is expecting you, you get concerned.

'I read about ya in *Practical Classics*, love the trip – I knew you'd have to come to see me when ya got to Darwin and I've been looking forward to meeting ya.'

We weren't aware we had been in the magazine, but his enthusiasm for our trip meant that he got our paperwork expedited within a day and ready to sign the next morning. We just had to sort out our MOT and we'd be away – if they were as nice as these guys, we thought, it'd be a doddle!

'I probably shouldn't let you drive outta here.'

We had failed most of the tests. Getting the cab out of the container with no power for the steering had wrenched all the steering rods out of line. The brakes stopped the car safely enough, but only three of them were technically working when put on a rolling road; the windscreen had a few big cracks made worse by the overeager power-washing earlier; a glance under the car revealed chronic rust in the body work (although the bombproof chassis was still fine); and the indicators had stopped working – again.

The big chap in overalls who was testing the cab as part of the Northern Territories Vehicle Testing Centre handed us back the sheet covered in red crosses and instructed us that we could only legally drive to and from a mechanic's. I was glad he didn't actually take the car for a drive; otherwise he would have discovered that our gearbox had almost given up, too. Terrible Coventry-made brakes, made for the streets of London, and the largest mountain range in the world do not go well together so we tended to use engine braking wherever possible. The gearbox had taken the brunt of the abuse and made a disgusting whirling crunching sound if the car was doing anything other than accelerating in second or third gear.

When we left to find a garage I thanked the mechanic and told him I'd see him on Tuesday, in four days' time, for the retest.

'Make sure you do.'

'Why wouldn't I? I don't really have any options.'

'Well this German couple with a camper van came through a couple of months ago, and when they heard that Queensland state doesn't need to test your vehicle, they just left.'

At this point, the GetTaxi deal was still a long way from being confirmed. Although Nimrod had given it the go ahead, it had to go up the ranks to all their investors and was by no means a done deal. We had to prepare for the likelihood that Sydney was the end of the trip, as we couldn't afford to invest thousands of dollars repairing a car that was going to have to be scrapped by law in a month's time. To make things worse, Leigh's girlfriend was flying into Cairns in six days' time – a five or six-day drive away. We had also arranged our arrival date in Sydney and had people flying in from the UK for it, meaning little wiggle room on our schedule. Things looked bleak, but we had one more option. I told the lads what I'd heard about the German couple and we started to plot and plan.

With our taxi not technically road-legal and the windscreen spiderwebbed with cracks, we tried desperately to look cool and not to draw attention as the cab slowly pulled through Darwin.

Even though we were covered for third-party damage in Australia on our insurance policy from home, legally we were only allowed to drive to or from a mechanic's without the MOT. So we did the only thing we could do and booked ourselves into a mechanic's and set off to get the car fixed.

Ahead of us lay the famous Outback. Ridiculously hot and unrelentingly inhospitable, stories were always surfacing about tourists going missing out there. The mechanical voice of the satnav rang out, 'Continue straight for five-hundred-and-sixty miles, then turn left…'

Nobody said the mechanic had to be in Darwin.

CHAPTER 44

ALWAYS TIP YOUR MECHANIC WELL

The roads were good, the scenery was unexpectedly green and bushy, and the engine was running well (well, in fifth gear anyway). Stocked up with three days' worth of water and supplies, we camped in a national park with famous swimming holes. We rose at sunrise for a quick dip in the clear waters, nervously avoiding the deep black bits for fear of the crocodiles. Although apparently there were none in the area, as soon as someone mentions it, you just get that little bit nervous and make up excuses as to why you're sitting in the shallows.

Australian birds are stupid. I can now comment with a fair amount of authority on international bird behaviour as a 1992 black cab drives towards them (although this is hardly the best speciality topic for *Mastermind*). Whereas most birds fly out of the way, Australian birds fly straight up and hover around the cab windscreen, blindly waiting to be hit. Leigh hit a small one on the drive to the campsite, which fuelled an evening of relentless bird-murdering jokes from his unsympathetic teammates.

As Johno was driving out from our camp spot, a much larger bird decided to play chicken (no pun intended) with the cab. There was a screech of brakes (or there would have been if they worked) and a momentous thud as irony struck. Johno and I in the front seats rose from behind the dashboard, where we had instinctively ducked, to find that our previously cracked windscreen had been damaged to the point where we couldn't see through it. Leigh was laughing away in the back seat at the karma he had just witnessed. The culprit-turned-victim, a bush pheasant, about the same size as an English pheasant, lay very dead, by the roadside. Fortunately the driver's side of the screen was clear, but with the nearest settlement 60 miles away, and the chances of them having a spare London taxi windscreen slim, we were forced to push on to Cairns in an even worse state than before.

Until you have driven in the Outback, it is difficult to really get a grasp of the true desolation. The country is vast; the roads are straight and go on for as far as the eye can see, blending into a hazy mirage when they meet the sky. Dead wallabies and kangaroo litter the roadside every few miles, mown down by the huge 'roo-bars' attached to the front of buses and road trains. Huge termite mounds stand like pillars beside the road, along with the occasional derelict wind-powered water-pump at some long-forgotten cattle station. The heat pounded down as we drove for about 12 hours every day.

Drive, stop, camp, repeat.

The process was only interrupted by the odd 'road train' every few hours. They're about 50 m long and consist of three articulated trucks bolted together that thunder along at 70 mph. These monsters are downright intimidating, especially as they cruised faster than our top speed and overtook us on roads barely wide enough for them, shoving us into a nerve-wracking battle to hold the line with half the cab on the road and the other in the dust.

Every day we drove through scorched desert scrub, every night a huge thunderstorm raged. This was typical luck for us. Rain in the desert; yet again we cursed our bloody single-skin pop-up tents, thoroughly fed up with being perpetually moist.

We eventually made it to Cairns, and realised that all the hard sections were finished; all we had to do was drive to Sydney. We were on the home straight and in a jovial mood. This was allied with the near-confirmation of a new sponsor getting on board and the chance to extend the trip beyond Sydney.

We arrived in Cairns looking feral and smelling worse, but our interviews with various Australian TV channels throughout Asia had come up with an unexpected benefit. The hostel company Base had offered to put us up in their establishments for free all the way down the coast and what's more they had mentioned, 'We often have wet T-shirt compos. D'ya wanna be pourers lads?'

If we had translated this correctly it definitely sounded like a good idea for three red-blooded 20-something males – although not so much for Leigh, whose girlfriend had flown out from the UK to visit him for the final leg.

With Hannah safely in the hands of a seemingly friendly mechanic, we went to explore the nightlife. One of our friends from back in the UK happened to be in the same town and before long our catch up had degenerated into one of those nights similar to the one that spawned the whole stupid taxi idea in the first place. Paul jumped up on our table and danced for approximately eight seconds before a bouncer appeared.

'Get the bloody-hell darn from there mate, where'd y'think you are, the bloody Woolshed?'

'The Woolshed? What's that?'

'It's the pub where everyone dances on the tables, mate!'

'Where's that?' the entire group chorused.

It turned out the Woolshed was only a few streets down and even had little shelves high on the wall of the pub designed to hold your drink while you boogied on the tabletops.

Now that the sponsorship with GetTaxi was looking more like a dead cert and we knew that Hannah had to go further than the

1,300-mile push down to Sydney, we got Brando the mechanic to work hard on getting her in shape. To say thanks, we went to his with a couple of crates of Oz's finest Castlemaine XXXX beer.

Six months later, we received an email from Queensland Police. It turned out that our helpful mechanic had murdered two of his customers; a couple who had taken their vintage camper van into his garage for some work. The details were sketchy but what we did know for certain was that Brando was in custody and refusing to tell the police where the bodies were. An Internet sleuth had tracked down the blog we wrote about that afternoon, and passed the details on to the police who now wanted to question us about the photos Brando had shown us of his two-year-old daughter holding a .22 pistol.

It later emerged that the couple had paid Brando thousands of dollars to restore their beloved van but he had spent the money on himself instead. When they had disputed things he killed them, shooting the man in the back of the head and stabbing his partner before dumping their bodies on the edge of the rainforest. He was convicted 18 months later and given two life sentences with a minimum of 30 years behind bars. We were suddenly awfully glad we hadn't got on the wrong side of him.

We headed south for a spate of reunions with old friends. Lila, a friend from university, and Leigh's girlfriend, Char, joined us in the cab for a few days. My parents had flown over to see us briefly before the big arrival in Sydney. Once in Brisbane, we found ourselves at a press event arranged by the dean from Queensland University of Technology – a partner institution to our old university, Aston – who we had met on the day we left campus. Unlikely as it had sounded nine and a half months earlier, he had promised us a big celebration including all the tea and scones we could scoff upon our arrival.

The jovial mood was further reinvigorated when we received an email; GetTaxi had signed the contract: we were not finishing in Sydney. We were now circumnavigating the world!

CHAPTER 45

- - - - - - - -

THE END IS NOT NIGH

The journey so far had left us all shattered, and boarding the 22-hour flight home with a savage hangover, gained by trying to spend the last of the free bar tab we had been given by the hostel, didn't do much to make things better.

It was strange to step from the sun-kissed sand of Bondi Beach into the damp sub-zero conditions of Manchester, England, but I was grinning my head off as I appreciated all the little things I had been missing for the past ten months.

Hannah was now safely on another container ship and sailing her way slowly across the Pacific Ocean from Sydney to San Francisco. The plan was that we would pick her up when she arrived there in a month or so and then drive across the USA from coast to coast.

From New York we would then air-freight Hannah over to Israel before finally steering her back up to London, having driven all of the way around the world.

Christmas flew by in a haze of family gatherings, lie-ins until lunchtime and turkey sandwiches. All of our family members asked one of the same two questions when we told them about our cross-USA extension.

'Are you sure this GetTaxi company is legitimate? What if they're trying to get you to carry drugs for them?' asked the mums, aunties and grannies.

'When are you going to get a real job?' the dads and uncles half-jokingly enquired, the concern barely masked in their voices.

By the middle of January we were itching to get back to our day job and start the process of driving Hannah another 13,000 miles.

'This bag is three times the maximum weight allowed per individual item, I can't let it go.'

Bright mid-morning sun shone through the glass roof at Heathrow airport and the three of us were reeling to find ourselves where we were. Who would have thought exactly one year since we were arguing about taxi parts in the bowels of Aston University's engineering department, we would be arguing about them again in Heathrow Airport.

It was time to implement our well-honed blagging skills – if we could do the Chinese driving test then sweet-talking a check-in girl at Heathrow should be child's play.

Leigh began telling our story, smiling sweetly and doing the male equivalent of fluttering his eyelashes. The girl behind the desk was playing ball.

'I'm not sure there's much we can do... wait, so you're transporting charity medical equipment?'

'Um, no, it's brake parts and a steering arm for a nineteen-ninety-two London taxi, I've just told you...'

'OK, so, charity m-e-d-i-c-a...' she started to type it into the machine, giving us a sly wink.

'Ooooh, yeah. Medical stuff... for kids mainly... saving lives and all that.'

'Well now, actually there will be no charge, we don't charge for excess baggage if it's medical equipment,' she beamed back at us before wishing us well.

We hitched the bag on to the conveyor belt, passed through security and headed to the pub.

We had stayed in some pretty atrocious conditions over the past year – Russian crack dens, grass verges in industrial parks,

Iranian artillery fields – but a flight from Heathrow to Baltimore could give them a run for their money. The cabin was cold, the coffee was cold, and the food and drinks (which you had to pay for) were rudely distributed with as much finesse as a workhouse chef. However, after one more flight we were in San Francisco, munching away on real American pizza.

Hannah was delayed on the ship, so we busied ourselves by preparing for our trip across the States, buying SIM cards and tracking down a workshop to do the mammoth amount of work needed on the car.

There are worse places in the world to be stuck. San Francisco's hilly streets, changeable weather and charming people meant that when we weren't carrying out taxi-related paperwork, we were very content visiting Alcatraz, wandering around Fisherman's Wharf and even sampling the city's excellent local brew, Anchor Steam, while watching the Super Bowl in a real sports bar.

Days passed as we waited for the news from our shipping agent that we'd be able to collect Hannah. We eventually got the call and were informed that the car had been selected for special investigation by customs and that *we* had to pay for the truck to ship the container to the customs yard. We ended up having to pay fees for the search *and* for the cost of them storing the car in their yard *and* the fines for whatever random things they could find wrong with the car. Shipping Hannah from Australia to America cost four times the original value of the cab – a vehicle that was ready for the scrapyard and wouldn't pass any of the MOT tests.

'But I'm a ten-hour drive away,' he pleaded down the phone. 'OK, I'm leaving now. DO NOT sell it. I'm driving all the way from San Francisco for it!'

Jon closed his 1990s flip-phone. 'Um… does anyone want to go to LA?'

Jon was an American student we had met at the Sufi festival in Lahore, Pakistan, who had come to meet us in San Francisco. He'd begged to join us across America when he heard we were extending our trip, and I had jokingly replied that we had no space and we only travel with other taxis, but if he could get his hands on a New York yellow cab then he would be welcome to come along. A few weeks later, here he was, following up on an ad for a yellow cab he'd seen on Craigslist. Even though Jon had transferred the deposit to the seller, he'd just heard that they were going to sell it to someone else unless he picked it up that day.

Leigh was lying on his bed, watching action films on his laptop, headphones in and Johno was absorbed in a book.

'Err, sure,' I responded – this sounded like it had the potential to be a random adventure within an adventure.

'Leigh, we're going to LA to buy a New York taxi from some gangsters, back sometime tomorrow.'

He looked up from *Zombie Brain Robots 7*.

'Cool.'

Jon and I picked up his car in the Oakland area of San Francisco (somewhere I made a mental note never to return to, filled as it was with unsavoury characters). It was a mid-1990s Jeep Cherokee, and it was filled to bursting with crap.

'Bloody hell, it looks like you've been living in here!' I said.

'I, err, kind of have been... for a bit,' he replied sheepishly.

'But, mate, it looks like you've been living in here for a year.'

Old food wrappers and tools carpeted the floor, along with vast quantities of cigar ash, and the entire back of the car was filled with bags and luggage.

'Yeah, best part of a year actually.'

It turns out there was a lot about Jon we didn't know.

The next thing I found out was that he is incredibly tight. We stopped at an In-N-Out Burger chain, which Jon had raved about, but as I tucked into the most delicious burger and fries I'd ever tasted I looked across and saw Jon was just sipping on a Coke.

'Don't you want any?'

'Yeah, but I'm trying to save money.'

Jon was so tight he made Johno (the tightest Northerner in the entire world) look like Jenna Jameson. He only had a limited amount of cash to last him across the States, so that meant In-N-Outs and beers were out of the question.

I could feel his pain; we had made it from England to Australia on a budget where the cost of that one roadside In-N-Out would last for three days. We would camp, skip lunch, Couchsurf and take advantage of every free meal we were ever given. Yes, we went out and partied quite a lot during the trip, but those nights would happen every few weeks, and often included free or ridiculously cheap booze.

But in the USA, with the new sponsor on board and a healthy living allowance, money wasn't as much of a problem anymore.

We headed south-east through rolling landscapes, topped by wind turbines. The sun was setting behind us, bathing the I5 Freeway in a rich orange glow. Big '76' petrol towers advertised fuel stops, roadside diners advertised burgers and chain motels advertised cheap rooms. This was the real America.

Time was ticking, and Jon kept calling the seller to ensure he hadn't sold the car and to update him on our progress. It all sounded very unreliable if you asked me. I took over driving and got my first feel for the American roads. It took no time at all for it to become clear that Americans are atrocious drivers. It's a bold statement to make – I'm not the best driver in the world by any stretch of the imagination – but having driven most of the way around the world by this point, I could comment with some authority on the topic and make sweeping generalisations about national driving ability.

Apparently, there are no lane rules – one can weave in and out of lanes, depending on which moves fastest at the time. Lorries are vast and are allowed to drive at whatever speed they want and big 4x4 pickup trucks seemed to have the right to mow down all other road users with impunity.

The cab-seller called threatening to sell again. We told him we would be there around 2 a.m. and hoped that was cool. I envisioned an elderly taxi driver being kept up late waiting for us to arrive.

'Err… I don't think that's the case. This guy sounds like a gangster; he's Armenian and he lives in Pasadena.' Wherever that was.

'So this guy's possibly a gangster, and we're turning up at 2 a.m. with two grand in cash?'

There was silence for the next few minutes as we contemplated our situation. The chances of us getting beaten up by angry mobsters looked high. Just before we got to our destination I pulled over, opened the toolbox and took out the tyre iron to place by my feet, at the ready.

There she stood – a bright-yellow New York taxi with an advert board on the roof advertising 'Skinny margaritas – iced low-calorie margarita mix'. We pulled up and Jon headed out to make the deal as I clutched my tyre iron. There were four men standing next to the cab, looking pretty intimidating in their best leisurewear, but it all seemed legit so I went out and said hello. They seemed uptight as they showed us the car, and I wasn't getting good vibes off them. Jon went and drove it around the block while I stayed as collateral. I nervously tried to make small talk while we waited, which they responded to with unimpressed grunts. Then I casually dropped into conversation that I was in Yerevan the year before.

'You've been to Armenia?' they exclaimed, incredulous smiles transforming their faces. 'NO WAY! We're all Armenian! How did you like our country?'

When Jon came back I can only think how surprised he must have been to find me and the four tough gangsters catching up like old friends.

The car was a Ford Crown Victoria that had been a police squad car for ten years before being converted into a taxi. On the road back, I quickly discovered a few of its quirks. The back seats were separated from the front by a thick plate and criminal-proof PVC screen. The taxi radio was still in place and there was even a mount for a shotgun. It also turned out that the lights had been linked up to the old police siren – a fact we discovered when we pulled into a gas station to replace a headlight bulb. I went to get back in the car to find a way of stopping the siren only to discover the automatic locking must have clicked on, and we had no way of getting back into Jon's new steed.

After 15 minutes of trying everything to no avail, we were just about to break a window when a man came over and asked if he could help. He just happened to be a highway support mechanic, who had his truck and all his gear just down the road. He had us back in the car in no time.

He asked what the story was with the yellow taxi so we told him.

'That's you guys? Oh. My. God!'

He called his girlfriend out of the petrol station.

'Remember those guys we saw on the news who were driving around the world in a taxi? This is them!'

He decided to waive the extortionate fee he normally charged for people who lock their keys in their car in return for becoming friends on Facebook.

I walked into the dorm room in our hostel approximately 30 hours after I'd left for LA.

'Alright.'

Leigh looked up from the film on his laptop.

'Get the car?'

'Yep.'

He returned his attention to *Zombie Brain Smashers in Space 4*.

'Cool.'

CHAPTER 46

CHIMICHANGAS, FORTIES AND WRENCHES

We finally got word to head to a yard in Oakland to collect Hannah almost two weeks after arriving. Even though we had been told it would never happen, customs had 'unusually' found nothing wrong with the paperwork. We'd got the car through over 40 borders to this point, so although we could be complete idiots with many things, border paperwork was not one of them. Frustratingly, it seemed like we had wasted precious time and money just to be told, 'Yes lads, you did everything correctly, well done, now give us a few grand for us to tell you this.' Fortunately it was now GetTaxi's money, but a cap had been set on our budget and the importing process had already eaten most of the contingency buffer we had agreed on.

While Leigh and some mechanics at the yard attempted to bump-start our beloved old girl by pushing her along with a forklift truck, I filled out the remaining paperwork in the office and was handed a piece of paper that clearly said: 'Amount owed: $0.00'. I blinked a few times, checked they were our Hannah's details, and stared at the amount again. It seemed like we were back in luck!

I signed the papers quickly, exchanged a cheeky, 'Let's get out of here' expression with Leigh and we headed off in a triumphant clatter of metal.

It later transpired that, of course, it had been a mistake and we really should have been fined a couple of thousand dollars. However, we were of the opinion that if it was their mistake they obviously couldn't have wanted the money that badly in the first place.

Before we could set off across America, Hannah had to be rebuilt from the bottom up. A friend of a friend put us in contact with a specialist British classic car restoration business called On the Road Again, an hour or so south of San Francisco. The owner kindly agreed to give us full use of his garage after usual business hours, and Dane, one of the mechanics, offered to put us up on his sofas during our stay. The workshop was filled with the most beautiful vintage cars I have ever seen: MGs, Austin-Healeys, E-types... and Hannah.

We worked like demons over the next few days to get Hannah back up to speed and before long she had a new gearbox and fixed brakes, and was generally ready to tackle the hills of San Francisco and beyond. On our final night, Dane and his wife set about making us some authentic American food. We had discovered that far from the stereotypical steaks and double cheeseburgers, the best food in California was basically Mexican style but with more meat and cheese.

Huge 'forties' – 1.5-pint cans of beer – were pressed into our hands and the feast began with a completely new culinary experience: chimichangas, a sort of deep-fried burrito stuffed with meat that had been marinated in Sunny Delight and Dr Pepper. It sounds like a disgusting combination but they were utterly delicious. It finally felt like we were seeing the real America.

CHAPTER 47

'YOUR GUYSES TAXI IS SICK'

Being back on the road was always a great feeling for us, especially after all the delays and false starts of the past two weeks. Now we were a gang of six, the original three, plus Texans Jon and his friend Drew, and our long-term passenger from the China leg, Matt. He was over in America visiting his new girlfriend, a girl he had met a few months earlier in Laos while tubing down the river with us. The scruffy yellow cab and the even scruffier Hannah, now rebranded a lovely GetTaxi yellow, must have presented a strange sight as we convoyed down Highway One, the supremely beautiful southern California coast road. Still, the sight of a London cab pulling up and offering a lift didn't seem to faze a group of unwashed hitchhikers we picked up halfway along the route. Initially I just saw one guy, standing next to what I thought was a pile of rubble, but on closer inspection we saw that two more men were snoozing under a filthy blanket, along with a mangy dog. Having raised their hopes we felt like we couldn't now abandon them so we squeezed them in and had a slow, spaced-out conversation about nothing for most of the way south.

Our new hitcher friends smelt. They smelt so bad that they made Hannah – after 30,000 miles and a year of sweaty boys on top of a lifetime of drunken revellers and kebab wrappers – smell fresh in comparison. We dropped them off as soon as we could.

Our destination for the night was the college town of Santa Barbara, 100 miles along the coast from Los Angeles. Matt had visited here in his younger years and vaguely knew someone connected to one of the frat houses, so we soon found ourselves knocking on their door, cap-in-hand, and asking if we could sleep on their floor.

We were shown around the huge mansion, although it was more like a run-down nightclub. The entire stock of furniture in the downstairs communal areas amounted to a stripper pole on a small stage and a torn-up pool table. The place was filthy and the stinking toilet was caked in dried vomit.

Still, we cracked open some beers and learned about our new hosts. All of our previous knowledge about the fraternity system came from Hollywood movies and from what we gathered from these frat boys it was pretty much spot on. Male undergraduates are selected to join a frat after applying in Rush Week, a sort of US Freshers' Week, and undergoing various initiations, often of questionable moral standing.

Once someone had joined a frat they were expected to socialise only with members of their frat. Rivalries were high and it was highly frowned upon to hang out with people from other frats. Each frat also had a corresponding sorority house, the female equivalent with whom they partied and socialised in a somewhat inbred system.

'Hey, is that your guys' taxi out there?' babbled the bubbly Valley Girl who had just strutted through the door. 'That's sickasfuck! Do you wanna come see the sorority house?'

As we were led over the road to another large mansion we were assured that this was not normally allowed but as we were British things would be OK. We walked through the door and immediately the difference from the frat house was staggering. This place looked like a Beverly Hills mansion. It was spotless and furnished with mammoth sofas, fluffy rugs and enough scatter cushions to keep a small Chinese upholstery factory in full employment. Wandering around were scores of model-like girls in various stages of undress from full catwalk regalia to those wrapped up in towels the size of a duvet. I blinked in disbelief.

'Hullo,' announced Matt in his hammiest accent, 'we're British!'

The tour round the stately home and the introductions to the sea of giggling college girls led to a swift invitation to a frat party that night: our ultimate goal.

'You're technically not allowed as you're not in the frat,' explained the self-appointed head-girl, 'but it's OK; you're British.'

If you've ever seen a generic American coming-of-age movie you'll have seen those crazy college parties that you think are just the stuff of Hollywood legend. The ones where huge houses are completely trashed and jammed full of drunken college students doing keg-stands while a supercool DJ spins an unfeasibly loud soundsystem. The place is totally banging; red cups of 'liquor' are being passed around like water and there are unfathomably hot girls wearing next to nothing and people doing crazy shit everywhere. They do exist and this was one of those parties.

We had heard about the power of the British accent second hand but this was the place where we realised it was all actually true. Even just asking someone the way to the bathroom resulted in an instant crowd of cheering girls swooning.

'Wait a minute,' one of the swooners suddenly asked me, feigning flirty suspicion, 'you're not really British, you're just a frat guy pretending so you can chat up girls!'

We all woke in various strange places; Leigh in the back of the cab and Paul was covered in paint and wrapped up in a tarpaulin underneath the frat-house pool table. Once we had regrouped we hit the glorious beach that lay just behind the college.

'I just can't believe that this is their university.'

'I know mate, we went to the derelict centre of Birmingham and they live on the Pacific coast in southern California.'

'Let's stay another night.'

We had been in LA on the day of the Oscars, which unexpectedly meant the whole city was completely dead, but we cruised around pretending to be Brad Pitt, got the picture of the taxis below the Hollywood sign at dusk and then got on the road.

Driving late into the night, we eventually stopped in a tiny town on the foothills of Mount Whitney. Leigh, Matt and Johno crammed into the town's only available room and Drew, Jon and I drove for a few miles into the desert in the dark and parked up to camp. We awoke in the cold and beautiful hills, the high peaks of the Sierra Nevada shrouded in cloud and the rolling dusty foothills spread out below. Most importantly, given our run-in with the Iranian secret police, our view contained no police officers. We breakfasted on a slice o' pie from a proper local diner before saddling up and heading east.

We stopped again at a tiny rest stop on the edge of the Death Valley National Park and I ran into a store to find something to sate my thirst. The shelves were stacked with bottle after bottle of bright, sugary beverages, but to my surprise a simple bottle of plain water was nowhere to be seen.

Eventually I found the next best thing – a bottle of crimson Vitamin Water – and took it up to the counter where the cashier rung up a completely different price to the one on the label. We had found that most American shops had the confusing practice of only adding sales tax, which varied in each state, once you got to the checkout, meaning that you never knew exactly what you'd end up paying until the last minute.

I peered at the pile of change in my hand as I counted out the coins and apologised profusely as I tried to make sense of the quarters, dimes and nickels.

'There's nothing to be sorry for,' grinned the clerk sincerely, looking around his completely empty shop with a look of utter contentment, 'I have all the time in the world.'

CHAPTER 48

PORN STARS AND BURGERS

'Guys, wake up, I've been robbed!'

We all stirred slowly. Leigh was frantically searching around the room.

'Someone has pickpocketed my phone!'

I started chuckling involuntarily, 'Leigh, you were hammered last night and then you texted me at 5 a.m. trying to get me to go with you to buy another bottle of rum. I'm pretty sure you probably just lost it after that.'

The previous day we had arranged to meet 'John' from the Vegas chapter of the Ferrari Club of America for a grand drive down the Vegas strip. His recommended meeting place was Sheri's Ranch – a fully functioning, legal brothel. None of our group had any intention of using the services available, but that didn't mean we weren't intrigued. John told us we could get a tour, 'and more... if you know what I mean'.

It was slightly awkward. We were quite clearly not the type to go in for prostitutes, but John kept dropping hints. It got to the point where we told him not to let us stop him and that we would wait in the bar.

'Oh guys, don't worry about me, I got here three hours ago. I am... shall we say... a, err... happy man... if you know what I mean.'

Even the inanimate furniture in the room knew what he meant.

Our guides, a brunette with a friendly demeanour and physique that didn't lend itself to the corset she was wearing, and a blonde approaching her twilight years, tottered around on inordinately high heels.

'Gentlemen, my name is JR and this is our menu.'

She presented a specials board in the atrium, faux-antique chaise longues and ornately framed prints of baroque paintings hung from the wall and gave the room the air of a period hotel lobby. Except, instead of announcing the breakfast times, the board outlined a list of sexual deeds in ornate gold leaf.

'So this area is the ranch. You can see the special private rooms over there. You hire those for the night and get unlimited champagne, steak, lobster and sex. That's the pool, for you know, pool parties...'

The audience of awkward Texans and Englishmen nodded and murmured their approval. The whole process was more like an estate agent showing us around a flat than a guided tour of a house of sex. More baroque fittings surrounded a table made up for two with pressed napkins and sparkling silverware. The only thing to remind us that we weren't in a premium restaurant was the helpful notice on the side: 'Please use condoms'.

Johno whispered as we were led into the next room. 'I know her, the blonde. I think she's a porn star. I think I've seen... um, I think I recognise her, um, face.'

'And next, we have the Budweiser Jacuzzi room.'

'Budweiser sponsors a room in a brothel?'

'Oh we have all sorts of corporate clients. We have a very normal company name so they can just put 'entertainment' on their expense account. We also do a lot of divorce parties.'

'Divorce parties?'

'Yeah – they're like bachelor parties, but you're celebrating your freedom.'

As it became clear that we genuinely meant it when we told them we just wanted to have a look around and nothing else, they quickly started to lose patience.

Our 12 hours in Vegas were an experience. As none of us had been there before, it should have been dazzling and glittery, but we found that, seeing as none of us were big gamblers and £25 a day doesn't go very far in Vegas, it quickly lost some of its allure. The casinos were filled with kids in shirts, blowing their minimum-wage pay cheques on bottles of champagne in an attempt to live like Jay Z for one night; mortgage payments placed on roulette tables to impress mercenary girls in short skirts; people buying expensive liquors in an attempt to convey some semblance of class, but only achieving the opposite.

We found a corner of a casino that did karaoke and had a bar that had a twister board with various drinks on. Every half an hour they would spin the wheel and the drink it landed on would be $1 for the next 30 minutes. The only gambling any of us did was Johno, who discovered that if he fed change into a blackjack machine on the bar, then he would get free drinks, drinking $15 worth of beer for the $8 he put in.

We decided to eat off our hangovers in true Las Vegas style, by completely overindulging.

The Heart Attack Grill is a burger joint in the seedier area of the city that especially prides itself on being particularly unhealthy. Fries are cooked in pure lard, salad is specifically excluded and diet sodas are not allowed. The chefs are dressed as doctors and the (remarkably slim) waitresses as nurses who rather unconvincingly swear that they eat the speciality burgers on a regular basis. What's more, anyone over the weight of 350 lbs (25 stone) eats for free and an industrial-sized weighing scale is placed in pride of place in the centre of seating area.

After donning the obligatory hospital gown, I was disappointed to see that I came in at under half the weight requirement, although we all applauded a hefty chap who easily topped the scales soon after with 371 lbs.

We were all feeling a little fragile so we plumped for the two-burger 'Double Bypass' option, with no extra bacon. All except

Leigh who was brought out the calorific Quadruple Bypass, replete with 20 extra rashers of bacon, apparently a whopping 8,000 calories in total.

As he tried to get his mouth around the giant handful, grease dripped uninvitingly out on to the table and he had soon attracted an audience of passing tourists who were gawking through the window, laughing and taking pictures. Half an hour later he threw in the towel with about a quarter of the last patty still uneaten, and another half an hour later the first three-quarters of the burger reasserted themselves on a Vegas sidewalk. He didn't eat another burger for the entire time we were in the States.

The next item on the whistle-stop tourist checklist was the Grand Canyon, and although we had chosen a southerly route across America we soon discovered that it was way too cold for our plan to camp near the rim. The next best option was to all squeeze into one cheap motel room and wake early in the pre-dawn chill for the ride down to catch the sunrise. Fortunately, given this plan, it was time to see Drew off at the airport, so there would be one fewer sweaty body to squeeze in.

Ice encrusted the floor of the motel parking lot the next morning as we gingerly walked over to the two cars, bleary-eyed. A mixture of extreme cold and tiredness meant that I was concentrating on peering out through a patch scraped in the ice and following Skinny Marge in front when Leigh looked over and saw to his alarm that the engine temperature was spiking right off the scale. We stopped immediately and, upon opening the finger-numbingly cold bonnet, were engulfed in a cloud of steam; it was a strange juxtaposition of severe temperatures. We figured that the cooling water in the radiator must have frozen, and I cursed myself for not being vigilant enough and for this happening at the worst of times.

As it was still dark and we were in sub-zero conditions we parked up on a side road, scribbled a hasty note to leave on the windscreen and all piled into Skinny Margarita, the yellow cab, for a morning walk around the chilly and slippery Southern Rim. We could deal with Hannah when the sun had warmed things a little.

CHAPTER 49

- - - - - - - -

THE MOST HEAVILY ARMED MAGAZINE IN THE WORLD

When we had started the trip, and indeed for most of the journey so far, we had had no idea what we were really getting into or how to actually do any of it. We had no clue how to get corporate sponsorship, ship foreign vehicles across seas, fix mechanical problems in wholly inappropriate places or deal with the media. But along the way we had slowly been learning on the job, and as we got further round the world more and more people started following our story, and asking us for advice for their own trips. One of these groups was *Overland Journal*, a magazine dedicated to the burgeoning lifestyle of overland travel. They invited us to their headquarters to take a look around, show off our car and see their range of much more impressive and appropriate vehicles. It was when we were talking to these guys that what we had achieved so far really started to dawn on me.

'You know, you guys are famous? You've probably done more for overlanding than anyone in the past ten years.'

Maybe they were being tongue-in-cheek but I suppose they were right. Now that we were three-quarters of the way around the world in a completely unsuitable car on an unsupported expedition, people were starting to take notice. The fact that someone was now paying for us to complete our adventure and that the story was starting to be picked up by major newspapers and TV stations showed that we were doing something remarkable, even if it was really just an excuse to go travelling and party on an overextended road trip with our best buddies.

For now, we were only thinking about a statement their digital editor Matt had made to us before our arrival.

'So we hear you like guns in Arizona?' we had said.

'Are y'all kidding?' he replied. 'We're probably the most heavily armed magazine in America – no, the world!'

Reminding him of this, he walked over to a towering safe behind the iMacs and the filing cabinets.

He swung the door open and our eyes widened.

'Is that,' faltered Paul, '... a grenade launcher?'

'Yeah-huh, but you can't buy grenades for it.'

'What's the point in having a grenade launcher and no grenades?'

'I put golf balls in it and shoot them... that's how we golf in AMERICA.'

We loaded up a humongous pickup truck called a Dodge Power Wagon that the *Overland Journal* was testing, hopped in the flat-bed and drove into the wilderness. An AK-47, a Walther PPK (the gun used by James Bond), a vintage World War One bolt-action rifle, and boxes and boxes of ammo later, we felt like virile, masculine and manly real men.

None of us are particularly into guns and we had been a little shocked to find a whole aisle of them at an American supermarket earlier that week. Sure, we've grown up around Action Man and Arnie films but we all found the stereotypical American obsession with firearms a little strange. However, when you're in the scrubland of the American West with a veritable arsenal of weapons it's hard not to see at least some of the appeal.

Although Matt and I had done a fair amount of shooting in our RAF days we quickly found that there's a definite difference between a straight-down-the-line warrant officer giving you commands to fire single shots down a military firing range, and between spurting bursts of AK-47 bullets at empty beer cans in the desert.

'It looks like that's nearly all the ammo guys,' announced our de facto range supervisor after a good few hours. 'Y'all should shoot your car with the last few rounds of the .303.'

There was a palpable pause.

'Shoot... Hannah?' Leigh looked worried.

'Yeah, just somewhere inessential, it's not like she's not battered already.'

Grins started to spread on our faces; all of them but one.

'You know, it might actually be pretty good for the pictu—'

'We are not shooting Hannah!' Leigh burst in, glaring at the group.

'... but it would be a funny story for the...'

'Guys! There's no way we're shooting our own car,' he pleaded, looking around desperately for a face of reason but finding none.

'Come on mate, just through the bonnet, it might even help with the cooling.'

After a moment's thought he groaned and grabbed the remaining clip of bullets. 'Fine!' he huffed, marching off towards our baby. 'But I'm doing the shooting!'

So, with a couple of new cooling holes in the bonnet to help the weary engine, we said goodbye to our new buddies and headed south to Tucson.

Although we had negotiated a living allowance with GetTaxi, we quickly realised that we did this back when we were surviving on less than £5 a day in Asia and had a different perception of budgets. This meant that even with multimillionaire backers, we still had to save as much money as possible. Jon simply had no money and my tightness seemed to have rubbed off on the other two. This usually resulted in us haggling hard for a £20 motel room then sneaking the five of us in when the concierge wasn't paying attention. By this point in the trip we had shared beds with each other more times than we cared to count.

Tucson would be the eastern terminus of what we had dubbed The Megadrive: a 900-mile slog through prime Texan ranch country over to Jon's hometown of Houston. We aimed to cover it without stopping for anything other than food or fuel. But before the start of the marathon interstate session we checked out an interesting attraction.

A consequence of a government having defence spending that is more than the next 20 countries combined is that the Americans have lots and lots of spare planes and helicopters – more than they know what to do with, in fact. In the dry desert air near Tucson, spread over a plot of land larger than 1,500 football pitches, sit rows and rows of over 4,000 aircraft – from Vietnam-era B-52 bombers to attack helicopters stripped of their rotors and sealed up tight. Some are simply mothballed in case of future emergency while others are cannibalised for spare parts or slowly chopped up for scrap metal. The 'Boneyard' was basically a giant open-air museum. The main drag even had a hall of fame with the entire aeronautical history of the USAF spread along one road, although, amusingly, the space behind the 'F-117 Stealth Fighter' sign simply had a trio of wheels and some mounting steps that led to nothing.

We had so much to see in the States and with our shipping already booked from New York we perfected a travelling technique where we would drive through the night, sleep in the cars and have action-packed days.

Nearly a thousand miles of good, straight AMERICAN roads later and we were in San Antonio at dawn on a bright Saturday morning. As we had got closer and closer to Texas, Jon had started to get giddy and excitable – whooping like a cowboy as we passed the state line – telling us all about how it was Texas Independence Day.

Jon and I arrived in the faster NY taxi a good few hours before the others, so we ate a wonderful breakfast at a famous Mexican foodstop with cracked Formica tables and a rotund, sweaty chef without a word of English. Independence Day is also the anniversary of the end of the Battle of the Alamo, and the local vintage re-enactment club would be doing their thing around the grounds of the old building. Jon explained the story to me over the theatrical gun and cannon fire, the cloud of cordite getting thicker and thicker as the 'battle' went on.

As far as I understood, and any Texans reading this will disagree, the whole battle went like this: some white guys who wanted slaves were told they couldn't have slaves, so they went to Texas (which was part of Mexico) with their slaves. The Mexicans took exception to this as slavery was forbidden (plus it was part of their country), and gathered an army to attack 'The Alamo' (a small fort/house where the slavers were living). They offered reasonable treaties to the Texans, who refused, and everyone died.

Perhaps Jon was explaining it wrong, but it's a big deal in Texas. If it's a big deal in Texas – the home of BIG – then there would be some big parties. And where better to party in Texas than 'the live music capital of the world', Austin.

We pulled up outside Jon's cousin's flat, which was to be our home for the night, and started to interrogate him on the nightlife. Aged 20 and a few years into university, the ridiculous American drinking laws meant he still, apparently, could not be trusted to drink beer. So his knowledge of the famous Sixth Street party scene was non-existent.

Being the kind-hearted, altruistically natured individuals that we are, we felt this needed to change. A five-minute brief on how to speak like an Englishman and how to look bouncers in the eye (as well as taking my UK Driving Licence as ID) and we headed to Sixth Street.

He was like a child in a sweet shop, especially when the first bar we walked into suddenly erupted and every girl in there climbed on to the bar and started to dance and take their clothes off (this actually happened – we have no idea why, but that doesn't mean it wasn't fantastic). In the next bar he was using the superpowers an English accent gives you to chat up American girls and in the next he pulled together the guts to go to the bar and buy beers, which he enjoyed so much that he refused to let anyone else buy any drinks for the rest of the night.

A short hungover hop the next morning took us down to Jon's college town (the imaginatively named 'College Station') to check out his friend's ranch. We were joined by a coursemate of Jon's, a Marine officer on his way to joining the FBI. In the back of his Tom Petty-blasting Mustang, he had brought an arsenal.

'You Brits don't have guns so I figured you might like to shoot some on the ranch. I've also got some zombie clown cut-outs to use as targets.'

We made our way to Houston that evening, where we stayed for a few days, and without doubt our highlight was the Houston Rodeo.

The huge, 70,000-seat arena fills up every night for a few weeks in the summer. Everybody gets dolled up in their best cowboy outfit and heads down to eat some Tex-Mex and watch the show. We got in just as they were doing some bull-riding, followed by some incredibly impressive speed/obstacle course horse-riding, but then things started to get *really* Texan.

The next event was the Calf Scramble. The basic premise of this is that 50 kids are put in the arena with a few calves, with a large square set out in the middle of the pitch. The kids have to lasso a calf, rope it up into a holster, and then drag it into the centre square. This is easier said than done – especially if you're a petite 15-year-old girl, desperately clutching the large calf's tail and being dragged around the arena as the poor animal casually saunters around. We weren't sure whether we felt more concern for the animals' well-being or the frantic teens desperately clutching at them. However, I did find out from a large Texan man sat beside me that the prize for the kids who get their calf in the square is full payment for their college education. Given that most of these kids were from under-privileged inner-city schools, we thought this was a pretty great prize. Apparently a Texan scholarship has nothing to do with grades, it's all about roping cows in front of 70,000 people.

But that wasn't the best event. After 20 minutes of calf scrambling, the arena was cleared and a small sheep pen was brought out.

'Ladies and Gentlemen, time for the event you've all been waiting for... MUTTONNNNNN BUSSSSSSTINNNN!!!'

I'd happily have waited my entire life for this glorious spectacle.

The competitors were brought out – three- or four-year-old kids in full-face hockey masks and protection – and introduced to their fluffy steeds. The competition, no joke, was that the child who rides a sheep the furthest distance wins.

This was amazing.

When it was all over the 'riders' were lined up in front of the cameras, almost all of them crying their eyes out, and given a rosette. The winner, however, received a big cup, and immediately stopped crying, posing for the camera with his very proud parents beaming behind him.

This was followed by an awful (but apparently very famous) country and western singer so we went to the pub – once we'd seen Mutton Bustin', even the Beatles coming on stage would have been an anti-climax!

CHAPTER 50

COLESLAW WRESTLING IN THE US OF A

We reached the heart of American voodoo late at night, crossing the straits of deep marsh and swampland on the outskirts of New Orleans. The only light came from the interstate, packed with trucks, while to either side dead trees loomed up eerily out of the darkness. It was a pretty creepy introduction. We stayed at a rundown motel surrounded by buildings with hints of the French architecture we were expecting in the city.

In the daytime we visited the city's sights, and I met up with my great uncle who emigrated there 30 years ago. He regaled me with stories of his time in the RAF over po' boy sandwiches – a Louisiana speciality – and told me tales of how he kept getting into trouble when he used to work for a mafioso running party flights to Mexico before settling down as a teacher.

However, New Orleans isn't a city for the daytime – it's a city for whiskey and sweat-soaked nights. In the evening, we watched a comedy night, and somehow ended up drinking bourbon with the performers, cruising from one incredible live music venue to the next in the French Quarter. One bar had a blues three piece, another a jazz quintet; there was even a 1930s big-band ensemble and an incredible blues man with a lap-steel guitar – all within 50 yards of each other. Unsurprisingly, the company was also hilarious, and we were sad that we'd have to leave so soon – the clock was ticking and we couldn't afford not to stick to our schedule.

It's quite a long drive to Memphis, and our fuel pump started to fall off halfway into the journey, leaving a trail of diesel for 40 miles. An hour of roadside repairs meant that, again, we arrived at night. We headed to Beale Street, which is the musical hub of the city, and made a beeline for a free bar with a rockabilly band tearing up the stage. This was where we bumped into one of Jon's friends from university, recognisable by his matching signet ring – which was handy as we hadn't arranged anywhere to sleep.

When we looked at the map of America and plotted our straight lines from city to city we failed to really comprehend the massive distances involved, even after our experiences in Australia: land of the never-ending road.

This was presumably why we decided to drive from New Orleans to Florida via Memphis and Birmingham, Alabama: a detour of over 500 miles and two states. Still, at least we got to see Elvis's house and experience some true Deep South accents. The decision to tack Birmingham on to the route was solely due to it being the namesake of the place where we came up with the idea for whole taxi trip. When we arrived, we were pleasantly surprised to find a thriving hipster pub where a moustachioed man was carrying around a wooden goose under his arm and the patrons brought their rare-breed dogs along for a pint. It wasn't quite the same as the Birmingham we knew.

The next big push was down to Florida where we had heard Spring Break was just about to hit with full-force. We all had visions of pretty college girls partying on the beaches of Daytona while 'roided up bros chest-bumped each other and chugged crates of Bud Light, and we were sure Hannah would make quite a splash. As we inched closer to the warm Atlantic sands we got more and more pumped up for another few days of partying, but as we hit Daytona and cruised along the strip we noticed there were surprisingly few keg-stands and sorority girls. Instead there was only sand. Sand and lots and lots of traffic.

The road was packed, but not with the ubiquitous American pickup trucks or even regular cars. Hundreds of middle-aged men with moustaches, ample beer guts and leather jackets with little flowy tassels were sat upon large, noisy motorcycles; their legs wide apart and held up as though in medical stirrups. Tattooed women occasionally sat on the back, their pale wrinkled love handles spilling out of their leather. Sat in solid traffic, these hundreds of bikers would constantly rev their machines to ensure everybody knew that they were there.

We pulled up on to the beach to find it almost entirely deserted. There was nothing but sand. We checked the dates – we had got it right, but maybe the revellers had all been scared away by the bikers. Sad and disappointed we decided we were going to embrace Bike Week instead. We headed to an interview that had been arranged with a local TV station.

We got the lowdown from the cameraman. 'Yeah, the best thing to see this week is the coleslaw wrestling.'

Our faces spoke volumes.

'Yeah, they get the biker wives to wrestle in a huge vat of coleslaw.'

'But aren't the biker wives a bit, um...?'

He read our minds. 'They sure are buddy! They're all machines, they would tear you in half, they're worse than most of the guys. And speaking of the guys, if you see patches or colours, you just walk the other way; all these guys are armed and won't think twice about shootin' ya in the face!'

The bar he directed us to was some miles out, and was halfway between Orlando and Daytona Beach, so we had to beware the rival biker gangs. It was odd that, although we had driven through some of the most supposedly dangerous places in the world, it was in the apparently civilised America that we were most likely to get shot. We drove for an hour or so and found the bar, where we also found out that the wrestling didn't start for two days.

CHAPTER 51

- - - - - - - -

HOW TO RACK UP
A $100,000 TAXI FARE

We were now left with just two days to reach Pittsburgh and Jon's uncle and aunt's house. It was the most intense driving session of the trip; stopping only for a three-hour roadside kip and hot-seating between the two cars so that we could get to Jon's relatives' house just in time for dinner.

Jon had warned us that his uncle and aunt were very right wing ('militant Catholics and single-issue voters'). I had always been under the impression that far-right Americans are ignorant, pig-headed and racist idiots, and so I was expecting to spend an evening biting my tongue. When I found that they were a kind, loving family and that their politics were just what they thought, not a way of life, I was both relieved and humbled (although the anti-abortion picketing placards stored in the toilet did give me a jolt). The next morning we waved our goodbyes to Margarita the yellow cab – we were leaving her with Jon's uncle and aunt, mainly so as not to have to worry about (or pay for) parking for two cars in Manhattan – and set off towards another new country: Canada.

A thick layer of fog had blown across Lake Erie, rendering our top speed to a walking pace and forcing us to camp up in an Indian reservation, the eerie mist clutching low to the dewy grass where we parked the cab. At dawn the mist still hadn't lifted and we crawled to the border town of Buffalo in upstate New York. We couldn't risk taking Hannah out of the country, after it had taken such an effort to get her here in the first place, but parking was incredibly expensive, especially for the whole night. However, we had a plan.

We pulled Hannah up outside the front of a huge casino that towers over Buffalo and gave the keys to the valet, quickly briefing him on her driving quirks, and headed inside. Walking through the casino and out the side door, we crossed the river on foot and into Canada. We took the bus (public transport felt like a novelty after a year of driving Hannah) to Toronto, where we met my cousin and his girlfriend and all their Irish friends for some St Patrick's Day celebrations. Since the recession it appeared as though the entire youth of the Emerald Isle has migrated to either Canada or Australia – I'm not sure I spoke to a real Canadian other than bar staff the entire time we were there. The Irish were identifiable by the fact that they were the only ones *not* dressed up in lewd green outfits and orange wigs; the other revellers were seemingly under the impression that wearing something bearing the corporate logo of 'Guinness' is synonymous with wearing something saying 'Ireland'.

We even got to squeeze in a quick trip to Niagara Falls, where the mist finally lifted to give us some spectacular views. Less than 24 hours later we crossed back into the USA, hopping through the casino side entrance and handing the slip to the valet, who obviously thought we had returned from an epic night of gambling. They had no idea we had actually been to another country and back.

As part of the sponsorship agreement we struck with GetTaxi, we had promised to do a load of publicity for them in New York. Saying our goodbyes to Jon, we made the nine-hour drive down to Manhattan, parked up and slept, ready for a few days of interviews.

We had done a lot of interviews by this point and most of them were fairly repetitive for us as everyone wanted to know the same things. However, one particular interview stood out; it was with Angus Loten, a journalist from the *Wall Street Journal*, who turned up convinced that we were just doing this for a publicity stunt. After he heard our stories about Hannah's adventures, however, he quickly changed his tune and was eager to find out more.

'So what's the meter on now?' It read somewhere around £60,000.

'That's about a hundred thousand dollars – it's important I get the facts right,' he said, scribbling down notes as fast as he could.

'Why, where's it going to run?' I asked.

'On the front page!'

The next morning our inboxes were full up with contacts, interview requests and some incredibly kind well wishes. What had started as a drunken plan in a pub had become front-page news in one of the biggest newspapers in America – we could barely believe it! As we drove around Manhattan people flagged us down to point at the newspaper in their hand and to try to hitch a ride. We managed to cram in an interview with ABC's *Nightline* before grabbing one last slice of New York pizza; I had to drop off Hannah at Lufthansa Cargo at JFK Airport by the afternoon, to take her across the ocean once more to the Middle East.

But there was a problem. When we had collected Hannah and got away without paying the customs agency, they hadn't given us the import document. Without the import document, we couldn't export. However, we were dealing with a whole different calibre of people to the imbeciles in Oakland Docks. Our NYC shipping agents were used to shipping Lamborghinis for sheikhs and vintage multimillion dollar Mille Miglia race cars (I must admit, they were a bit shocked to see our battered black cab) and tackled the problem head on by calling a high-up official.

'Hey, Joe, got a problem,' we overheard him saying down the phone. 'No import document on this car but it's got everything else... yup, got all the ownership docs... yeah, actually it's pretty famous... you got a copy of the *WSJ* there? Yeah, right, front page, see that headline that says, "$100,000 taxi ride?" It's that!'

And just like that we were done.

A few hours later and we were on a flight back to London for a couple of days of seeing family and stocking up on taxi parts, because before we knew it, we would be following Hannah to Israel.

The beginning of the end of the trip was upon us: we were going to bring Hannah home – the longest way possible, of course.

CHAPTER 52

THE LITTLE TOWN OF BETHLEHEM

'Which countries have you visited in the past ten years?'

I felt deflated.

'It's quite a lot,' I warned, 'do you want me to list them all?'

Before I had even entered Israel I had been pulled aside, to be questioned intensely about minor things such as how long I had studied my degree for and the names of my former housemates, not to mention the exact purpose of my trip to Israel.

The immigration clerk's eyes grew wider as I reeled off the 40-plus places Hannah had passed through over the previous year and she looked like she was going to faint as I got to the Arab states.

'... Turkey, Iraq, Iran, Pakistan...'

She stopped me. Israel is rather twitchy about letting in travellers who have visited any of the countries on the other side of the conflict, and vice versa. That had been one of the reasons for our original change of route the previous year, and why we had avoided Israel up until now. However GetTaxi had offered to pay to ship Hannah over, to put us up and show us around all at their expense, and it seemed too good an offer to refuse. Nimrod had been enthusiastic to say the least, singing the praises of Israel's nightlife, beaches, food, women and much more.

'And what exactly are you doing in Israel?'

I took a deep breath.

'We're driving around the world for charity and we're being sponsored by an Israeli company; our car is waiting in Tel Aviv.'

'So there are more of you?' she asked. 'Why aren't you travelling together?'

'Look, can you just take a look at this.'

I produced a copy of Israel's main national newspaper, in Hebrew, complete with a story on us and our pictures and offered it to her.

She studied it for a while.

'Wait here.'

Eventually she reappeared with my documents and sent me to a special line of 'suspicious' travellers, to be searched extra carefully, until they were satisfied that I was telling the truth. I later found out that Leigh and Paul had gone through the exact same overblown procedure at their respective airports, and we were reminded why we had thought the bureaucracy might not have been worth it.

Nimrod had been right about the food – it was truly incredible – but we started to think he had oversold us on his other promises; the beaches were rocky, the women were aloof and strangely immune to the British accent, the nightlife was cripplingly expensive and the drivers' bad habits easily kept pace with the rest of the Middle East. Still, we were probably always going to be in for a heavy landing after we left the USA, and we were happy to be in such a unique place where the combination of the ancient Middle Eastern setting and traditions with modern-day Western-style culture and values intrigued and impressed us.

Since GetTaxi had come on board, the atmosphere on the expedition had changed, strangely. No longer were we three mates on an adventure – sleeping on floors and changing plans at the last minute for a possible random excursion. Now, we were in a hotel and doing interviews as part of a PR machine. This was the price we had to pay in return for the chance to circumnavigate the world, and we understood that and appreciated the chance we had been given, but airlifting the car to Israel for two weeks – just to then ship it out again – seemed so against everything that had come before. The air freighting alone cost more than our entire fuel bill to Australia.

The chance to get away from it all came in the shape of a cancelled interview, so we loaded up the tents and headed out to the Dead Sea. Hannah plodded along over the low rolling hills and fruit fields of Tel Aviv, past Jerusalem and numerous checkpoints, and we wild camped and cooked over a fire. It felt like we were back to our old ways and the realisation that it was coming to an end started to sink in.

The next morning, after a short and painful dip in the Dead Sea (we read the 'DO NOT submerge head' sign after we'd gone swimming and discovered what happens when that concentration of salt gets in your eyes) we got ready to go. Johno and Leigh had a flaming argument over whether we should go and check out a nearby waterfall or leave straight away for a PR call that, Johno insisted, would inevitably be cancelled. Leigh and I had showers to wash the thick salty water off, but Johno – still smarting from the argument – sat in the taxi looking surly while he dreamt of distant waterfalls. We started to drive back to the holy city and as the cool air flowed into the car, the gloopy seawater started to dry on Johno's skin, leaving behind a thick layer of salt. By the time we reached the Wailing Wall his hair had dreadlocked and his skin appeared to have developed a serious flaky condition, and anybody unfortunate enough to walk behind him when he ran his hand through his hair received a face full of crusty salt.

The city itself is incredible – old winding streets where the clash of cultures and religion blend. We wandered the streets and enjoyed cool drinks in the baking heat, before returning to where we parked Hannah in the Hasidic Jewish area. We arrived to find a gang of lads in dark *rekels* and black hats, with their long sideburns peeking out, laughing and posing for pictures next to Hannah.

One of Hannah's quirks after so many rebuilds and roadside repairs was that her alarm system was now hardwired into the car's horn – it meant that we could hear if there was any trouble with the car from about four streets away as the horn was so loud. It also meant the horn was set off whenever we locked or unlocked the cab.

Sneaking up and hiding behind a wall, we pressed the unlock button on the keyfob. Two loud horn blasts blared, and the local lads who were posing were sent three foot in the air in a mass of hats and curls. They looked around just as we locked Hannah again – the look of puzzlement on their faces as this black cab turned Herbie on them was priceless.

We crossed into Palestine through the famous 'security wall'. The difference between the two sides was stark – the Israeli side was immaculate; the Palestinian side was strewn with litter and detritus, and was covered in the most incredible graffiti – mainly political, but some just for the sake of it. We photographed Hannah by some of the most interesting ones (and even a few Banksy pieces) before heading to Bethlehem – we wanted to check out Jesus's birthplace before heading back to our hotel.

The only thing that stood between us and our room in Tel Aviv was a short 50-mile drive, and of course the 8 m-high concrete wall. We had just passed through it with no problems but now, on our return trip, we seemed to have an issue.

As we waited in the queue of slowly moving cars, trundling past the 20 m-high sentry towers and lines of barbed wire, I fished around for Hannah's registration papers to show to the weary recruits manning the checkpoint.

'Er, guys, where's the *machina passporta*?' I asked Paul and Leigh, as I leafed through the mountain of documents but came up empty.

'The V5? It's in the documents folder,' replied Leigh, 'where it always is!'

'Um... no it isn't, any ideas Paul?'

'Yeah, it should be in there,' he confirmed. 'Let me have a look... it's the only logical place it would be.'

Leigh and I had learned that Paul never 'lost' anything; he merely misplaced things in 'logical' places that often showed a remarkable lack of any sort of logic.

We inched closer to the checkpoint as he hurriedly flicked through a year's worth of unpaid (and hopefully untraceable) parking tickets and short-term insurance policies.

'You're right, the bloody shippers must've lost it,' he concluded just as we got to the soldiers, 'just play it cool.'

Thankfully our smiles and passports were enough to get us back over the border into Israel, where we met up with a guy called Eyal who had emailed us with an unusual problem.

Eyal was an Israeli student who had visited Belgium the previous summer in order to study French. He met a Latvian exchange student there and they had a bit of a whirlwind romance. After visiting him in Jerusalem, she accidently left her favourite straw hat at his. He had read about our journey in the newspaper and sent us a nice email asking if we could possibly stick the hat in the back of the cab and hand deliver it to his Latvian sweetheart, Laila. Who were we to refuse to such a romantic request?

When Hannah and Laila's hat were loaded into the ship that would carry them from the northern port of Haifa up to Athens, the V5 was still nowhere to be seen. It was a pretty essential document we needed for taking the car over international borders, but with most of Israel shutting down for a long Passover weekend it seemed there was nothing we could really do apart from wait for the car to arrive in Greece and try to blag her into Europe.

I had volunteered to fly ahead of Leigh and Johno to sort out importing the car. It was 4 a.m. and I had arrived in plenty of time for my flight to Athens. The young conscript whose unenviable job it was to interrogate foreigners started to go through the questions.

'Have you ever been to the Middle East?'

'Yes.'

'When?'

'Well... apart from being born in Bahrain? Lots of times, you have my passport, it's probably best if you look for yourself.'

The guard had my British passport that I had generally reserved for Western countries, like America and Australia, and after looking through it thoroughly he couldn't find the stamp he was after.

'I can't find the stamp... do you have a second passport?' he asked.

My Irish passport was in my back pocket, containing stamps and visas from Israel's worst enemies. But there was no point in lying – Mossad probably knew what I ate for breakfast. Reluctantly, I handed it over. He opened it, and, by complete chance, it landed on the worst possible page:

VISA: ISLAMIC REPUBLIC OF IRAN

The guard's mouth fell open and his face showed a look that said, 'This is way above my pay grade'. He couldn't even string a sentence together, just mumbled, 'errrrr', and disappeared around the back at a brisk jog.

Ten minutes later, my palms were flat against a wall of a curtained-off cubicle.

I was wearing nothing but my tatty, ripped boxer shorts and a gloved hand was examining my manhood.

As I zipped myself up after my strip search, I attempted to be jovial – as much as I didn't want to be strip searched in Tel Aviv Airport at 4 a.m., I knew that my searcher had probably never harboured dreams of nightshifts searching foreigner's privates. Ready to go, I grabbed the pile of change I had emptied out of my pockets and gave him a mischievous smile.

'How about a tip?'

He looked me in the eye and in a flat voice without the slightest hint of humour, said, 'I'm sorry, it's against regulation for me to accept that,' and returned to his form.

CHAPTER 53

TROUBLE AT THE BORDER

Leigh and I hitchhiked up to the airport and waited for the flight to Greece in a McDonald's, chosen for the trusty free Wi-Fi. It was peopled with teenage conscripts horsing around, with their assault rifles piled up next to the straw dispensers and ketchup sachets.

After arriving in Greece, the next task was to get the car released from the port, albeit with no registration document, no insurance and, worst of all, no vehicle owner, as our rendezvous with Paul hadn't gone to plan.

All we had was a colour photocopy of the elusive V5 document that Leigh had printed at the airport. Somehow, that, along with our dubious English charm, was more than enough for the relaxed Greek customs agents to let us retrieve Hannah. We loved the laxness of the Greek authorities.

The Romanian and Bulgarian borders also accepted the forged V5 with no problems and we started to wonder what all our worries had been about as we whizzed past the many roadside prostitutes and up to Bucharest. We had missed Eastern Europe's bizarre quirks dearly. The hearty, fatty food easily gave America a run for its money and the cheap and tasty beers knocked anything Israel had to offer right out of the bar. With only four new countries left to go what could possibly go wrong?

'This is copy.'

'No, it's not.'

'Yes, this photocopy, I can tell from the lines. It's forged.'

The Moldovan border guard in his big, flap-eared Soviet woolly hat was, of course, right.

The Romanians who had just let us out of their country had also noticed this small hiccup, and now they wouldn't let us back in. We were, quite literally, in no-man's-land between the countries and royally stuck.

The Israelis swore blind that the Americans had lost the original V5. The Americans said they handed the documents over, and seeing as their job is shipping multimillion-dollar vintage sports cars, and having seen the chaotic Israeli shipping office, I was inclined to believe them.

I had ordered a brand new V5 from the UK to replace the old one but it still hadn't been printed, let alone shipped out to us. Until we got that, we weren't going anywhere. Besides, where would we ship it to?

Three Unwashed Idiot Boys
Pink & Leaky Pop-up Tent
London Black Cab
Somewhere between Romania and Moldova

We had nothing but a packet of crisps and a cold hot dog. This was also pretty embarrassing as an old Moldovan friend of ours from university had offered to put us up that night. Well, technically her mother had, as Nelly was still back in Birmingham doing her finals. Her mother had insisted that we stay with her and was already cooking dinner, while her cousin came to meet us at the border – the border we couldn't get through because we didn't have the right paperwork. We had driven around the whole world, but we couldn't get into Moldova. Leigh made the call to Nelly to apologise.

'Hey, guys, hang fire,' she said. 'I'll make a few calls and see what I can do.'

'I'm not sure you can do anything without this document; it's like trying to cross a border without a passport. You'll have to be the Queen... or a president or something. Plus we've tried to do it on forged documents, we're... er... kinda in trouble!'

'OK, I understand. But just wait there while I make some calls – don't go anywhere.'

We couldn't.

Twelve hours later, Leigh had almost run out of action films to watch and we'd caught up on writing all the blogs we needed to write, when the boss came over.

This wasn't the boss of the guards; this was the boss of the whole border post. She efficiently strode towards our stinking tin hovel.

'Passports, paperwork?' We handed them over.

'We... um don't have... um... *nyet machina passporta*,' I tried to look apologetic.

'I know. I also speak English. I'll be back. Don't go anywhere.'

There was still no risk of that.

She returned 15 minutes later with our passports and ushered us into the main queue.

'Hey – she's given us visas,' Johno piped up after checking his passport.

The cars in the queue of traffic in front of us were unceremoniously ordered to pull into the side and we were directed through the gaps. This was either going really well, or we were about to get into even more trouble.

The guard grabbed our passports again, which were promptly stamped before being handed back to us with a flourish, a smile and a simple, 'OK!' as she pointed us through the border.

Waiting on the other side was a brand new Mercedes and out stepped a leggy blonde, who said, 'Hi, I'm Lena, Nelly's cousin. I'm the host of Moldovan *Top Gear*.'

We were a little bit impressed. 'Hi! Great to meet you!' we enthused. 'So it was you who managed to get us through the border?'

'Oh no… that was Nelly's mum. She called the President.'

'The… President?'

'Yes, he has given you a pardon – now we must move, dinner is getting cold.'

Nelly's mother was an absolute saint. She invited us into her home and made it her job to ensure we all put on a stone each from all the wonderful food she cooked for us. We celebrated Easter with her, acting as surrogate children while her own were still studying abroad.

But there was a problem – even with the President's blessing – as without our V5, we were still stuck in Moldova indefinitely, unable to enter any other countries. It could take weeks to be processed by the good old DVLA in Swansea (perhaps their employees were too busy trying to have sex with black cab exhaust pipes at Full Moon parties…) and there was still no sign of the old one in Israel. I tried one last-ditch attempt with the Israeli shippers, insisting categorically that they lost it and mentioning the damages they may be liable for, in a desperate attempt to persuade them to take their feet off the desk, stop smoking and start searching their office.

'OK, OK… we look again.'

And, all of a sudden, it materialised. I expect they never bothered to look in the first place. But this wasn't the end of our problems – we now had to get the document from Israel to Moldova, hardly a route regularly serviced by DHL, and it was still the Passover week in Israel, so no couriers were working. The fastest we could get it was a matter of weeks and we were due in Moscow as GetTaxi's guests of honour at a huge tech conference in a few days. A load of interviews had been scheduled soon after that, along with various flights, meetings, visa restrictions and our imminent arrival back in London.

But we had one characteristically convoluted option. Fini, an overworked PA and general saviour at GetTaxi who had had the unenviable job of translating my constant requests to the shipping agents to 'search harder', had an idea. Her father was flying to Romania the next morning for business. With a few calls and some favours, the V5 was on its way to us via a rather unusual route. Fini drove from the shipping agent to her father's house and handed over the document. He flew to Bucharest and handed the document to his secretary before going to his meetings. A courier collected it from the secretary, took it to the bus station and handed it to a bus driver. The bus driver drove his bus from Bucharest to the border with Moldova, where he dropped his passengers off, and handed the document to another bus driver. The second driver then drove to Chisinau, the Moldovan capital, where he was met by one of Nelly's mum's employees (we weren't allowed to go as a feeding was due), who then drove the document up to Nelly's house and dropped it off just in time for tea.

The Moldovan border guards couldn't stop laughing at our rubbish car as they stamped us through. The Ukrainian officials weren't quite so jolly and unceremoniously demanded to know whether we had any pistols or narcotics as they led sniffer dogs around the back of Hannah.

One police stop later we were back in Kiev, back in Joanna's hostel – where we had celebrated our first month on the road – catching up on the last year and a half and drinking vodka. It was like déjà vu but this time the birthday boy changed from Paul to Leigh.

'I don't want to go to exactly the same bars and do the same as Paul on his birthday, I want a different experience,' he said.

But before long we were back in the same underground bar, again a little worse for wear, watching the same barmaids breathe shots of fire over a very jolly Leigh's head.

CHAPTER 54

- - - - - - - - -

THE 'FILTHY RAVE CLUB' — TAKE TWO

Last time we were in Moscow we didn't see too much apart from the inside of a police station and a few hazy clubs. This time we were determined to actually see the sights, after first spending a night camping on the vast Russian steppe. Driving in Russia had reminded us how much we hated the bumps, and the appalling drivers, but it also gave us the chance to partake one more time in that Russian tradition.

In the morning, three huge guys in a gleaming BMW stopped to take photos with us and chat, all smiles. One of them asked, 'Is it too early?'

'Erm, for what?'

'Vodka! It is Russian tradition!'

We informed them that 9 a.m. was slightly too early for us and they accelerated off in a screech of wheels.

Russia passed in a flash of interviews, meetings and press engagements with GetTaxi and the crew in the Moscow office. The Russia we saw was slightly different than the one we had seen before, but there was a friendly face waiting for us; we had met a photographer called Rob in Ukraine, 13 months earlier. He was now teaching English to the kids of oil billionaires in Moscow and jumped at the chance of another international trip in Hannah.

In ancient China a unit of distance known as the *li* was used to measure the difficulty of a journey, rather than the actual physical distance. So in one direction two towns could be 100 *li* apart but going back might be 200 *li*, if, for instance, it was all uphill. Using the *li* would have been useful in Russia where one moment we could be zipping along on autobahn-like highways and the next bouncing around on India-esque tracks.

We had one day to get out of Russia and a mere 200 miles to go. For most of the way we were blessed with empty, arrow-straight and surprisingly smooth roads. We even took some leisurely stops where we saw, at what could barely even be called a hamlet, a well-tended war memorial next to a couple of tumble-down houses. A fatherly statue of Lenin quietly watched over them while a lonely pigeon sat perched on his head. The extensive lists of names were testament to how thoroughly the war ravaged this area of western Russia and every falling-down barn and dilapidated house represented someone's destroyed future. Each pile of decaying beams was once someone's dream; thought up and painstakingly built, but then left to rot by a builder who would never return. With every mile closer to the Estonian border, I felt more and more relaxed. Now we would definitely make it out in time, short of a major disaster – a major disaster like a two-day long queue of vehicles at the border.

Like the one that greeted us around the next corner.

The whole car winced.

'Just go around, it might be for trucks or Russian cars only,' I said hopefully, but as we rolled along slowly on the opposite side of the road it was clear that the line was for all vehicles and that it was at least two or three miles long.

We crept forward, and within sight of the border there was a break in the line of cars. We pushed in, using all our British arrogance and Rob's passable grasp of Russian to skip hundreds of waiting people.

'We just drove all the way around the world!' we explained, to the angry glares as we passed through the checkpoint and out of Russia.

The first flowerings of spring were blossoming and I quickly remembered why I loved the Baltics. Rob described them as 'like Russia but with smiles and Jägermeister'. It certainly was good to be back in Europe.

We reached Latvia and reunited a bemused Laila with her lost straw hat, before meeting one of the last Couchsurfers of the trip. Ance lived with her family in a beautiful house in the forest, complete with a sauna outhouse of which we soon sampled the delights. It was like our relaxing break in Finland but without the snow, and we each had our own bedroom for the night – exactly what we needed after rattling through Russia.

We drove all day and crashed out in fields and on Couchsurfers' sofas at night all the way through Latvia, Lithuania, Poland and Germany on our way home. The typical European scenery rushing by was comforting after spending so long on the other side of the world, and we were relishing the sense of familiarity that being so close to home brought. We paused only for Leigh to purchase a questionable rubber phallic-like object from a Polish service station to be our new taxi mascot.

We arrived in Berlin mid-afternoon in an attempt to experience properly the nightlife we had tried so desperately to find last time we were in the city – although this time hopefully we wouldn't wake up the next morning and find our taxi had been lost.

It was a Friday night and we were staying at Anne's again. We learnt from our previous mistake and dressed as 'hip' as we could before we headed out. The next morning we found ourselves swinging in a rowing boat pirate ship that was strung between the trees in the garden of an ex-brothel-turned-electro-nightclub. We were suitably satisfied that we had 'done Berlin'.

Driving out the next day, we stopped to prepare our road sandwiches in the usual way – using the bonnet as our picnic table – and planned the route west, when there was a shout.

'Hey! Hey, taxi boys.'

There, out of the blue, was Felix; the German guy who had hitched a lift from Georgia to Armenia with us. We were in his home city, and after catching up briefly we were back on the road, amazed at the odds of the chance meeting with someone we had met half a world away.

A friend of ours was living on an army base just outside of Hamburg and had invited us to dinner in the Officers' Mess. After cruising down the autobahns, we were uncharacteristically on time – and everything was going well until we heard that familiar 'pop' and crunch, as what felt like the hundredth ball joint of the expedition failed. A roadside bodge job allowed us to limp to the base to find the officers of Her Majesty's Mercian Regiment drinking gin and tonics and awaiting our late arrival.

It turns out the damage to the cab was more substantial than we had initially thought and soon after dinner, as Leigh and Johno worked on the cab, Captain Martyn Fulford and I were searching through rows of huge battle tanks trying to find a bolt of the right length and thickness.

We failed, and the next morning took a trip to the other side of the base to the mechanic's, manned by a combination of British soldiers and local Germans. They carefully examined Hannah's knackered front end before trying to remove the shattered ball joint, amid an unceasing barrage of World War Two-based banter from the British mechanics.

'No wonder you lost the bloody war, you can't even remove a simple ball joint!'

The German mechanic gave a few more heaves on a huge spanner and the parts plopped out on the floor.

'We may have lost the war,' he started, standing up and wiping his hands, 'but we have better women, beer, cars and economy. Now,' he smirked as he tossed the bits over to his British counterpart, 'be kind enough to press this joint back together so your countrymen can be on their way.'

CHAPTER 55

HOMEWARD BOUND

Suddenly it was all upon us; the final stretch of road before Hannah would be reunited with the beloved Tarmac of Blighty. At this point I could hardly wait to complete the trip, and Leigh must have felt the same as he drove Hannah up the autoroute at the fastest speed we ever hit, a pant-wetting 85 mph.

We were swallowed up into the Channel Tunnel somewhere around Calais and spat out at the other end 40 minutes later on to our dearly missed homeland.

Even the miles of barbed wire fences around the Eurotunnel exit and the inevitable rain couldn't dampen our spirits. Finally, after a year and three months on the road we were home. Even the familiar road signs made me smile.

The most important thing at that moment was to order a true English pint, so we headed to the White Horse in Dover, the little pub where we had our leaving pints two cold Februarys ago. Up above the bar, amid the scrawlings, lay a familiar sight: a postcard of Hannah in front of the Sydney Opera House that we had sent six months previously.

Suitably refreshed we started the ride up to London.

A tiny 80 miles was all that now separated us from our final destination. Compared with driving the length of America or crossing India, it seemed so insignificant. Britain felt so small.

As part of the world record attempt rules, the taxi had to be a fully registered taxi in the country it departed from. However, before we had left the UK, Transport for London or any of the other taxi-licensing authorities wouldn't grant Hannah a licence. I had called up just about every licensing authority in the country, coming up against typical bureaucratic public sector inflexibility at every turn.

'Hi, can we register the taxi for an expedition to raise money for the Red Cross? It will never actually be used as a taxi and never collect any passengers?'

'Will it have child-friendly seat belts?'

'Err… like I said it won't actually be used as a taxi so therefore it won't carry any children.'

'I'm afraid child seatbelts are a must on all taxi vehicles due to the Hackney Carriage Act of 1831. Does the vehicle in question have child seatbelts tested to 2001 European standards, part 17, appendix D?'

'No, not exactly… but it does have a winch and a really big sound system.'

This went on and on, until about two weeks before our departure I eventually managed to persuade Gloucester City Council to waive the vehicle requirements (at the time we hadn't even fitted seatbelts!) in return for placing their logo on the cab.

However, when I went to collect the taxi badge she realised she had forgotten a rather vital question. 'You are a registered taxi driver, right?'

'Err… not exactly. Why?'

'You know it's illegal to drive a registered taxi unless you're a registered taxi driver for the local council, according to the European Mandate of blah-blah-blah, Part 192738 Section C?'

At the time this seemed pretty insurmountable. Without the registration, there was no world record. But if the taxi was registered, we couldn't drive it without passing the registration test – an impossible task to accomplish in a fortnight.

In the end we had hatched a convoluted plan and the evening before the departure we parked the taxi (which was still a private vehicle at the time) near Covent Garden, and at exactly midnight the taxi registration kicked in. The next day we waved our goodbyes and drove away from the cameras with me at the helm, then turned a corner and stopped before we reached public roads.

I hopped out and swapped places with Steve – the head of the Gloucester Taxi Drivers Association and a fully qualified taxi driver. Once we were on the ferry, the taxi ceased to be under the law requiring a registered driver to drive it, but it was still registered in the UK and therefore legitimate for the world record. It was to become synonymous with the kind of bizarre kinds of creative work-around logistical solutions we would have to continuously create as the expedition progressed.

Now we were back in Blighty, the same problem presented itself but we conveniently ignored both Hannah's lack of MOT roadworthiness certificate and the fact we weren't officially licensed taxi drivers. What had seemed like such an important technicality at the start of the trip now was a trifling rule that could be bent.

As we approached our final destination, I felt a huge rush of emotions. We were all glad it was over and felt like the adventure had run its course. Fifteen months of travelling had worn us down to the bone; staying in a different place every day or two, continuously making new friends only to have to immediately say goodbye, living from a rucksack and never being truly clean certainly had its effect. Suddenly feeling emotionally and physically drained, we had the crushing realisation that none of us had any idea what we wanted to do with our lives. How could we assimilate back into normal life after so much had happened? My plan to return to the City of London when we left now felt ridiculous and the lads felt the same. We had no money, no desire to do anything more with the taxi, and life was moving on.

But first we had one last short drive to complete.

London was grey, wet and beautiful. We pulled on to Trafalgar Square, where 15 black cabs were waiting for us, and we paraded down the Mall for GetTaxi's photographers with them in procession.

We reached Covent Garden, where the whole trip had begun, at around 10 a.m. on 11 May 2012, 450 days after we had departed from the exact same spot. When we finally stopped the meter it read a total of £79,006.80, but thankfully Leigh, who was driving at the time, agreed to waive the fee.

We had managed to raise £20,000 for the Red Cross, and after we had presented them with an oversized cheque, an official from Guinness World Records stepped up to present us with not one, but two world records.

Guinness World Record for the Longest Journey Completed by Taxi

Guinness World Record for the Highest (Altitude) Reached by Taxi

We were double world record-breakers – one for a truly ridiculous and pointless journey, and another for what sounds like drug consumption in a taxi (but was actually for the mountain pass in Tibet).

Our friends and family came rushing over to welcome us back home and I think all three of us felt like we couldn't have driven a mile more. We were exhausted, but we had made our dreams come true.

And another dream was about to be made. Way back during one of the pub-planning sessions almost five years previously, we had talked about what would be the dream indicator that the expedition had been a success. I said being featured on BBC News would be the biggest thing I could imagine.

As we pulled up outside the gates of Broadcasting House, I was as nervous as could be. Leigh could see this as the colour drained from my face while we waited, 30 seconds from going on air. He was typically understanding.

'So, how many people will see this?' he asked the assistant as he grinned and winked at me.

'Oh, at this time of day? Something like seventy or eighty million.'

Whatever colour was left drained from my cheeks and we walked on to the set. Thanks Leigh, you bastard.

But strange opportunities started to appear. When people heard about our expedition we had a wonderful email asking whether we would like to take part in the London 2012 Olympics Closing Ceremony. However, there was only space for one driver and we were three. As with everything else on the expedition, we decided in the fairest manner. Rock, paper, scissors. And as luck would have it, I found myself driving out with the Spice Girls to 80,000 screaming fans. Zig-a-zig-ah!

Soon after we finished, when Hannah was rusting in retirement in GetTaxi's car park in London, a journalist asked me what I had learned 'about all the people of the world you met'.

I felt such a general question could only be answered with a correspondingly massive generalisation and told him that I had gleaned that people everywhere were usually kind and that most people wanted the same basic thing out of life: the opportunity to share a small corner of the world with the people they loved, free from conflict or persecution.

'That's not interesting for my readers,' he retorted, 'why would anyone want to hear your story if you say that everyone is the same?'

After thinking a short while the only thing I could reply was that adventures are what each person makes of them. That maybe his readers should get out and explore the world themselves. Clashes are inevitable when the differences between people are so huge. Perhaps if more people tried to understand these differences then the world would run more smoothly.

But is it smoothness we want? The German autobahn is frictionless and recognisable, but it is also bland and monotonous. The rutted track slows you down and rattles you around, but it affords you adventures you would never imagine. Where would the fun be in life if all of our roads and our paths were smooth and familiar?

We could have stayed in our local pub on a Friday night, but the fun came from discovering that you should never challenge a seven-foot Viking to a drinking competition, that Dina and Sasha chase vodka with pickled gherkins not Coca-Cola, that cha-cha doesn't really make you go blind and that Special Brew is the drink of choice in dry Iran.

We could have driven on our safe and ordered English country roads, but would we have figured out how to avoid potholes the size of watermelons, how to dig a car out of a seven-foot snowdrift or that the police in Berlin don't take kindly to you leaving your car parked in the middle of a street on a Monday morning?

I spent a good chunk of my adult life studying engineering, but picked up more about mechanics from the radiator blowing up in the desert, from the ball joints snapping in the mountains of Nepal and from sharing some beers with Brando the mechanic, even if he did later turn out to be a multiple murderer.

A lifetime of walking past British bobbies and the occasional traffic stop were no substitute for finding out how to bribe your way out of a Russian police station, fobbing off the Persian secret police, ditching armed escorts in lawless Baluchistan or blagging through borders with the arrogance of youth and friends in high places.

We could have read all the guidebooks we liked but they would never take the place of hearing Russian dirty jokes from the horse's mouth, or shooting guns with locals in the backcountry of the USA. All the nature documentaries in the world couldn't compare with seeing the Arctic sky lit by the Northern Lights, stepping out on to the base of the world's highest mountain or really comprehending the vastness of the Australian Outback by chugging through it for four days.

It is often said that people only show their true colours in times of great stress and conflict. Arguing with gun-wielding guards and escorts and countless border guards really let us see ourselves, and each other, more clearly than ever before. Spending 15 months cooped up in a car with Leigh and Paul allowed me to grasp why we were such good friends, and to learn a lot about myself along the way, too. I'm honoured to have spent so long with two great travel buddies and friends.

As our story comes to an end, I hope we managed to give you a taste of the adventure. We loved our expedition precisely for what it was: a ridiculous pub idea that got out of hand. It was a road trip with three best friends, parties, mistakes, mischief, breakdowns, jokes and everything you would expect from three 20-something males on the road. Except ours went on for almost a year and a half, and involved a cast of hundreds of some of the most amazing, kind and unique people I will ever have the pleasure of meeting.

Jasper, the Dutchman with the horny cat, told us that bad decisions make for good stories. We made countless bad decisions and foolish mistakes along the way but the best decision we ever made was to try.

We three intrepid idiots, bluffing our way around the world and learning as we went, managed to drive a black cab purchased on eBay the entire way around the globe. So go out and buy that vehicle, or book that flight, or plan that route for your own adventure. It will be the best thing you will ever do.

Because if *we* can do it, believe me, you certainly can.

AFTERWORD

By Leigh Purnell

*This book is dedicated to all the people who thought
we were bat-shit crazy, but supported us with food,
floors, finance, friendship and spare parts anyway*

Sitting back and thinking about it, a lot changed in the 15 months since we left Covent Garden, with a half-working taxi that didn't even have functional wiper blades. We waved goodbye to our friends, family and sponsors, who honestly didn't even think that we would make it out of Europe, let alone circumnavigate the world.

Stuck in the basement at Aston University, desperately working on Hannah just days before launch, 50 hours into a 54-hour workathon, I was just thinking of all the things that needed to be finished otherwise we would fail before we even began. I was sat there with a welder I had just learnt how to use, thinking that the people who had said we were crazy might have just been right.

Buying any vehicle from eBay has its risks; buying a car from eBay that you expect to take you around the world was maybe a stretch too far. When we were trying to figure out what vehicle to use, we immediately went with the iconic London black cab and focused on finding one with a manual gearbox, as the roads that we aimed to traverse were not as forgiving as the busy streets of London. We then began to convert Hannah into a steed that might stand a chance in the conditions we were going to put her through. The ideal donor car to use for these modifications was the Land Rover Defender; nearly all of the parts we used were taken from this vehicle and they served us well. Here is a full breakdown of what we changed on Hannah:

- Added a roof rack and roof box
- Added adjustable suspension and raised the height by 60 mm with custom springs
- Replaced all ball joints on the wheel assemblies
- Replaced clutch and fuel sensors
- Added winter tyres and upgraded brakes
- Added a cable winch and bull bar to enable recovery
- Welded in a new driver's seat and added a passenger seat
- Installed air intake snorkel for better air filtration and to prevent engine flooding
- Welded new floor in the boot to replace the almost completely rusted-through existing version
- Installed new silicone engine hoses for high temperature tolerance
- Increased the capacity of the stock radiator and added electric fans for increased cooling
- Installed custom high-power output alternator and extra fuse box for additional electronics
- Created and welded custom roll bar to replace partition normally found in taxis
- Created a custom storage unit (The Bar) for secondary back-up battery and mains power invertor
- Added new electrical spool and high-intensity lights for night driving

- Installed alarm and immobiliser system
- Fitted insulation for sound dampening and thermal protection
- Cleaned and painted all the underbody for rust protection
- Finally, we added a sweet sound system.

Looking back at what we had just accomplished, I would not have traded it in for the world. We went from being three students, who knew a little about fixing cars, had ran a few events and travelled a little, to becoming seasoned explorers, who had just traversed 50 countries, in some of the harshest weather conditions that humans could tolerate, and hadn't managed to kill each other in the process. It was a life-changing experience and it made me feel a whole new respect for Johno and Paul, not to mention all the amazing people we had met along the way.

The previous record for the longest journey by taxi was set in 1994 and was a 21,691-mile, four-month taxi ride from London to Cape Town, South Africa, and back, by Jeremy Levine, Mark Aylett, and Carlos Arrese. The trip ran the meter up to $64,645 (around £40,000). When we saw that mileage figure all those years ago, drawing our fingers across a map of the globe, it seemed a simple task; they had just gone to South Africa and back, easy right?

But after nearly 15 months, 43,319.5 miles, 8,000 litres of diesel, 50 countries and four continents, I had a newfound respect for people who go out and try to achieve something that is truly a world record, that somebody has never been able to accomplish before or is striving to beat, always pushing yourself to be the best that you can be. To Jeremy, Mark and Carlos, well done in 1994; it must have been far from easy and I now have the utmost respect for the three of you.

Below are some facts and figures from along the journey and I hope that by the time you finish reading it will generate a spark that might put you on a path to achieving something great:

AFTERWORD

- Total cost of taxi fare: £79,006.80
- Total distance travelled: 43,319.5 miles (69,716.12 km)
- Amount of money raised for the British Red Cross: £20,000
- Number of litres of diesel consumed: 8,000
- Total spent on visas: £3,345
- Highest altitude above sea level: 5,225.4 metres (17,143 ft)
- Lowest altitude below sea level: -423 metres (-1,237 ft)
- Number of passengers: 102
- Number of times Hannah was repaired: 97
- Highest temperature recorded in taxi: 60.4°C (140.72°F) Zahedan, Iran
- Lowest temperature recorded in taxi: -19.4°C (-2.92°F) Rovaniemi, Finland
- Number of countries visited: 50
- Number of languages experienced: 46
- Number of sponsors to help us on the way: 27
- Number of times Hannah was welded: 24
- Number of police fines issued: 6
- Number of times we used the winch: 3
- Number of bullet holes in Hannah: 2
- Number of times arrested: 2
- Number of times Hannah's wheels fell off: 1
- Number of times the engine failed: 0
- Number of people who woke up to a picture of Hannah on the front of their morning *Wall Street Journal*: 2.1 million

APPENDIX

– – – – – – – –

THE CHEERS GUIDE

England – *Cheers!*

France – *Santé!*

Belgium – *Santé!/Proost!/Prost!*

Netherlands – *Proost!*

Germany – *Prost!*

Denmark – *Skål!*

Sweden – *Skål!*

Finland – *Kippis!*

Russia – *Na zdorovie!*

Belarus – *Ŭra!*

Ukraine – *Boodmo!*

Poland – *Na zdrowie!*

Czech Republic – *Na zdravi!*

Austria – *Prost!*

Liechtenstein – *Prost!*

Switzerland – *Prost!/Salute!/Santé!*

Monaco – *Santé!*

Italy – *Salute!*

San Marino – *Salute!*

Slovenia – *Na zdravje!*

Croatia – *Nazdravlje!*

Bosnia and Herzegovina – *Živjeli!*

Montenegro – *Živjeli!*

Kosovo – *Gëzuar!*

Macedonia – *Na zdravje!*

Greece – *Yamas!*

Turkey – *Şerefe!*

Georgia – *Galmajuice!*

Armenia – *Genatzt!*

Iraq – *Noş!*

Iran – *Salâmati!*

Pakistan – *Kha sehat walary!*

India – *A la sature!*

Nepal – *Subhakamana!*

Tibet – *Tashi deleg!*

China – *Gān Bēi!*

Laos – *Cap-ey!*

Cambodia – *Leuktukchet!*

Thailand – *Chok dee!*

Malaysia – *Sihat selalu!*

Singapore – *Sihat selalu!/ Cheers!*

Australia – *Cheers (mate)!*

USA – *Cheers (buddy)!*

Israel – *L'chaim!*

Bulgaria – *Nazdravey!*

Romania – *Noroc!*

Moldova – *Noroc!*

Latvia – *Uz veselibu!*

Lithuania – *Į sveikatą!*

Luxembourg – *Prost!*

ACKNOWLEDGEMENTS

First and foremost thanks have to go to Leigh, and to Paul and Johno respectively, for being such great travel buddies and friends, and for putting up with living in a cramped, hot, noisy and smelly metal box for 15 months.

Thanks also go to our families, and to Char, Katie and Lindsay for being so understanding and supportive.

Huge thanks to everyone at Summersdale and co., especially Debbie, Sophie and Emily for great editing and general helpfulness. Thanks to Jennifer also for originally seeing the potential in our story.

Thanks to all of our friends for their support during the planning and execution of the trip, in particular, to Pete, for bringing the car up to scratch and teaching us how to 'fold pizza'; to Chops, for the charity advice, general words of support and for being such a great first passenger; to Sam for letting us stay on her floor for so long; to Sarah L. for support and generous use of her office; to Dave P., for excellent China advice; to Nick, Katy and James W. for listening to the taxi spiel repeatedly; to Rachel at UK2Oz; and to everyone else – you know who you are.

Thank you to all of our sponsors, particularly Matthew, Rob, Matt and Duncan with Performance Direct; and Nimrod, Fini, Sofia and co. at GetTaxi (now Gett). The other vital sponsors included Aston University and Aston Business School, CabCard Services, Queensland University of Technology, Modis, WOSP, NGK Spark Plugs, Bloc Eyewear, Gloucester City Council,

ACKNOWLEDGEMENTS

Gloucester Taxi Drivers Association (especially Steve), Gaz Shocks (Gazzmatic International), Fenchurch, Synthotech, Cygnus Automotive, MaxSport, Flip Video, JBL, Sat Nav Warehouse, Samco Sport, Hotcourses Abroad, Skrapbook, The Roof Box Company, Club 9, Mac Tools, Base hostels and UKHost4u.

Thanks to Ranulph Fiennes, Boris Johnson, Suzanne McTaggart, Ron Miller, Danny Wallace, Bill Bryson, Frank Turner, Peggy Fok, Colleen Sollars, *Overland Journal* and all the other many media folks who helped support the trip and raise awareness.

A huge thanks to all the Couchsurfers and other generous folk who gave us advice, showed us their city, bought us food, let us sleep on their floors or otherwise opened their homes to us; we couldn't have done the trip without you. Thanks to all the people who gave us directions (except those Georgian farmers), gave us food and water, beeped and waved at us on the road, and took pictures and spread the word about us in their own country.

Thanks to the mechanics, armchair and otherwise, who got our heap of rust all the way around the world, in particular the technicians at Aston University and the students who gave up their free time to help us; the friendly folks at the Erbil Auto Bazaar; Brando in Australia, even if he did turn out to be a murderer; the guys and families at Back on the Road Again in California; and the mechanics at the military base in Germany.

Thanks to all the passengers and hitchers; especially Craig, who refreshed our company, stopped the three of us killing each other and was a vital link in getting through Pakistan; to Matt for the endless supply of comedy catchphrases and Swamp-Donkey anecdotes; and to Rob for being an all-round great dude and amazing photographer.

Thanks to everyone who took an interest in the trip, told their friends and donated to the Red Cross.

Finally, thanks to you for reading this book!

Have you enjoyed this book?
If so, why not write a review on your favourite website?

If you're interested in finding out more about our books,
find us on Facebook at **Summersdale Publishers** and
follow us on Twitter at **@Summersdale**.

Thanks very much for buying this Summersdale book.

www.summersdale.com